mDh0280

D0025451

Basketmakers

Meaning and Form
in
Native American Baskets

Copyright © 1992 Pitt Rivers Museum

ISBN: 0 902793 26 8
ISSN: 0141-2477

Printed in England by
Stephen Austin and Sons Ltd, Hertford

Cover illustrations:

Front cover: **USA, Arizona, Third Mesa, Hotevilla, Hopi.** Detail of wicker plaque by Abigail Kaursgowva, 1991. Design in natural dyes representing the *sipápuni*, the opening through which the Hopi people emerged from the previous world. 1991.35.17

Back cover. **Surinam, Tiriyo.** Tiriyo man plaiting a disposable palm leaf basket. Photograph by Peter Rivière.

Basketmakers

Meaning and Form
in
Native American Baskets

edited by

Linda Mowat, Howard Morphy and Penny Dransart

Pitt Rivers Museum   University of Oxford
Monograph 5

Acknowledgements

We would like to express our thanks the following individuals and institutions for the assistance and advice they have provided towards the production of this book:
The Area Museums Service for South Eastern England; Dail Behennah; Laurence and Mary Ellen Blair; Rowena Bradley; Joanne Segal Brandford; Gerry Brush; Betty DuPree; Linda B. Eaton; Elizabeth Edwards; Geoffrey Fouquet; Catherine Griffin; Maggie Henton; Joyce Herold; Sarah Hill; Clara and Rocky Keezer; Abigail Kaursgowva; Tamara Lucas; Bessie Monongye; Alexandra Morgan; Stan and Sherri Neptune; Malcolm Osman; Lydia and Melanie Pesata; Alison Petch; Polly Pollock; Qualla Arts & Crafts Mutual, Inc.; Pauline and Eleanor Quiyo; Shuna Rendel; Bob Rivers; Margaret Saguin; Sally Seguin; Birgitte Speake; Sue Walker; Amanda Wallace; Lynne Williamson.

Illustrations

All baskets illustrated are in the collection of the Pitt Rivers Museum unless otherwise indicated.

All photographs of Pitt Rivers Museum baskets by Malcolm Osman. All other illustrations are credited in the text with the exception of the following:
Maps by Amanda Wallace; drawings for Figs. 3, 124, 125, 144, 155 by Penny Dransart; photography for Figs. 23-26 by Robert J. Bitondi, courtesy the Connecticut Historical Society, Hartford, Connecticut.

Notes on Contributors

Stuart Carter is a D.Phil. student at the School of Anthropology, University of Oxford.

Penny Dransart is Departmental Demonstrator at the Pitt Rivers Museum, University of Oxford.

Claire Farrer is Professor of Anthropology at the University of California, Chico, USA.

Rayna Green is Director of the American Indian Program at the Museum of American History, Smithsonian Institution, Washington, DC, USA.

Andrea Laforet is Chief of the Canadian Ethnology Service at the Canadian Museum of Civilization, Hull, Quebec, Canada.

Sally McLendon is Professor of Anthropology at Hunter College, City University of New York, USA.

Ann McMullen is a PhD student at Brown University, Providence, Rhode Island, USA.

Howard Morphy is Curator of Anthropology at the Pitt Rivers Museum, University of Oxford.

Linda Mowat is Assistant Curator (Documentation) at the Pitt Rivers Museum, University of Oxford.

Peter Rivière is Lecturer in Anthropology at the Institute of Social and Cultural Anthropology, University of Oxford.

Marianne Cardale Schrimpff is an archaeologist and associate of the Gold Museum, Bogotá, Colombia.

Contents

Native American Baskets at the Pitt Rivers Museum

by Linda Mowat

The visitor looking for baskets in the Pitt Rivers Museum will be directed to a series of large Victorian mahogany showcases. These are crammed with scores of baskets displayed according to technique of manufacture. American baskets jostle for position with examples from Ancient Egypt, Australia, Nagaland and Sarawak.

This arrangement is the legacy of General Pitt Rivers, who gave his collection to the University of Oxford in 1883. The collection contained almost every kind of object made by man, ancient and modern: it ranged from weapons to walking sticks and from fans to fire-drills. One of the conditions attached to the gift was that the artefacts should be arranged typologically rather than culturally or geographically, to show:

the succession of ideas by which the minds of men in a primitive condition of culture have progressed in the development of their ideas from the simple to the complex (Lane Fox 1874:2).

Historic now, the arrangement of the Museum still holds relevance for the modern visitor, who can compare the ways in which men and women from different cultures have found answers to the broadly similar problems confronting them. It is surprising how often the answer has been a basket.

The General loved to collect ordinary, everyday objects and many baskets are exactly that. Yet, had he been a serious student of basketry, he might have paused to think about just how they fitted into his evolutionary scheme of things. Is a coiled basket simpler than a twined one? Is plaiting a basket with no tensioning mechanism any less skilled than weaving a textile on a loom? How is it that a single group of people, presumably at the same stage of development, can produce a whole set of baskets ranging from the simple, quickly made and disposable to the complex, highly skilled and deeply symbolic?

Setting aside these problems, one advantage of General Pitt Rivers' arrangement is that it allows us to look at baskets in quantity. And if this is not enough, their nature is such that we can turn away from the Basketry cases and still find baskets - American baskets - all over the Museum. Here they are with Cradles: baskets for babies from California and the Great Basin. There they are with Agriculture: a Choctaw winnowing tray from the Southeast. Nearby we find them with Food Processing: acorn hoppers, cooking baskets and soup bowls from California, a long tubular cassava squeezer from the Amazon. Displayed with Clothing is a beautiful painted hat from the Northwest Coast, and with Textiles a woman's sewing basket from a Pre-Columbian burial. There are burden baskets for garden produce, berries and firewood; there are storage bins, water jars, fire fans and rattles; there are children's toys, trinket boxes, fish traps and weapons. Baskets are woven from the strands of life itself.

It is our privilege as curators of the Pitt Rivers Museum to select material from time to time for special exhibition. The density of the permanent displays, while providing the visitor with almost endless scope for observation and reflection, can sometimes by its very diversity obscure the qualities of individual objects, drawing attention away from their cultural context. By concentrating purely on Native American basketry, it is our aim to devote to one section of our vast collection the attention we feel it deserves. The scope of American baskets is tremendous in terms of technology, all the basic constructional techniques being represented and

Fig. 1 White River Apache basketmaker.
Photograph by Beatrice Blackwood. Copyright Pitt Rivers Museum, BB B1 98.

1

Fig. 2 Photograph taken by Barbara Freire-Marreco on the Yavapai reservation, McDowell, Arizona, in 1910. Photographer's caption: *Mídamapúla, Yuma Frank's wife, making a large basket, on which she has already worked for two months. Martynia wrapped in a cloth near her. Willow twigs lying near. Water in a saucepan for moistening the work.* Copyright Pitt Rivers Museum. V.125

a wide variety of exquisite forms being produced. The range of basketry materials used across North, Central and South America is extensive. The cultural groups involved are extremely diverse and we have taken the opportunity to examine each culture area separately with the help of the experts who have contributed chapters to this book.

It is relatively easy for museums to acquire baskets. They are attractive enough to appeal to the most casual of collectors. They are often inexpensive: basketmaking remains an undervalued craft even today, even in our Western society. Baskets are light, flexible, virtually unbreakable, easily accommodated in a traveller's luggage. They come in various sizes so that the smaller ones can be (and often are) selected for easy transport home.

This selection process works two ways. Travellers choose what will fit into their baggage:

basketmakers, sensing a good market, develop ranges of small, fancy baskets made especially for sale. The forms and patterns may start out as copies of larger baskets in regular use, but often they move in completely new directions. The tourist does not need a burden basket, but she might use a shopper. Shapes are more appealing if she can relate them to something in her own culture. Patterns are insignificant so long as they are believed to be "Indian", so tourist baskets can become a vehicle for experimental, non-traditional designs. Many of the American baskets in the Pitt Rivers Museum's collection were made specifically for sale to Europeans, but this does not make them any less interesting.

The Native American baskets in this exhibition have been acquired gradually throughout the century of the Museum's existence. While many of them form part of comprehensive collections made in particular areas, there was no attempt in the early years to collect systematically from the Americas as a whole. Our baskets reflect the travels and experiences of their collectors and a certain degree of bias is therefore inevitable. Some cultural groups are well represented, while for others we hold sparse collections or nothing at all. Efforts to redress the balance were made by Beatrice Blackwood in her wide-ranging acquisitions from Denver Art Museum in 1946 and 1948; contemporary collections made in 1991 by Ann McMullen, Penny Dransart and Linda Mowat have also helped to expand our Northeastern, Southeastern and Southwestern holdings. However, there are still no baskets from the Plains, where the art of basketmaking disappeared early, leaving few traces; our Californian collections are not comprehensive; and there is only one Inuit basket in the collection (Fig. 7). While recognizing these deficiencies we nevertheless hope to present a broad overview of Native American basketry, yesterday and today.

The collectors of our baskets represent many walks of life. Some of the earliest pieces were collected in California by Captain Frederick William Beechey during the exploratory and scientific voyage of HMS "Blossom" in 1826-27. Dr. Frederick Dally, a dental surgeon and a talented photographer, collected around Vancouver in the 1860s. Missionary collectors include the Rev. Charles Harrison, who worked with the Haida in the Queen Charlotte Islands of British Columbia in the 1880s; and the Rev. James Williams, who lived among the Macusi Indians of Guyana from 1907-1913. Important collectors of material culture in addition to General Pitt Rivers himself include Dr. C.F. Newcombe, H.G. Beasley and J.T. Hooper.

Early anthropological collectors include Franz Boas, who visited the Northwest Coast in the 1880s and 90s; and Barbara Freire-Marreco, one of the first students of anthropology at the Pitt Rivers Museum, who went to the Southwest between 1910 and 1913. Freire-Marreco's documentation of her collection is particularly detailed and sensitive (Fig. 2). Beatrice Blackwood, who devoted her whole life to the Museum, made collecting trips to Canada, the United States (Fig. 1) and Mexico during the 1920s and 30s. Contemporary anthropologists Audrey Butt Colson, Marcus Colchester, Peter Rivière and Marianne Schrimpff have made collections for the Museum in South America.

These scholars have provided detailed documentation for their collections. They remind us that behind every basket is a basketmaker: the woman or man who gathered the raw materials, prepared them with care and constructed the form that, whatever its original purpose, has now become in addition a work of art, a piece of sculpture. But many of the old basketmakers are anonymous. Like most of the artists who made the beautiful objects in the Pitt Rivers Museum, their names were never recorded or thought important. They passed on the skills and traditions of their people from generation to generation, but the signatures on their work - a particular start to a coil basket, a particular finish to a rim - remain illegible to the uninitiated. Contemporary basketmakers, maintaining and reviving skills that in some cases have faced extinction, are at last beginning to receive some of the acclaim due to their craftsmanship and that of their ancestors. It is our hope that this exhibition and this book will bring more people to understand, admire, respect and ponder the art of the basketmaker.

Fig. 3.1 Wicker weaving

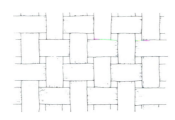

Fig. 3.2 Chequer weaving or plaiting

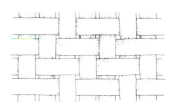

Fig. 3.3 Twill weaving or plaiting

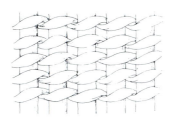

Fig. 3.4 Twining

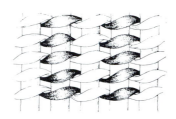

Fig. 3.5 Twining with wefts of different colours

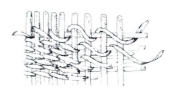

Fig. 3.6 Wrapped twining

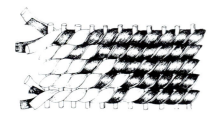

Fig. 3.7 Twining with overlay

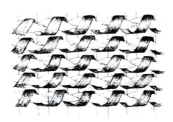

Fig. 3.8 False embroidery

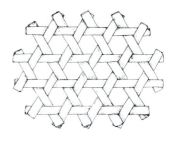

Fig. 3.9 Hexagonal plaiting

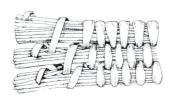

Fig. 3.10 Coiling

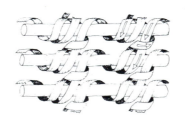

Fig. 3.11 Space coiling

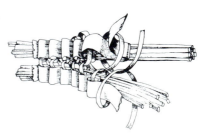

Fig. 1.12 Imbrication

A Guide to Basketmaking

by Linda Mowat

Before a basket can be made, its components must be gathered and prepared for use. For a Native American basketmaker this can take as much time as constructing the basket itself, or even longer. Materials must be gathered at the right time of year and it may be necessary to travel a considerable distance to find them. Hard physical labour can be involved in collecting wood, shoots, roots, bark, grasses and leaves. Removal of extraneous matter, splitting or gauging into suitable widths and dyeing with natural or even chemical dyes are all time consuming processes. Prepared materials must be dried and stored correctly so that they do not decay and before use they may need soaking to restore their flexibility. Only after all this preparation can the business of basketmaking begin.

Many excellent publications already in existence (e.g. Adovasio 1977; Boas 1928; Emmons 1903; James 1909; Larsen 1986; Mason 1904; McMullen & Handsman 1987; O'Neale 1932; Tanner 1983; Roth 1924) describe and illustrate basketmaking techniques in considerable detail and it is not the aim of this chapter to attempt a complete survey of basketry technology. The basic processes will however be briefly outlined as a guide to understanding the construction of the baskets described in this book.

One problem with any guide of this nature lies in the terminology to be employed. While makers and students of basketry are in general agreement concerning the concepts of basketmaking, no universal set of terms has been adopted. This problem becomes particularly acute when preparing a catalogue of American baskets in a British museum, as terms tend to vary on both sides of the Atlantic as well as among scholars, between scholars and basketmakers, and among basketmakers themselves.

Another problem with a brief guide is that it can make the processes themselves appear more simple than they are. While the principles are easy enough to understand, their application is a different matter. A skilled basketmaker has had years of practice, the learning process often beginning in early childhood. Although still universally undervalued, the art of the basketmaker merits equal status with that of the potter, weaver, sculptor, metalsmith and painter.

Weaving Processes

In broad terms all baskets are often described as "woven" and "weaving" may be synonymous with "making" when basketry is loosely discussed. More accurately, weaving is a process where two sets of elements are interlaced at right angles, one set (the **warp**) remaining passive while the other set (the **weft**) passes actively over and under the warp in various ways. Basketmakers often refer to the weft strands as "weavers"; the warp strands may be called "standards". Warp and weft may be of the same or different materials and widths. Baskets are woven without the aid of a loom to keep the warps under tension.

In **wicker weaving** a weft row passes over one warp or group of warps and under the next, over, under, over, under. In the next passage the weft reverses this action, passing under, over, under, over the same warps. The third row repeats the action of the first, and so on to produce an interlaced fabric. This technique is also called "stake and strand", the stake being the warp and the strand the weft. In wicker the weft is thinner than the warp (Figs. 3.1, 116).

Chequer weaving is exactly the same as wicker but warp and weft are the same width, giving a pattern of squares or checks (Fig. 3.2).

Twill weaving is a variation where the weft passes over and under a certain combination of

5

warps, e.g. over two, under one. Each successive row shifts to the left or right, resulting in a diagonal pattern on the basket (Fig. 1.3)

Overlay may be used to decorate woven baskets by inserting an extra element, usually a weft, into the structure. Looping and twisting of the overlay can produce three-dimensional effects such as the "curlicue", "wart weave" or "porcupine" baskets of the Northeast (Figs. 4, 29-30, Plate 2).

Wicker, chequer and twill baskets are woven over wooden moulds in the Northeast of North America. Wicker is also found in the Southwest, particularly on the plaques made by the Hopi of Third Mesa (front cover, Figs. 96-97, Plate 7), in the Southeast, in Middle America, in the Andes and occasionally in the Amazon.

Twined Weaving Processes

Twining is a weaving process using two or more flexible wefts simultaneously which cross at intervals between the warps. In the simplest form of twining two wefts cross between each warp (Fig. 3.4). If the two surfaces of the weft are of contrasting colours (as when the bark is left on), twisting on the inside of the basket can bring either colour to the outside as desired. Twining with wefts of contrasting colours results in the colours showing alternately on the surface of the basket (Fig. 3.5).

In **twill twining** the wefts cross between groups of two or more warps. Each successive row shifts to left or right, resulting in a diagonal pattern on the basket (Plate 1, Fig. 48).

Wrapped twining is a variation in which one weft element is passive while the other binds it to the warps (Fig. 3.6). This technique is employed with different coloured wefts on the tiny souvenir baskets made by the Nuu-Chah-Nulth of the Northwest Coast (Fig. 41).

Overlay may be used to decorate twined baskets. The structural ground wefts are doubled in places by overlaying with weft of a different colour or material. Ground or overlay colour

6

can be brought to the surface as desired by twisting the wefts as they cross (Fig. 3.7). This technique is demonstrated by the Hupa, Karok and Yurok baskets of Northwestern California (Figs. 5, 78-80).

False embroidery is another decorative process. Twining proceeds with two wefts as usual but a third, decorative strand is wrapped around the weft between each cross on the outside of the basket only (Fig. 3.8). False embroidery in elaborate patterns can be seen on Tlingit baskets from the Northwest Coast (Fig. 46).

Twined baskets, particularly on the west coast of North America, may be so finely and tightly made that they are watertight. In California they were used for cooking with hot stones, and for serving soup. Twined baskets are also found in the Southwest, Middle America, the Andes and the Amazon.

Plaiting processes

Plaiting produces a similar effect to weaving but there is no distinction between warp and weft. In plaiting, all elements are equally active and tend to be of the same material and width. In diagonal or bias plaiting the elements which form the base of the basket are also plaited together to form its walls. However, many baskets with plaited bases have walls woven with additional wefts, thus combining two constructional techniques.

In **chequer plaiting** each element passes over one, under one of the opposing set, resulting in a pattern of regular squares or checks (c.f. Fig. 3.2).

In **twill plaiting** each element passes over and under a certain combination of the opposing set, e.g. over three, under two. Each successive row shifts to left or right, resulting in a diagonal pattern on the basket (c.f. Figs. 3.3; see also Fig. 8).

Hexagonal plaiting or **three strand plaiting** involves three active sets of elements interlocking with one another (Fig. 3.9). Four strand plaiting is also found (Fig. 159).

Doubleweave is a complex version of diago-

Fig. 4 **Canada, Nova Scotia, near Monkton, Northeast Woodlands.** Woven basket of ash splints with sweetgrass trim on rim and handle. Overlay decoration in pink splints (aniline dye). H: 100 mm; dia: 100 mm. Probably early twentieth century. Donated by Anne Walker, 1991. 1991.23.2

Fig. 5 **USA, NW California, Hupa.** Twined basket with warp of hazel shoots and weft of split conifer root. Overlay pattern in bear grass (white) and maidenhair fern (black). Used for serving acorn soup, traces of which adhere to the inside. H: 120 mm; dia: 205 mm. Collected in 1889 by J. Curtin for the US National Museum (No. 131152). Donated by the Royal Gardens, Kew. 1892.2.2.

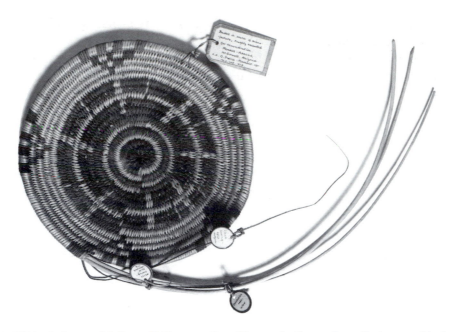

Fig. 6 **USA, Arizona, McDowell Reservation, Yavapai.** Start of a coiled tray with three-rod willow and cottonwood foundation sewn with split cottonwood and martynia. Coiled to the left, showing the stitches passing through the uppermost foundation rod of the preceding coil. Dia: 165 mm. Labelled by collector. Collected by Barbara Freire-Marreco, 1910. 1911.86.110.

Fig. 7 **Canada, Northwest Territories, Cumberland Sound, Inuit.** Oval coiled basket of grass, with bundle foundation. Coiled to the right. H: 30 mm; L: 125 mm. H.G. Beasley collection (formerly in the colection of York Museum). 1954.9.109

nal plaiting particularly favoured by Southeastern and Mexican basketmakers. A double-walled basket is plaited by beginning with the base of the inner layer and ending with the base of the outer layer (Fig. 13, Plate 6).

Plaited baskets occur throughout Middle and South America. A wide range is produced in the Amazon region, where palm leaves are often used to create unusual shapes (Fig. 158). They are also found in the Southeast of North America, in the Southwest and on the Northwest coast. Plaiting is used for bases in the Northeast.

Sewing Processes

Coiling is a sewing process in which baskets are built up spirally from the centre (Figs. 6-7, Plate 5). The two elements involved are the **foundation**, which may be a single rod, a group of rods, a bundle, or a combination of rods and bundle, depending on resources and the function of the basket; and the **sewing material** used to simultaneously wrap the foundation and stitch the coils together (Fig. 3.10). The structure of the foundation and the manner of stitching can provide valuable clues to the provenance of a coiled basket. An awl is needed to pierce the foundation so that the sewing material can pass through it. Baskets may be coiled to the right or to the left, depending usually on cultural preference but also sometimes on whether the maker is right or left handed. The direction of coil is always determined from the working surface of the basket which may be inside or outside, depending on shape and function. Coiled baskets, particularly in California, may be so tightly made that they will hold water. Decoration may be applied by the use of different coloured sewing material (Figs. 89-92, 99-104) or by attaching feathers, beads or shell pendants (Figs. 66-67).

In **closed coiling** the foundation is completely covered by the sewing material. This is the case with most old and traditionally made coiled baskets (e.g. Figs. 92-93)

In **open coiling** stitches are spaced to reveal the foundation as a design feature. Spacing the stitches speeds up construction, but the end product is not as strong as a close coiled basket. Open coiled baskets for the tourist trade are made by the Tohono O'Odham of the Southwest (Fig. 108), the Coushatta, Seminole and Miccosukee of the Southeast and also by the Inuit and Tlingit of Alaska.

In **space coiling** the foundation is wrapped with the sewing material a number of times between each stitch, producing an openwork effect (Fig.3.11). This technique is clearly shown on Otomí baskets from Mexico (Plate 10, Fig. 119).

Imbrication is a decorative process used on coiled baskets. An element of bark or grass is incorporated into the structure as sewing proceeds, being caught by each stitch and then pleated to cover that stitch completely on the outside of the basket only (Fig. 3.12). This technique is peculiar to the Plateau peoples of the Northwest and can be seen in the baskets made by the Chilcotin, Salish and Klickitat (Figs. 34-37).

Hats are made in Middle and South America by coiling plaited strips of palm leaf. The coils are overlapped and joined with flat stitches rather than being wrapped with the sewing material (Figs. 128-131).

Coiled baskets are found among the Inuit in Northern Canada and among the Plateau groups of the Northwest. They are also found in California, the Southwest, the Southeast, Middle America and the Andes.

9

Red Earth People and Southeastern Basketry

by Rayna Green

My people are rivercane and palmetto people, people of buckbrush and honeysuckle, people of oak, maple and hickory. Southeastern peoples always made baskets, no matter whether we lived in the lowland deltas and swamps or in the upland mountains and hills. In some ways, our baskets were homely things, never developing into the finely detailed, feathered works of the Paiute and Pomo, the minuscule twining of the Athabaskan and Yurok, or the elaborate ornamentation of the Mohawk. Our baskets sifted flour, sieved cornmeal and seined fish, they held eggs and fruit and trapped eels (Figs. 9, 10). Later, the people converted old burden or pack baskets into large "market" baskets for a modernized life where cars, not mules and horses, carried them into town (Fig. 11). Not much delicacy in these baskets. Still, Cherokees made the frail twined baskets of honeysuckle and buckbrush (Fig. 12) and the demanding, indestructible and complex double-weaves (Fig. 13). The huge Choctaw rivercane carrying or burden baskets with lightning designs cannot be matched anywhere for size and strength and startling design. It's not the complexity or elaboration that matters, however. Southeastern baskets are the very essence of functionality. Solid and sturdy, they do the jobs for which they were intended. They are durable, like the women and men who weave them, Red Earth People, Oklahumma, from Georgia and Louisiana, from Mississippi and the Carolinas.

The names of these Red Earth people populate the landscape of the Southeast, even though many of those peoples no longer exist on the Red Earth. Alibamu, Atakapa, Coasati (Coushatta), Catawba, Choctaw, Cherokee, Creek, Opelonsas, Seminole, Houma, Ofo, Chitimacha, Acolapissa, Guale, Biloxi, Monacan, Pamunkey, Powhatan, Mattaponi, Pascagoula, Timucuan, Natchez. In the old times when we were what scholars call Mississippian peoples, much of the basketmaking skill went into the making of mats, for bedding, for flooring, for seating, for lining walls (Fig. 8). Almost all the peoples of the Southeast used rushes and cane, found in and near the waterways of the South. They lined the walls of ceremonial houses with these mats; often the cane or rush splints were dyed and arranged in designs on the mats. Women brought beautiful mats for visitors to seat themselves, and mats kept the rain from coming in ceremonial and ordinary houses alike. As times changed the way they lived, however, the brush arbours, chickees and open-sided houses yielded to the log cabins and frame structures of the white man, houses with walls and floors that did not require matting.

Later, they made every kind of basket imaginable, from "elbow" baskets to carry small items, to medicine gathering baskets for taking plants used in healing, to baskets used to carry a portable meal, the first lunch baskets. Still later in the nineteenth century some basket forms, made since the coming of Europeans, show European forms and both Indian and white basketmakers made these. The ridged saddle or pack basket, the double bottomed egg or "Granny's Fanny" - these oak and hickory baskets are shared by Indians and their white neighbours and methods of making and finishing them are the same (Fig. 14). Similarly nowadays, people make market and purse baskets with handles, laundry baskets and hanging baskets for walls.

Fig. 8 **USA, North Carolina, Cherokee.** Twill plaited mat of rivercane. Pattern in natural dyes: black (butternut root) and red (bloodroot). L: 380 mm; W: 390 mm. Made by Mrs. Rowena Bradley, 1991. Collected by Linda Mowat. 1991.35.34.

Fig. 9 **USA, Louisiana, Choctaw.** Twill plaited basket of rivercane. Design in natural dyes: green (peach leaves), yellow (wild coreopsis) and brown (walnut leaves). For carrying corn meal. H: 140 mm; dia: 350 mm. Purchased by Beatrice Blackwood from the Indian Arts and Crafts Board, Golden Gate Exposition, San Francisco, 1939. 1939.8.9B.

Fig. 10 **USA, Louisiana, Choctaw.** Plaited sieve of undyed rivercane. Used for sifting corn meal after pounding in a mortar to remove the husks. L: 350 mm; W: 340 mm. Purchased by Beatrice Blackwood from the Indian Arts and Crafts Board, Golden Gate Exposition, San Francisco, 1939. 1939.8.13B

Fig. 11 **USA, North Carolina, Cherokee.** Market basket of rivercane with plaited base and twill woven sides. Pattern in natural dyes: black (walnut bark) and red (bloodroot). Rim lashed with hickory. Hickory handle. H: 370 mm; L: 510 mm; W: 310 mm. Purchased by Beatrice Blackwood from the Indian Arts and Crafts Board, Golden Gate Exposition, San Francisco, 1939. 1939.8.6B

Fig. 12 **USA, Oklahoma, Cherokee.** Round wicker basket of buckbrush woven in double-wall technique with scalloped rim. H: 210 mm; dia: 330 mm. Purchased by Beatrice Blackwood from the Indian Arts and Crafts Board, Golden Gate Exposition, San Francisco, 1939. 1939.8.5B

Fig. 13 **USA, North Carolina, Cherokee.** Twill plaited basket of rivercane. Double-weave technique with two layers plaited as one, beginning in the centre of the inner layer and ending in the centre of the outer layer. Design in black (walnut bark dye). H: 123 mm; dia: 205 mm. Purchased by Beatrice Blackwood from the Indian Arts & Crafts Board, Golden Gate Exposition, San Francisco, 1939. 1939.8.4B.

Fig. 14 **USA, North Carolina, Cherokee.** Rib basket woven of white oak. Design in natural dyes: black (walnut) and red (bloodroot). Made by Mrs. Annie James, 1991. Collected by Linda Mowat. 1991.35.37.

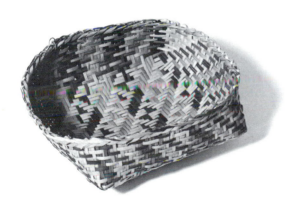

Fig. 15 **USA, Louisiana, Chitimacha.** Square shallow twill plaited basket of rivercane. Design in red (probably bloodroot) and black (walnut bark). H: 50 mm; L: 140 mm. From Denver Art Museum by exchange. 1948.12.75.

Fig. 16 **USA, Southeast, Houma.** Coiled oval basket with bundle foundation sewn with palmetto. Coiled anticlockwise. Plaited handle. Design of four diamonds in pink. Used as a woman's work basket. H: 200 mm; L: 275 mm; W: 153 mm. From Denver Art Museum by exchange (F.G. Speck collection). 1949.3.27

Fig 17 **USA, Louisiana, Choctaw.** Twill plaited "heart-shaped" basket of rivercane with design in natural dyes: yellow (wild coreopsis) and black (walnut bark). Used for giving presents. H: 375 mm; W: 350 mm; D: 155 mm. Purchased by Beatrice Blackwood from the Indian Arts & Crafts Board, Golden Gate Exposition, San Francisco, 1939. 1939.8.10B

Fig. 18 **USA, North Carolina, Cherokee.** Deep storage basket of white oak splints. Plaited base and woven walls. Design in black and brown (walnut bark dye). H: 270 mm; rim dia: 240 mm. Purchased by Beatrice Blackwood from the Indian Arts & Crafts Board, Golden Gate Exposition, San Francisco, 1939. 1939.8.7B

14

But other shapes and certainly designs remained distinctively tribal (Figs. 15, 17).

Southeastern Indian women, and occasionally men, wove and now weave baskets using several methods: wicker and checkwork weaving (Fig. 18), twilling (mostly for cane baskets), coiling with grasses and rushes (Fig. 16) and plaiting. For these baskets, they made splints stripped out from the surface of cane and from the trunks of white oak, bark from the hickory tree, honeysuckle and buckbrush branches stripped of their bark and leaves, pine needles from the white pine. The people made dyes of black from sumac and black walnut, brown from the butternut tree, purple from the berries of mulberry, pokeweed and maple, red from the "hair plant", wild peach and red oak, yellow from "puccoon" (bloodroot) roots and coreopsis flowers, green from peach leaves. And they wove designs into the basketry that were often as old as their Mississippian ancestors: designs at Eastern Cherokee, for instance, with names like "Flowing Water", "Chief's Daughter", "Thunder and Lightning", the "Big Diamond", "Man in the Coffin", "Broken Heart", "Cross on the Hill".

Some forms - once needed for carrying and serving breads, flour and grain sifters of all kinds, certain kinds of burden baskets and fish traps - these have virtually disappeared though they were staples of basket making even through the nineteenth century. Other kinds disappeared or have been threatened because the materials from which they are made are threatened. Rivercane, for example, is a highly endangered resource, threatened by the extensive building of roads and the destructive properties of carbon monoxide emissions from automobiles which attack and destroy cane. The Eastern Cherokees have had an agreement with people in Kentucky since the 1950s to come and gather cane there, the resource being virtually depleted in the Carolinas.

Still, the people have revived some types and forms of basketry because they found an external, usually a tourist market for some of the old

forms. In the sixties and seventies, economic development and cultural revival projects sponsored by the government and by tribes brought many back to basketmaking. Today, Southeastern Native peoples, primarily those in North Carolina, Louisiana, Mississippi, East Texas and Oklahoma, make baskets. While the majority are made for the tourist or external trade, once again they can be created for internal use. Increasingly today, Native peoples themselves want the old and new forms of baskets, so basketry is a healthy art form in the Southeast in spite of the losses in the forms and practices. Basketmakers occasionally produce the old forms, just like jewellery makers have revived the older shell jewellery and potters some of the Mississippian styles and designs (Figs. 19, 20). Some revival is, without doubt, connected with religious, linguistic and other forms of cultural revitalization; some revival connects itself with an art market deeply self-conscious about innovation and tradition; another piece connects itself to economic imperatives; yet another part of revival reflects a profound drive toward cultural nationalism in American Indian cultures. Whatever the impetus, in Cherokee country, both in North Carolina and Oklahoma, in Choctaw, Houma, Alabama-Coushatta and Chitimacha country, basketmaking thrives in the Southeast. As long as there is fibre, there will be baskets.

My grandmother could make baskets; though she made fewer and fewer of them as I got older. When I was a little girl, I would go with her, down in Southeastern Oklahoma - with my other grandmother, who was German, and my young Choctaw friend, Pete (a girl) - to gather dye plants and buckbrush and honeysuckle. Those were the kind she made. I saw her use sifting baskets for some of the cornmeal we got, for the hominy flour she used to use in bean bread. She was a midwife, a "granny woman", as they called them in the Upland South. So, besides her skill in making baskets, plants were part of her life. Some she'd make medicine out of; others were for dyes. She didn't like to talk about these things much, and I wasn't supposed to ask, just watch and observe and, I suppose, learn if I wanted to do so. So, I followed her - she was called Gahno, Cherokee for sister, sometimes Dude, because she'd run away to the city. Gahno and Mommy and Pete and I would go out in the brush to pick wild plums and other things. I hated gathering black walnuts because they would stain my hands and clothes with a sticky substance, and because they were hard to crack and eat. But mulberries tasted wonderful and the pokeberries were juicy and fat and I loved the purple stain they both made on my fingers.

I got to hold collecting baskets, but I didn't get to pick plants because that required special knowledge about how to take them from the ground or the main plant. I know a few words of the prayers she said when gathering plants, some fragments of the chants she would make so that the medicines would be good and do their work. If we were gathering honeysuckle, I could coil it in a circle for storing and carrying. Then, I helped strip the honeysuckle of its leaves and twigs, and later, after it was soaked and boiled, I could strip it off bark. We did the same thing with hickory. My Grandmother later in her life took the Baptist church more seriously than before, and she quit making medicines because the preachers told her it was heathen nonsense. Then arthritis made her hands hurt and she stopped making baskets. I don't even have one of my Gahno's baskets. They were given away, one by one, but I remember her hands, the feel of the baskets I held for gathering, the stains of walnuts and pokeberries, the stories they would tell when we were out together some forty years ago.

Even if I don't know all the words to say for the plants and if I don't know how to make the baskets, I am still part of the world that weaves these things of the past, for the future. My house is filled with baskets, old and new, from Red Earth People. I use them; still, you might call them art. Those baskets hold flowers and dried herbs now. One holds cornmeal from home. When I have guests, I serve bread in some of them, just as they did in Tsa-la-gi country a long time ago. A pine needle armadillo and turtle keep guard over other animals made from pottery. They tell histories. On a rainy day, a smell comes up from them that is the smell of Red Earth, of swamp and mountain, a smell of pokeberry and peach trees. I hear the women talking about making conuchi (a porridge of hominy and hickory nuts), about someone's hard pregnancy, about the Choctaw brush arbour sing we'd go to next month over in McCurtain County. Not ever simply utensils, they hold memory and prayers for an Indian future.

16

Fig. 19 **USA, North Carolina, Cherokee.** Lidded basket, twill plaited from rivercane in double-weave technique. Pattern in natural dyes. This basket dates from the 18th century and is one of the oldest known Cherokee double-weave baskets. British Museum: Sloane Collection 1218.

Fig. 20 **USA, North Carolina, Cherokee.** Lidded basket, twill plaited from rivercane in double-weave technique. Pattern in natural dyes. H: 195 mm; L: 380 m; W: 200 mm. Made by Mrs. Lottie Stamper in the 1940s, based on a photograph of an 18th century Cherokee basket in the British Museum (above). In the collection of the Indian Arts and Crafts Board. W-52.19.64.

Fig. 21   Donald Sanipass, Micmac, beating black-ash splints to separate the annual rings, or "grains". Robert Abbe Museum, Bar Harbor, Maine, summer 1991. Photo by Ann McMullen.

Talking Through Baskets:
Meaning, Production and Identity in the Northeast Woodlands
by Ann McMullen

[It is] difficult to speak of Native American bas-ket-making as just a craft or an art form. To view basketry from merely one perspective is to see only the material world and to forget about the spiritu-ality of its making (Lamb Richmond 1987:127).

Since first seen by Europeans, Native bas-ketry has been a source of wonder. That Native Americans, "living on the edge," skilfully wove baskets was not surprising; that they *decorated* objects was remarkable and helped convince early writers of Native peoples' humanity. Today, Native basketry is no less remarkable; where women decorated grass bags, today Native people make baskets as survival and expression: where meaning was embodied in designs, today basketmaking itself allows Native people a voice in society.

This paper explores changing function and meaning of Northeastern basketry. Within the context of material culture analyses and colo-nialism, I discuss the "origins" of woodsplint basketry and later commercialization, commer-cial and utilitarian basket traditions and their economic and symbolic position. The Native conception of baskets as a link to tradition will be explored along with learning basketmaking as a family and group tradition and the objectifi-cation and curation of baskets by Native people.

While artefact studies have increased recent-ly, not all regions and traditions are viewed equally; some categories must overcome invisi-bility or perception as "tourist" arts or intro-duced traditions. Woodsplint basketry has been so stigmatized, and has only recently been rec-ognized as potentially meaningful (McMullen and Handsman 1987). A key problem in Native American studies has been consideration of "decorative arts", earlier differentiated as undecorated versus decorated (Speck 1976), no matter what their use. Similarly, collectors' and curators' preference for decorated objects led to museum bias against "ordinary" material (King 1982:9; Porter 1990:10). Since objects made for sale often lack provenance, they can bc seen as art, further dehumanizing them. While such per-ception has "ennobled" objects in the minds of collectors, categorization as "primitive art" leads to neglect of history, change, and the role of individuals (Handsman 1987:147; Price 1989:5).

Recent Northeastern material culture studies have focused on Native people - "extinct" or assimilated - who maintained a regional pres-ence and significant aspects of culture (Porter 1985; Lester 1987a; McMullen and Handsman 1987), increasing recognition of "invisible" Native communities (McMullen 1991). Baskets, especially, have proved important in exploring everyday life (Porter 1985:25; McMullen and Handsman 1987). While scholars have fought "invisibility", decades of work label Northeastern baskets artless products of cultureless remnants:

The Algonquians in early historic days were expert basket makers. The excellence and vari-ety of the old basket work of the New England Indians ... is represented to-day only by the degenerate splint basketry which is not worthy of a place upon the shelves of a museum (Willoughby 1902:31-32).

This view is not confined to the early twenti-eth century: "Eastern North America is a region in which basketry is of comparatively minor importance ... Woodsplint basketry has become an Indian art, though its origins are plainly post-European" (Feest 1980:107). Feest and others seldom illustrate splint basketry, calling it degraded: "In all this area, decoration is practi-cally non-existent. The art is now purely utili-tarian" (Feder 1933).

Disregard for splint basketry stems from its identification as introduced. Jonathan King cites the "apparent reluctance of [European] collectors to obtain material showing evidence of European materials and ideas", including splint baskets (King 1982:10). As the label "forgery" changes critics' opinions (Price 1989:21), the perception of splint basketry's introduction has affected scholarship. While European influence on other Native arts has not made them disreputable, many consider splint basketry a bastard child of colonialism despite its position in Native societies.

While basketry is a symbol of identity, baskets as sale items provided a bridge between worlds. Native people reacted to consumers, but production helped maintain Native identity, serving as a double reference to Native and Victorian ideas (Brandford 1984:10; Dixon 1990:11). European reactions to Native basketry were diverse: baskets were utilitarian products of fringe members of American society, oddities signifying Victorian perceptions of Native people (Phillips 1989:52; Porter 1990:3) or fitting Euro-American expectations about primitive art (Price 1989). Anthropologists saw basketry as a marker of traditional culture, but anthropology's power to construct as well as record images suggests that historic photographs of Native people with baskets and museum collections require critical scrutiny.

Despite the interpretative potential of material culture to inform everyday life, meaning depends on contexts of production, use, and sale. Setting baskets within economic and social contexts is necessary: baskets are part of the history of capitalism, and "may reflect how Native Americans thought and behaved during this period of profound change" (Handsman and McMullen 1987:23). Style changes must be contextualized to analyze Native reactions, for instance, the growth of eighteenth-century amalgamated communities often yielded individual rather than group reactions (Brandford 1984:7; McMullen and Handsman 1987).

20

Basketry at contact and the origins of splint basketry

Since 1975, the origins of woodsplint basketry have been hotly debated. While early students admitted splint basketry's historic spread, Ted Brasser (1975) stated Swedish and German settlers introduced it before 1712 in the mid-Atlantic, tracing its spread throughout the Northeast. Brasser's work is not without its critics. Although he used linguistic evidence (Algonkian words for "basket" are similar; names for splint containers different [Brasser 1975:7]), Ruth Whitehead (1980) claimed a Micmac word for making splints as proof of Native origin. Whitehead (1980) and Kathryn Bardwell (1986) challenged Brasser's statement that splint basketmaking was impossible without metal tools, also publishing splint basketry examples predating Brasser's references for specific locales. Others have brought Native people into the argument: some contradict Brasser (Holland 1983:1; Lester 1987a), while many disagree over the aboriginality of splint basketry (McBride 1990:11). Whitehead, Bardwell, and others would like to *prove* splint basketry existed before European contact, but the evidence does not hold up, except fragments from seventeenth-century Seneca and Susquehannock graves (Bardwell 1986; McMullen and Handsman 1987). Small narrow-splint containers, like corn-processing baskets (Fig. 27), may have existed before contact (McMullen and Handsman 1987), and splint basketry may have been *transformed* by European contact rather than *introduced* by it.

The impact of splint basketry on earlier technologies - twined basketry and birchbark containers - has seldom been addressed. While splint basketry replaced twining and birchbark artefacts (Brandford 1984:8; King 1982:25), evidence suggests Native people made splint baskets commercially, preferring twined baskets or bark containers (Morgan 1962:383; Parker 1983:57). There is a great deal to be done to

Fig. 22 Donald Sanipass, Micmac, using a drawhorse and drawknife to smooth the quartered log before beating. The same techniques are used in riving splints and shaping heavier handles and rims. Robert Abbe Museum, Bar Harbor, Maine, summer 1991. Photo by Ann McMullen.

Fig. 23 Mahican covered storage basket, 1800-1850, black ash splints with swabbed and stamped decoration. Typically, Mahican baskets of this period were rectangular, with high sides that tapered slightly toward the rim. The combination of wide and narrow weft splints in the body was common and preferred colour choices reddish-brown and either blue or black. In the collection of the Connecticut Historical Society.

Fig. 24 Wampanoag covered storage basket, c. 1800, ?hickory splints with hand-painted decoration. Unlike groups west of the Connecticut River who swabbed and stamped basket decoration, Native people in SE New England painted wide-splint baskets with multicoloured variants of the basic "medallion" or four-part design. Throughout the 19th century Wampanoag basket decorations were strongly zoned in horizontal bands, and were later separated by the insertion of narrow weft splints. While this early basket is painted with brown, green and pink, later Wampanoag basketmakers used only brown and black. In the collection of the Connecticut Historical Society.

Fig. 25 Schaghticoke covered storage basket, c. 1875, black ash splints with swabbed and hand-painted red-brown and blue designs. As a result of the creation of amalgamated communities in the 18th and 19th centuries, Schaghticoke basketmakers combined different "tribal" chatacteristics in their basketry, joining traditional rectangular Mahican forms with the tapered shoulder common to the Paugussett. This basket has been attributed to the Cockshure family, who moved from the Housatonic Valley west into New York State in 1799. In the collection of the Connecticut Historical Society.

Fig. 26 Pequot bail-handled work basket, black ash spints with pink and blue handpainted designs. Along with traditional forms like the covered storage basket, 18th and 19th century basketmakers created a variety of forms for home and farm use. Handled forms like this were commonly used in the home and made for sale to whites and were used for garden produce, berrying, etc. In the collection of the Connecticut Historical Society.

document survival of these industries.

Also, we can re-examine popular non-splint basketry traditions. As before, anthropological regard plummets for "tourist" industries, yet we should ask whether coiled grass and plaited straw basketry may, like woodsplint basketry, be transformed Native technologies rather than introductions. Coiled grass basketry, recorded among Great Lakes groups, the Gay Head Wampanoag, the Canadian Delaware and perhaps the Huron, was defended as a survival of a precontact industry. Similarly, Gladys Tantaquidgeon suggested that mass-produced Wampanoag rye-straw basket traditions related to those of the Delaware and Mohegan (Tantaquidgeon 1930a, 1930b). Some Wampanoag basketmakers also made splint baskets, but relations between splint and other basket industries must be clarified.

Technology and the Production of Woodsplint Basketry

Splint baskets were commonly made of black ash *(Fraxinus nigra)* or white oak *(Quercus alba)*, although other materials were used: white cedar, black spruce, or maple in the Maritimes (Whitehead 1980:57), and hickory or maple in southern New England (McMullen 1990). The Menomini were said to use black elm (James 1972:70; Hoffman 1970:259).

Different materials required different splint-getting procedures. Black ash, maple, hickory, and black elm logs were beaten to separate the annual rings (called grains), then smoothed with a knife. Some Maritime groups, especially the Micmac, quarter the log, trim it square, and beat each section (Fig. 21). White oak logs (and perhaps hickory) were split using a froe, then smoothed using a drawhorse and drawknife (Fig. 22). This process - riving - may have been introduced in the Pennsylvania Dutch country (Brasser 1975); Mason (1988:64-65) states that it was used by the Abenaki. Eastern New England groups used a horse and drawknife to prepare splints, while western groups beat black ash and maple logs. Bardwell (1986) has suggested that beating technology, not recorded in Europe, is purely aboriginal.

Whatever the origins of splint-getting technology, historic basketmaking developed from joining European and Native technologies (Bardwell 1986:63). As Brasser (1975:12) has suggested:

Swedish woodsplint basketry was near identical to the Indian product ... Both Swedes and Indians used special tools, manufactured wide splints, utilized these in identical techniques, creating the same forms in basketry, and both decorated the splints with painted designs.

While Speck called painted decorations "an early type of Algonkian art" (1915a:10), Brasser believes that "historical basket painting and stamping were European folk art techniques, adapted to an aboriginal decorative art tradition" (1975:4). Elsewhere, I have suggested that stamping (Fig. 23) grew out of painting as a labour-saving device (McMullen 1982:8). As above, the problem is not whether basket decorations were introduced, but what they meant to Native people. This idea will be explored in a later section of this paper.

Besides technology and decoration, some forms were also introduced. Although Brasser allows that covered storage baskets (Figs. 23-25) are early (I have suggested these were like *mokoks* - stitched bark containers [McMullen 1982]), the "melon" or "buttocks" basket, possibly introduced to the Micmac by Bretons (Gordon 1990:27), and other handled forms (Fig. 26) may have resulted from market demand.

The tools used in producing splint baskets show influence from contemporaneous industries. While some used only a knife to prepare splints (Speck 1947:6; Tantaquidgeon and Fawcett 1983, 1987), improved basketmaking tools increased quality and quantity (Speck 1947:5). Basket gauges were perhaps the most important tools, spreading to the Great Lakes and the Iroquois (Mason 1988:273; Lismer 1982:9), and becoming the "most important tools in the [Penobscot] woman's tool kit" (Speck 1976:124). Among the Iroquois and in northern New England, the splitter and the taper-vise became indispensable in producing fancy baskets (McMullen and Handsman 1987). The use of wooden moulds, called "blocks", also brought about uniformity in mass-produced baskets among the Penobscot, Passamaquoddy, and Abenaki (Fig. 28; Pelletier 1982).

Historic Production and Commercialization of Splint Basketry

By 1750 the production of splint baskets by Northeastern Native groups became commonplace, and many relied on their sale for cash if not survival, defining themselves by their ability to make baskets (McMullen 1990, 1991). Use of material culture to maintain identity suggests meaning hinged on how people constructed their group and the value of membership; if Native identity was valued and basketmaking was a signal of Native identity, basketmaking took on meaning as an ethnic symbol. Baskets became a mediating symbol between Native and white culture, and the production of baskets, as a way whites constructed "Indians" (Hicks 1977:13), often became an expectation. While Brasser (1971:86) characterized Native people of the eighteenth and nineteenth centuries as "detribalized tramps", many continued in their homelands with a "traditional" lifestyle and economy: making and selling baskets. Native people maintained distinctions between themselves and other groups through distinctive basket styles (Figs. 23, 26), used to make statements about identity or family lineages. Some used basket decorations as links to the past, including three-banded designs, older organizational principles such as the medallion, even with stamping (McMullen 1987:123), and a grid framework in designs, analogous to the structure of older twined designs (Fig. 24). Some nineteenth-century basketmakers, often separated from reservation economies, devel-
24

oped identifiable personal styles (Fig. 25). Others in southern New England continued within group styles until the early twentieth century.

While the reconstruction of splint basketry's spread after 1712 (Brasser 1975:3) contained references to the manufacture and sale of baskets, the earliest known fragments come from seventeenth-century Seneca graves (Bardwell 1986:60). These suggest that the Seneca made splint containers for their own use and may have sold small forms by the late 1600s (McMullen and Handsman 1987:19). Other commercial endeavours also existed; Whitehead (1980) and Pelletier (1977:6) cite seventeenth-century Micmac and Maliseet sales of bark containers and decorative items, while Native people in Connecticut wove chair seats in the 1730s (Butler 1947:41-42; Trent 1986, pers. comm.). By the mid 1700s Native people near Albany, New York sold narrow-splint baskets (Bardwell 1986:61), and the Moravians encouraged the Schaghticoke to sell baskets on the Housatonic River (Lamb Richmond 1987). The Pequot were also said to have sold baskets and other utensils in the 1800s (Guillette 1979).

Northeastern Native women loaded themselves with baskets and set out to sell them to neighbouring families. The Schaghticoke, separated from white settlements, sent baskets downriver in canoes (Lamb Richmond 1987). These picturesque peddlers were often the subject of artistic (Pelletier 1977; McMullen and Handsman 1987) and literary images:

Bending beneath a load of these fabrics, and often the additional weight of a papoose, or babe, deposited in a large basket, and fastened around the neck with a leathern strap, might be seen, walking through the streets of the town, after a weary journey from their own settlement, the descendants of the former lords of the soil, perhaps the daughters of kings (Sigourney 1824:135).

Basket sales became one way Native people, landless and often without means of support, survived the eighteenth century. In the mid-

Atlantic the Delaware and others, robbed of land by the Walking Purchase and other transactions, took advantage of settlers' need for utilitarian wares (Brawer 1983:72); Native people produced baskets cheaper than those made by settlers or sent from England. Native people were affected by European products, adopting the melon basket (Porter 1985:31) and cylindrical baskets like bandboxes (Eckstorm 1932:29). While changes followed white taste, Native people also tailored forms for wage work, such as harvesting potatoes (Fig. 27; McBride 1990:20). Adaptation was not confined to utilitarian baskets; fancy basketmakers exploited the Victorian penchant for novelty and excessive ornamentation to create unique styles (Fig. 29).

Many basketmakers did not think of basketmaking as separate from sale. Even at the traditional Mohegan Homecoming, baskets and other crafts were sold (Speck 1909:194). Among the Seneca, crafts for sale were seen as "our own work, our means of earning, our living" (Jesse Cornplanter in Hauptman 1979:303). There, sprinkling finished baskets with "basket medicine" ensured their sale (Lismer 1982:33). During the Depression, "[S]ome Micmac ... felt very degraded when they could not sell their baskets and had to trade them for food and clothing" (Pelletier 1979:66). In northern New England and the Maritimes, basketmaking has only recently been seen as other than economic (McBride 1990:ix).

The construction of basketmaking as Native tradition revolves around making baskets as a means of identity but also as survival. Basketmaking, broommaking (Jones 1934:25; Stone 1983); and woodenware (Speck 1909, 1915a; Voight 1965:73-74) allowed Native people to maintain separate lifestyles, supplementing subsistence farming and wage work. The persistence of craft production existed within the context of nineteenth-century Native communities which maintained contacts with whites despite physical isolation (Brasser 1975:30). Overemphasis on established reservations has led to

neglect of these communities and the assumption that Northeastern Native people did not survive into the nineteenth century. Since individuals who sought wage work left reservations (McMullen 1985b:7) and people on some reservations were not allowed to conduct business there (Guillette 1979), Native people and their work might be practically invisible. Despite a climate that discouraged crafts by making it difficult to gather materials or sell products, basketmaking and woodcarving continued into the early twentieth century, the interest of scholars and collectors encouraging production of "traditional" decorated forms through the 1920s (McMullen and Handsman 1987:121). Businesses like the Mashpee Manufacturing Company, which made and sold baskets, brooms, and woodenware (Weinstein 1986:97), continued traditional manufactures.

"We didn't make fancy baskets until we were discovered" (Eunice Crowley in Lester 1987b:48).

In the late nineteenth century, Northeastern tourism grew, encouraging the sale of small, decorated baskets called "fancy baskets" (Fig. 28). By the 1860s, some basketmakers already used decorative weaves - a second warp splint, looped or twisted into curls, rolls, or points - to decorate small commercial baskets (Figs. 28-30, Plate 2). Mass-produced baskets to be shipped were seldom decorated this way because of the risk of damage (Pelletier 1979:59). At about this time commercial dyes became popular on fancy baskets. Increasing use of decorative weaves and dyes was followed by the introduction of sweetgrass (also sweet hay), *Hierochloe odorata* or *Savastana odorata* (Eckstorm 1932:25; Pelletier 1973). The association between sweetgrass and women (Benedict 1982) and sweetgrass and the Longhouse religion (Adams et al. 1990:53) made production of baskets more than economic, and referred back to traditional activities.

Despite Native perception that made fancy baskets a Native art, baskets were commercially valuable and Native ideas about basketry were

25

Fig. 27 Contemporary work baskets.
USA, Maine, Wells, Penobscot. Potato basket by Leslie Ranco, "Chief To-me-kin". H: 280 mm; dia: 365 mm. 1992.1.10
Canada, Quebec, St. Regis, Mohawk Twilled corn washing basket by Cecilia Sunday. H: 275 mm; L: 315 mm; W: 300 mm. 1992.1.11
USA, New York State, Steamburg, Allegany Reserve, Seneca. Work basket by Ruth Watt. H: 190 mm; L 350 mm; W: 230 mm. 1992.1.12
Collected by Ann McMullen, 1991.

Fig. 28 Fancy baskets. Useful forms like the pocketbook and more fanciful shapes such as the cup and saucer are typical of 20th century manufacture. Continuity of production of earlier types and innovations like the vase continue side by side.
USA, Maine, ?Penobscot. Pocketbook of splints and braided sweetgrass. Made c. 1975. H: 260 mm; L: 200 mm; W: 100 mm. 1992.1.7
NE Woodlands, ?Micmac. Splint cup and saucer with sweetgrass trim. H cup: 55 mm; dia saucer 130 mm. 1992.1.1
USA, Maine, ?Penobscot. Vase of splints and braided sweetgrass. Glass liner. H: 115 mm; dia: 100 mm. 1992.1.5
Collected by Ann McMullen, 1991.

Fig. 29 Contemporary Mohawk fancy baskets.
USA , New York State, Hogansburg. Flower basket of splints and braided sweetgrass with "porcupine" overlay. Made by Agnes Garrow. H: 300 mm; dia: 320 mm. 1992.1.14
USA, New York State. Covered sewing basket of splints and braided sweetgrass with "porcupine" overlay. Made by Margaret Terrance. H: 165 mm; dia: 290 mm. 1992.1.13
Collected by Ann McMullen, 1991.

Fig. 30 Contemporary Micmac fancy baskets.
USA, Maine, Limestone. Covered sewing basket of splints with braided sweetgrass. Made by Frank Hanning. H: 170 mm; dia: 200 mm. 1992.1.4
USA, Maine, Caribou. Covered basket with points, lid trimmed with sweetgrass. Made by Jane Zumbrunnen. H: 130 mm; dia: 210 mm. 1992.1.2
Collected by Ann McMullen, 1991.

sometimes subverted by consumer demands (Mason 1988:270; Speck 1976:54; Lismer 1982:10; Carse 1949:45). To ensure sales, Native people travelled to resorts to sell baskets (Pelletier 1982:6; Lester 1987b), often playing on the public's notions and "dressing up" (McMullen and Handsman 1987:32). Basketmakers also made baskets for sale to non-Native catalogue wholesalers. Until 1920, resort and catalogue sales did not conflict, but economic changes in the 1920s eliminated travel, putting basketmakers at the mercy of middlemen who controlled resources and sales (Pelletier 1982). In the 1940s the catalogues and middlemen faded, leaving basketmakers demoralized; some continued to weave and sold their work in local craftshops. Many, lacking material or the means to get it, gave up basketry altogether.

While two traditions existed, "each apparently as old as the other but serving different ends and having different meanings for the persons involved" (McFeat 1987:62), women made decorated baskets, while men made sturdier, undecorated forms for outdoor work. These baskets, called "Yankee" baskets (McMullen and Handsman 1987), are practically indistinguishable from non-Native baskets used in farm and outdoor work.

While Native people in Northern New England, the Maritimes, upstate New York, the Great Lakes, Quebec, and Ontario still make baskets, production in southern New England and the mid-Atlantic ended in the twentieth century. Wage work and decreasing natural resources made basketmaking an occasional endeavour, with few opportunities to pass on the tradition (Porter 1990:8). While other crafts, such as rye-straw basketry, often replaced splint basketry as a survival strategy (McMullen and Handsman 1987), basketmakers on Long Island produced work baskets and perhaps miniatures into the 1940s (Butler 1947:5 4). In the twentieth century, it became increasingly difficult for Native people to succeed while maintaining traditional work and interactions with whites. As an economic venture that began when Native people lost other means of subsistence (Brasser 1975), basketmaking has almost always been a survival skill that yielded little profit:

Basket ash is very difficult to procure, and expensive. A single butt costs over a dollar, and sometimes as much as two dollars. From an ordinary-sized butt ... a smart Indian can make six baskets ... for these he gets forty cents each, $2.40, after having expended perhaps $1.50 for the butt. Impossible for them to make a living at basket making under these circumstances (Reverend John O'Dowd, 1887, in Eckstorm 1932:21).

Despite low profits, basketmaking was a means of support for many Native people after 1890. While some benefited (Pelletier 1982), basketmaking was often simple survival : "My grandmother taught me 'someday this will keep you from going hungry' and it did" (Madeline Shay, in Lester 1987a:37). For the Micmac and others, basketmaking was just one aspect of a modified "seasonal round" of varied, transient work (Konrad 1987:5; McBride 1990). A drop in demand and prices ($0.75 for a potato basket in the 1960s [McBride 1990:40]), led young people to reject commercial basketmaking as hard, demeaning work (Johannsen 1984:182).

Commercially Produced Baskets and their Meanings

In exploring commercial basketry, it is important to recognize the relation between baskets and the idea of traditional life. Basketmaking, foods, and language are seen as most important for judging Native identity. The link between language and basketmaking is specifically mentioned: "Basketmaking is the last of our traditions along with our Micmac language. It was passed down from generations to me and I will pass it along to my children" (Donna Marie Sanipass Stevens, in Sanipass 1990:33).

Like quilting and other arts that have become "Native crafts" because of designs and symbols used, baskets have been redefined as Iroquois crafts *"because they were made by Iroquois"* (Johannsen 1984:182). Tom McFeat defined "Indian work" as that linked to traditional life and the bush, including guiding sport fishermen, making rustic furniture and basketmaking (McFeat 1987:62; see also McBride 1990:33). While maintenance of tradition involves work patterns like those in the past, it is sometimes sufficient to *refer* to the past, i.e. to speak about natural dyes although commercial dyes have been used for decades (Johannsen 1984:134). Beating splints is also traditional behaviour (Johannsen 1984:133) although many now use gas-powered engines to beat or buy prepared splints. Splint-getting is connected to the relation of Indian work to the land - the inalienable rights of Native people:

The Indians were adept in making splint brooms and other articles of wood for household and farm, and were allowed by a sort of pre-emption title to good splint timber wherever they could find it, a practice not relinquished by those who follow the same craft today (Gold 1903; see also McFeat 1987:66).

Recognition of these rights ensures continuation of traditional activities, for commercial purposes or not (McFeat 1987); thus "outward appearance can hide a culture's sense of what constitutes tradition" (Dixon 1990:2).

Meaning in basketry was thought to have been lost through centuries of contact (Skinner 1913; Lismer 1982:32); aboriginal designs had been influenced by Euro-American designs. Analysts also felt that the basket designs were transparent: "The designs themselves ... are preeminently floral, the figures being highly conventionalized" (Speck 1915a:4; see also Tantaquidgeon 1935:44), failing to see that what looks like a flower is not necessarily so (Bedford 1985:9). Despite Speck's assumptions about basket decorations, he recognized stamping and painting as Native Algonkian art:

Strange as it may seem to find definitive material amid such deculturated surroundings, there can be little doubt that these tribes have

28

preserved designs of considerable antiquity. Perhaps they belong to an early type of eastern Algonkian art, consisting of curves, circles, ovals, waving lines and dottings forming floral complexes, having a general distribution in the north and east, from which the more elaborate realistic floral figures of beadwork have developed (Speck 1915a:10).

Speck suggested that double-curve and other "protective plant designs" provided "a therapeutic function subconsciously underlying their floral art" (Speck 1976:159). Gladys Tantaquidgeon also saw splint basket designs as symbolic: "The earth and the sky in all directions, growing things of all kinds, the spiritual force that is everywhere, man, and man's journey through life on this earth, all were symbolized by early Mohegan artists in their designs on splint baskets" (Tantaquidgeon and Fawcett 1987:101). However, Tantaquidgeon and Speck felt that decorations on later baskets replaced symbolic designs (Tantaquidgeon 1935:46; Speck 1915a:33), with largely aesthetic motivations: "You put on what comes to you to make it look nice" (Eben Queppish, in Tantaquidgeon and Fawcett 1983:2).

Other interpretations have been suggested for southern New England designs. Despite changes in technique, design structures - the medallion (Figs. 24, 26) and the stockade, use of a chequer-plaited grid, and specialized design use - persisted, suggesting basketmakers continued them intentionally. Correlations between design types and historic events suggest that designs figured as political expressions rather than statements about everyday life. These include design structures making statements about eighteenth-century movements to Brothertown, New York (McMullen 1987, 1990), Fort Shantok as a symbol of Mohegan identity (McMullen and Handsman 1987:34), and the designs showing ethnic difference at amalgamated settlements like Schaghticoke and the Pawcatuck Pequot Reservation (McMullen 1987). These interpretations suggest that basketry designs are far more than aesthetic.

Continuing Tradition and Maintaining Identity Historically

While splint baskets have been labelled an introduced, commercial tradition, such attitudes prevent us from seeing the position of splint baskets in the preservation of Native lifeways. Looking at splint basketmaking as a tradition *incorporated* into Native lifeways rather than one that replaced meaningful Native technologies allows us to see change rather than "deculturation". No matter what its origins, splint basketry was important to Northeastern Native peoples after 1750. East coast groups moving to the Great Lakes - the Delaware, Stockbridge, Mohegan and others - introduced utilitarian and commercial traditions there, maintaining these traditions to the present day. As will be discussed later, splint basketmaking is becoming a means of maintaining traditional life; revivals have contributed to increased participation in other activities, community pride and cohesiveness (Konrad 1987:1; Brandford 1984:6; Hauptman 1979:284).

Splint basketry as a means of maintaining Native identity is not new: nineteenth-century Native people used basketry to maintain separations between Native groups and with whites. Conscious emulation of the styles of earlier basketmakers such as Molly Hatchett (Fig. 25), the transformation of introduced folk-art motifs (McMullen 1990:64), the continued decoration of baskets despite loss of design knowledge (McMullen 1987:123); the adoption of economic shifts in colour choice as "traditional" (McMullen and Handsman 1987:82), and the use of watercolours to continue decorating baskets (McMullen and Handsman 1987:141) all allowed Native people to maintain tradition despite massive change.

With decorative continuities, the production of undecorated baskets and the teaching of Yankee and other basket traditions indicates basket-making's importance. Production and sale of decorated splint baskets gave way to souvenir forms and the development of undecorated utilitarian traditions. The continued production of baskets, whatever their form or decoration, helped reinforce Native ideas about identity and traditional life. For many, the tradition of sale integral to earlier production lost ground through mass-produced containers of the nineteenth century.

Utilitarian Traditions and the Meaning of Basketry

Several factors contribute to the neglect of undecorated baskets in the analysis of Northeastern material culture: undecorated baskets used for outdoor work were often discarded while decorated baskets were protected indoors; undecorated baskets may have provided significant income, but are poorly represented in museums (McMullen and Handsman 1987:21) or, lacking provenance, are seldom identifiable. These preservation factors, along with the tendency to collect decorated objects and ignore the utilitarian (King 1982:9; Porter 1990:10), hamper efforts to interpret utilitarian baskets which have not been extensively treated, with the exception of corn-processing baskets and non-chequer weaves.

Because of the relation between basketmaking and Native foods, the use of splint baskets in processing traditional corn foods is important (Fig. 27). While Speck suggested that splint basket technology followed the growth and spread of maize in the Northeast from the Iroquois (Speck 1920, 1926), corn-processing baskets probably predate widespread Iroquois influence. Although Willoughby (1902) saw later splint basketry as degraded, he recognized use of corn-processing baskets as a survival (Willoughby 1935). Among Iroquois groups and the Delaware, use of twill-plaited sifters and corn-washing baskets continued into the early twentieth century. Twined or plaited sieves of twigs or split roots were also produced by the Iroquois and the Canadian Delaware (Waugh 1973:61-63, Plate XXIII; Harrington 1908).

For Northeastern Algonkian groups, twill plaiting was less common than hexagonally plaited sieves. Hexagonal weaves - "old" and traditional - were used for making small gift baskets for the "little people" (Tantaquidgeon pers. comm. 1986). Some groups, like the Nanticoke, did not make sieves despite dependence on corn (Speck 1915b). Wampanoag groups, including the Gay Head, made beach-grass hulling baskets - "open work, very fine" - and pack baskets used to gather produce (Harrington n.d.).

While collection and preservation have slanted our perception of utilitarian baskets, there exists a strong photographic record of Native people pictured with splint baskets (Trigger 1978) which, although it may result from anthropological "fiddling", does show Native people using baskets supposedly made only for sale, illustrating large work baskets, eel traps, corn-processing baskets, pack baskets, round handled baskets, melon baskets, sewing baskets, and winnowing baskets. While some baskets were collected in the early twentieth century, collectors were usually more interested in "ancient technologies" than items that were actually used. Along with objects they made and used, Native people retained remarkable items, many of which held tremendous meaning, such as a twined hemp bag kept by a Mohegan family over 200 years (Butler 1947:42). Although reluctant to give up these things, Native people yielded, convinced that museums might preserve objects better (Price 1989:70). This "emptying of Native landscapes" occurred all over North America (Handsman 1987:157), but was particularly harmful in the Northeast because collectors carried away traditional technologies:

The old manufactures are also practically extinct ... There are still to be found however, or were until I made my house-to-house canvas, a considerable number of old specimens saved by
30

the Indians as mementos or on account of their intrinsic usefulness ... I had never ventured to hope that any of the fine baskets, evidently twined, mentioned in the early accounts as being used by eastern Indians, might survive to the present day (Harrington 1908:408-10, emphasis mine).

Harrington and others (Skinner 1924) not only bought objects, they searched Native settlements for "survivals", bemoaning the object's fate when their offers were refused. While purchase assured objects' museum preservation, it also assured their demise as technologies, since they were replaced by manufactured goods.

Because of concern with ancient technologies, anthropologists and collectors paid little attention to undecorated baskets. Most groups in southern New England maintained a specific non-commercial basket technology; on Cape Cod, women plaited splint or twined beach grass into pack baskets (Turnbaugh and Turnbaugh 1987; McMullen 1987:79), or plaited straw baskets (Tantaquidgeon 1930a, 1930b). These baskets, along with Yankee basketry, replaced older, treasured objects as connections with traditional life (McMullen 1991).

Baskets and Basketmaking Today

Today basketmaking involves not only baskets but also how people think and speak about basketmaking in the past. Even for groups not actively engaged, basket production is an image of the past and Native life. Basketmaking cannot be conceived of as introduced, or as tourist manufactures; fancy baskets are part of culture, even if they did not exist before 1850 (Coe 1986:17). Working within a tradition, and cultivating a "genuine knowledge of their culture with a deeply personal concern for its preservation" (Benedict and Lauersons 1983:7) is fundamental; Native people learn in order to make accepted traditional works (Johannsen 1984:139; Johannsen and Ferguson 1983).

Baskets - beautiful and durable - are a

metaphor for Native culture, and basketmaking and its transmission to younger tribal members ensures the survival of tradition. For basketmakers of the past their work was culture, not art, and baskets are testimony to the endurance and power of women of the past (Benedict and Lauersons 1983:7).

Basketmakers near the Great Lakes carry on ancient traditions: "I make only authentic Indian baskets same as my ancestors" (Edith Bonde, Ojibwa, in Coe 1986:94). A few Penobscot and Passamaquoddy women carry on the fancy basket tradition, because they enjoy it and to express identity. While these women sell their work, meaning is not diminished; proud to be basketmakers, they hope that young people will follow (Lester 1987b:46). Those who make baskets today do so because of special meaning, but also because of the freedom (McBride 1990). Many have taken up basketry after leaving other kinds of work (McBride 1990:55; Johannsen and Ferguson 1983), and because it allows women to work in the home, their traditional place:

Quick cash from a job off the reservation may appeal to both men and younger women, but to old-timers, like Mary Adams, it is better to stay on the Reservation, perfect your skills, and earn more in one day's sales than a wage earner brings in from a week's work. While phrased in terms of money, the real issue involves pride in being a Mohawk basketmaker close to her people's heritage, not just another wage earner in white society (Johannsen 1984:141-42).

In areas where basketmaking has ceased, there has been renewed interest recently (Lamb Richmond 1987), although it is seen as traditional activity rather than a source of income. While revival is possible, securing raw materials and the necessity of economic return will make revival difficult. In the late nineteenth and early twentieth centuries, individual families were instrumental in maintaining fading traditions (McMullen 1985a); it may be up to them to lead a basketmaking revival.

When we were young, we thought these were just wonderful stories, but as we grew older, we realized they were filled with information, and they shaped our lives ... It was not until we were much older that we realized how much we had learned, particularly about respect. It has affected our entire lives and our relationships with others. It lives at the center of everything we do

The sentiments expressed by Trudie Lamb Richmond (n.d.:11) on elders' philosophical and spiritual teachings are equally appropriate to Native crafts. In traditional societies, instruction is relatively informal, and young people learn by watching: "Nobody really taught me baskets. You weren't supposed to bother [adults] when they were working ... I just watched my mother ... picked up leftover wood she threw away and tried to make some little basket exactly like her. Mine looked funny" (Ruby Schillinger, in McBride 1990:48). Once they begin, children are encouraged and gently corrected (McBride 1990:63). Mary Adams (Fig. 31), whose basketmaking career started at age ten, recalls:

I learned how to make baskets from my grandmother and my mother ... I started with ... candy baskets ... then I started on the bigger baskets, the strawberry ones, that's the one I learned from my grandmother, she teach me to make them, 'cause they pay more for that kind of basket (in Hill and Semmens 1980).

While children eagerly learn baskets (Benedict and Lauersons 1983:7), it is difficult to sustain interest as they grow older. Many basketmakers today gave up basketry as hard or unprofitable, returning only when marketing made it worthwhile (McBride 1990:23). With this resurgence, Micmacs are learning or relearning basketmaking, but basketmakers regret their children are uninterested in basketry: "I taught my eight children baskets when they were little, but they don't want to do it, and you can't tell them what to do" (Jane Zumbrunnen, in McBride 1990:47).

I've got seven girls and five boys ... the oldest girl she knows how to make baskets ... I make her start to make the fancy basket, 'cause I got sick. I said if I quit my baskets, you going to keep on, so she learned how to make the fancy ones ... she knows how to make baskets but she won''t do it ... Maybe after we are gone, nobody will make the baskets again ... (Mary Adams, in Hill and Semmens 1980).

While basketmakers talk about cultural continuity, splint basketmaking is also spoken about as a *family* tradition (Plate 2). The pattern of traditional learning - by observing elders - reinforces family ties (Johannsen 1984:139) and conveys the importance of basketmaking, along with inherited tools and designs. Basketmaking is also a family business, work which all share: "In the winter everybody works at it, down to the kids" (Coe 1986:64). Families gather and prepare materials, weave and sell baskets; family members sell baskets for one another at their stands or elsewhere. Continuation of family crafts is primary, gender becoming unimportant: "I wanted to leave the tradition with someone, and it looks like he's the one" (Sarah Lund in McBride 1990:32). For the Sanipass family, Micmacs from Houlton, Maine, basketry is "a unique chain in our family" (David Sanipass, in McBride 1990:65). Roldena Sanipass states: "Mom and Dad are as proud of me being a basketmaker as they'd be if I'd become a doctor" (McBride 1990:67).

While baskets made by family members sometimes exist, Native people regret not having preserved work of earlier generations: "I started making baskets with my mother. She had made them all her life and told me her mother had made them too. I never saved one of my mother's baskets" (Elizabeth Knockwood Hanning, in McBride 1990:59). Producing the same styles as ones' parents or regaining them is important: "my mother ... could make the prettiest baskets you ever saw; I wish I had one of them today. I tried to buy some of her baskets back from people in Houlton [Maine], but they wouldn't part with them" (Joseph Sylliboy, in McBride 1990:53).

I still like working on baskets. If I were a million

32

years old, I'd still do it. Baskets are my life (Elizabeth Knockwood Hanning, in McBride 1990:62).

Although basketmaking was survival, others may not have seen it as an occupation (Pelletier 1979:52; see also Johannsen and Ferguson 1983:vii). Many made baskets occasionally as household work or in social networks (McBride 1990:32). Young women working in craft shops often did so because of the fun (Lester 1987b:57). In other situations, groups of women met to do crafts together (Johannsen and Ferguson 1983), creating new forms for the pleasure of it (Pelletier 1979:37; Johannsen and Ferguson 1983:22). For many, basketmaking is not necessarily a type of work Indians do, but just a fun way to make a living: "Baskets are good company" (Harold Lafford, in McBride 1990:45). For others " ... basketmaking has been elevated to a refined art by people who enjoy creating for themselves endlessly innovative designs - all still based on the use of traditional materials, methods, and styles" (Benedict and Lauersons 1983:8; see also Pelletier 1982:viii). Some basketmakers, like Mary Adams, whose work is coveted by museums and collectors, enjoy their renown, but the reason she continues is "because I like making baskets" (Fig. 31; Adams et al. 1990:53).

In traditional learning, the importance of elders is fundamental. In mid-Atlantic communities, reduced populations made continuity of tradition difficult (Porter 1985:35), while in southern New England, the movement of young families away from reservations, where elderly relatives stayed and lived off tribal monies (McMullen 1985b), made it impossible for children to learn basketmaking. Where basketmaking survived, elders are recognized for preserving basketmaking: "The majority of our basketmakers are the older people ... [I]f it wasn't for them the art of basketmaking would have died years ago" (Frankie Benedict, in Hill and Semmens 1980). The recognition that basketmaking is in danger has led to renewed hopes for the future.

While traditional learning has long sufficed,

Fig. 31 Mary Adams, Mohawk, Akwesasne Reserve, demonstrating basketmaking. Photo by Christina Johannsen, courtesy Association for the Advancement of Native North American Arts and Crafts.

other sorts of teaching, especially through tribal or other authorities, have grown. In the 1930s, national programmes such as the Seneca Works Projects Administration (part of Roosevelt's New Deal) and the National Youth Administration (Hauptman 1979) held basketmaking classes among the Iroquois, while convalescing Micmac veterans learned basketmaking in the 1940s (Pelletier 1979:73). The Homemakers, a Canadian women's organization, taught basketmaking and provided opportunities for social contacts (Johannsen 1984:41).

In the 1960s, traditional arts and crafts programmes sponsored by tribal organizations stressed the conjunction of tradition and personal creativity (Porter 1990:11), but in the Maritimes teaching programmes failed along with marketing associations (Pelletier 1979:173; Gordon 1990:37). Similar Iroquois programmes during the late 1960s and early 1970s were more successful because of the Mohawk Crafts Fund's work to provide a market (Johannsen 1984:81). In the 1970s, Title IV and Title VII legislation providing for Native education created children's language and culture programmes (Johannsen 1984:231). Unfortunately, the "Cultural Centres" created often replaced elders as teachers, and children lost contact with earlier generations (Johannsen 1984:252).

Today, Native people learn basketmaking and other crafts by a variety of means, including apprenticing, classes, books and examining museum collections as well as by traditional means (Lester 1987a:2). At Akwesasne, children are taught in organized basketry classes (Johannsen and Ferguson 1983:2); for adult education, the Akwesasne Museum offers classes (Benedict and Lauersons 1983), and prominent basketmakers take apprentices from other families (Benedict 1982:14), suggesting that basketmaking is becoming a tribal rather than a family tradition. The same pattern is taking shape in the Maritimes; the Maine Arts Commission now offers grants to support apprenticeships in basketmaking (McBride 1990:47).

34

As mentioned above, basketmaking in a number of communities has survived only because of strong marketing efforts. Although the Mohawk Craft Fund is now defunct (Johannsen 1984:141), other outlets such as Irocrafts at Oka, the Akwesasne Museum, and others have kept basketry viable (Johannsen 1984:82, 104). Akwesasne basketry has become globally known and Mohawk baskets now travel far and wide. Craft demonstrations outside Mohawk country reach the public, ensuring a future market (Fig. 29).

In Maine and the Maritimes, similar efforts have been made but with less success. The creation of Penobscot and Passamaquoddy craft co-operatives has failed (Lester 1987b:57-58), and basketmakers sell their work through demonstrations, Native and museum shops. Among the Micmac, sales through craft fairs increased after the Aroostook Micmac Council's creation of the Basket Bank in 1982 (Fig. 30; McBride 1990:21).

Native people today are more likely to create craftwork for themselves than twenty years ago. Although baskets were admittedly made for sale, this does not make them less important; contemplating baskets empowers the people of the present as it may have in the past (Handsman 1987:149). Native people have begun to keep examples of their work and that of other tribal members, displaying them in their homes (Johannsen 1984:37). Among the Micmac, concern over commercial loss of baskets has led to a collection and a travelling exhibit by the Aroostook Micmac Council, and a book on Maine's Micmac basketmakers (McBride 1990).

Native museums have served much the same purpose. One of the oldest, the Tantaquidgeon Indian Museum, opened in 1931 in Uncasville, Connecticut (Voight 1965:61). The Tomaquag Memorial Indian Museum in Exeter, Rhode Island similarly serves the Narragansett and the Niantic. With the help of the Massachusetts Historical Commission and the Town of Mashpee, The Mashpee Wampanoag Indian Museum opened in 1970, to "to preserve their history and culture through a repository for their art and artifacts" (Peters 1987:76). In the Maritimes, museums like Musée des Abenakis (Pelletier 1982) maintain collections, while smaller museums are planned by other groups in Canada and Maine.

Among the Iroquois, museums and cultural centres in Native communities preserve and encourage Native arts, including Caughnawaga and Oka (both in Quebec), Akwesasne Reserve (Ontario, Quebec, and New York State), Six Nations (Ontario), Oneida, Tonowanda, Allegany, Cattaraugus, Oneida, Niagara Falls, Buffalo, Rochester, Onchiota (all in New York State), and Oneida, Wisconsin (Johannsen and Fergu son 1983:x; Johannsen 1984:117: Benedict and Lauersons 1983). In addition to broadening public interest, at least two films have been produced on splint basketmaking: *Mohawk Basket Making at Akwesasne* (Hill and Semmens 1980) and *Our Lives in our Hands* (on Micmac basketmaking) produced by the North American Indian Film Company.

Conclusion

This essay has explored the many-faceted meaning of basketry in the Northeastern woodlands. As a bridge between cultures, baskets serve as meaningful objects to Native people and to non-Native purchasers. In each case, the historic and economic situations surrounding production and sale of baskets affects these meanings, and study of these contexts allows us to see changes in Native societies and their larger social environments.

Discussions of change require examination of the origins of splint basketry, whether or not splint basketry represents an autochthonous technology. Since proof of its origins may not exist, we should work toward evaluating splint basketry historically and humanistically rather than technologically (Handsman and McMullen 1987:23; Johannsen 1984:3). Earlier statements about splint basketry's spread should be taken with Brasser's work to interpret basketry's importance in Native economies and traditions, rather than labelling its spread as evidence of cultural disintegration (Brasser 1971).

Looking at splint basketry as a phenomenon arising out of colonialism and historic contingencies suggests that analyses of splint basketry and contemporaneous technologies can benefit from recent discussions on the invention of tradition (Hobsbawm and Ranger 1983). Recognition of traditions as introduced or "invented" does not invalidate them, obviously, but serves to remind us of the dynamic nature of culture.

In looking at "invented traditions", we must begin to rethink our reliance on "objective", "scientific" and obviously exterior views of Native societies, and place them alongside Native peoples' own views of culture and history. Doing so allows us to see perspectives within each point of view, to evaluate and learn from such accounts without judging or dismissing them. In a world where multiple perspectives are increasingly voiced, anthropologists, among others, are learning to speak about the lives and cultures of Native people in that changing world. However, our success in this endeavor can only be gauged by how well we learn to listen.

Acknowledgements

Many people contributed to this essay in a number of ways. My thanks to Penny Dransart, Steven T. Fish, Betsy Fox, Russell G. Handsman, Eldon and Frankie Hanning, Christina Johannsen, Diane Kopec, Joan Lester, Bunny McBride, Ruth B. Phillips, Lynne Williamson and Linda Mowat.

Fig. 32 **Canada, British Columbia, Lower Fraser River, Ruby Creek.**
Salish woman making a basket, c. 1890. Courtesy, Field Museum of Natural History, Neg. No. 9468, USA.

36

Windows on Diversity:
Northwest Coast Baskets in the Pitt Rivers Collection

by Andrea Laforet

The request to write an essay on any topic pertaining to Northwest Coast basketry illustrated by baskets in this collection is deceptively simple. There are baskets here from virtually every region of the coast, from Southeast Alaska, the Queen Charlotte Islands, the central coast, the west coast of Vancouver Island, the southern mainland and the central interior of British Columbia. There are baskets of spruce root, spruce root combined with cedar branch, cedar bark and grass, and cedar bark alone. The baskets represent at least four different twining techniques, in addition to simple plaiting and coiling. They were acquired by several different collectors, some well known for other work on the coast and some less famous, and they were purchased over a period of more than fifty years.

It is the very diversity of these baskets which provides the theme of this essay. The basketry of the Northwest Coast is difficult to fit within a single essay because it is far from being a single topic. Basketry was a medium for making not only containers, hats and cradles such as those represented here, but also mats, food dish covers and toys. Tough, delicate in form, precisely composed, colourful and above all useful, they gave both texture and substance to household furnishings and their geometric patterns were an art form developed and practised exclusively by women.

Before the arrival of European explorers in the 1770s and the development of intensive settlement after 1858, there was very considerable diversity in form and style, both within regions and from one region to another. In the post settlement period, diversity remained characteristic of Northwest Coast basketry.

The period in which the baskets in this collection were originally acquired, 1860-1920, was a time in which basketry was transformed from an element of domestic material culture which supported activities ranging from food gathering to the protection of pubescent girls, to a source of economic support for families in an altered economy. The transition was not absolute, many forms of basketry continued to be made for domestic purposes, but as the nineteenth century gave way to the twentieth, the shift in emphasis was nearing completion.

A time of substantial change in many sectors of Native life on the Pacific coast, these decades saw some previously made forms of basketry discarded and others given new emphasis, the adaptation of older techniques to accommodate changing purposes, the development of new traditions and changes in the geographic distribution of traditions long known in particular regions.

Collections of basketry from the Northwest Coast began to be assembled in Europe following the first voyages by Spanish, Russian and English explorers. As is true for all Northwest Coast artefacts, the collecting of basketry has followed the political history of the coast. Most collections now in North American museums were assembled at approximately the same time as the Pitt Rivers collection, during the late nineteenth century and the first three decades of the twentieth. None of the collections is fully representative. All were assembled by various collectors working independently, from an assortment of motives and with many different criteria. A full picture of basketry on the coast at this time can only be approached through comparison of all of the collections.

Among the collectors represented here are Frederick Dally, who lived on the southern coast during the 1860s and is still known in British Columbia as a talented photographer; Charles Harrison, who first went to the Queen

Charlotte Islands as a missionary to the Haida; and C.F. Newcombe, a Victorian physician who worked as an amateur ethnologist and collector and assembled collections which are now in many museums. Also represented is the Church Missionary Society, one of several Christian organizations in Britain which sent missionaries to the coast during the nineteenth and early twentieth centuries.

Catalogue records associated with all museum collections reflect the knowledge and perspective of the collector and the conventions of the day. For the Pitt Rivers collection, as for virtually every other collection, the catalogue records identify the collector, but not the person who made the basket.

With some exceptions, such as the records made by the Canadian ethnologist Marius Barbeau concerning the collection he made at Port Simpson in 1915 (Canadian Museum of Civilization n.d.) and C.F. Newcombe's records concerning the Haida basketmaker Isabella Edenshaw (Laforet 1990), basketmakers enter the archival record of the history of the coast as part of the photographic record. Even here, they are anonymous.

Some of the photographs of women making baskets, perhaps all of them, were posed. In each case the photographer's intent was to capture the process, to freeze it in time, and in each photograph as we see it now the basketmaker sits forever, work in hand (Fig. 32). The basketmaker and the process have become inseparable from each other in an image of the past.

In the villages of the coast virtually every woman made baskets, learning the rudiments in early childhood, becoming accomplished in adulthood, and able to devote long hours to basketry in late middle age. Nonetheless, basketmaking was only a part of their lives. To speak of "basketmakers" is merely to direct attention to that part of a woman's knowledge which she expressed when working in basketry.

The change in the Native economy which accompanied settlement of the coast by Euro-

peans brought significant changes to the role of Native women. In their case, however, "change" meant "expansion". Native women remained responsible for gathering and preserving vegetable foods, preserving and cooking fish and meat, raising and teaching children, catering for feasts and dealing with the multitude of organizational details that attended the frequent travel which was a feature of coastal life; but they also became responsible for bringing money into the household economy, either through wage work in canneries or the sale of basketry. Some domestic activities, such as the making of cooking baskets and cedar bark clothing, became much less important as these items of traditional material culture were replaced by factory-made counterparts, but there was a corresponding increase in the forms of basketry made for sale.

The Pitt Rivers Museum's collection is divided roughly equally between forms of basketry made primarily for household use, such as the Kwakwak'wakw (formerly called Kwakiutl) burden basket (Fig. 38), the Nuu-Chah-Nulth (formerly called Nootka) hat (Fig. 47) and the Nuu-Chah-Nulth cradle (Fig. 40) and forms made for sale (Fig. 41). By the time these baskets were purchased, the selling of baskets as curios and household objects for use by settlers was well established on the coast and in the interior of British Columbia and Washington State. Basketmaking became part of the tourist industry of the day to the extent that The Alaska Steamship Company of Seattle published a booklet on Alaska Indian Basketry in 1904 (MacDowell 1904).

The baskets from each region which can be found in the Pitt Rivers collection represent a much more extensive range of basketry which was characteristic of the production of coastal women of that time. The baskets exhibited can be arranged in four general categories: three geographical, i.e. the interior plateau, the southern and central coast and the northern coast; and one typological, i.e. hats.

The Plateau

A tall Klickitat burden basket from the interior of Washington State (Fig. 33), two Chilcotin baskets, one round (Fig. 34), one a classic burden basket (Fig. 35), two Interior Salish baskets made for sale, one a fishing creel (Fig. 36), the other a container trapezoidal in shape with a narrow pedestal at the base (Fig. 37): what do they have in common? They are all watertight, all made either of spruce roots or cedar roots, all decorated with cherry bark (red, the natural colour and black, dyed) or grass (white), and all part of a vast tradition of coiled basketry characteristic of virtually all the southern interior of British Columbia and the adjacent plateau region to the south. The Nlaka'pamux (Thompson) and Lillooet speak Salishan languages, the Chilcotin an Athapaskan language, the Klickitat a Sahaptin language. Coiled basketry was also made by the Shuswap, Okanagan and Kootenay and during the past one hundred and fifty years a distinctive Coast Salish coiled basketry tradition has developed to supplant, to a large degree, a Coast Salish tradition of some antiquity which was more clearly related to the cedar bark and open-meshed root and branch basketry of other regions of the coast.

How are they different? They all exhibit specific regional approaches to shape and design. In the case of the two Interior Salish examples, they show certain decisions which Interior Salish women made concerning the baskets they made for sale.

The most unusual of these baskets is the round Chilcotin basket (Fig. 34). There are several substantial collections of Chilcotin baskets in museums. Most are burden baskets (Fig. 35). Round baskets are not unknown, but are much less common. The Chilcotin Plateau in the central interior of British Columbia is a beautiful country of meadows, grasslands and forest. The traditional economy was based on fishing for salmon in the rivers and hunting deer, elk, caribou and beaver. It was an environment which

required constant care in the use of resources. Spruce root baskets were among the most distinctive forms of Chilcotin material culture. The late nineteenth century saw the settlement of the plateau by ranchers, who found the growing season desperately short and the living hard. Most of the Chilcotin baskets now in museums were acquired about this time.

Fig. 35 shows a definitively Chilcotin approach to design: a band of decoration immediately below the rim, bounded on the lower side by a reinforcing hoop of wood or metal, and below the hoop three bands of decoration, the first and third generally carrying the same motif, the middle different.

The principal decorative technique used on plateau coiled basketry is imbrication, in which a strand of decorative material is folded under and then over successive surface stitches, to make solid blocks of colour on the surface of the basket. Cherry bark in red (its natural colour) or black (dyed with mineralized mud or steeped in a mixture of tea and iron) and bleached grass are the principal materials although, on one dramatically decorated Chilcotin basket in a Canadian museum, the basketmaker has used bird quill in place of grass. Interior Salish design uses all three colours, red, black and white, often with red and black the principal colours and white the buffer. Kootenay baskets use black and white, Chilcotin baskets red and white.

There are well over 800 recorded decorative motifs used on Interior Salish baskets (Boas 1928). These are generally geometric, with some representational designs used by certain basketmakers. Chilcotin motifs are distinctive and include both geometric and representational designs. According to diagrams published by the turn-of-the-century ethnographer James Teit (1900:766), the motifs on Fig. 35 can be interpreted as arrowheads (above the hoop) and fish ribs (in the central band) while the first and third bands below the hoop may represent beavers. The central band of horses on the round

Fig. 33 **USA, Washington State, Klickitat.** Watertight coiled burden basket with foundation and sewing of cedar or spruce root, imbricated pattern in cherry bark (red) and bleached grass (white). Coiled to the right. Skin thongs for carrying. H: 250 mm; dia: 200 m. Collected by Dr. Charles Pope before 1865. 1886.21.15

Fig. 34 **Canada, British Columbia, Upper Fraser River, Chilcotin.** Coiled watertight basket with foundation and sewing of cedar or spruce root. Coiled to the right. Imbricated design of horses in cherry bark (red) and bleached grass (white). H:220 mm; dia:220 mm. Collected by Norman H. Lee in the 1890s; donated by Prof. R.W. Lee. 1950.3.5

Fig. 35 **Canada, British Columbia, Upper Fraser River, Chilcotin.** Coiled watertight rectangular burden basket with foundation and sewing of cedar or spruce root. Coiled to the right. Imbricated designs in cherry bark (red) and bleached grass (white) representing arrowheads, fish ribs and ?beavers. Reinforcing hoop of wood below the rim. H:210 mm; L:265 mm; W:210 mm. Collected by Norman H. Lee in the1890s; donated by Prof. R.W. Lee. 1950.3.3

Fig. 36 **Canada, British Columbia, Lower Fraser River, Interior Salish.** Coiled watertight basket made in imitation of a European angler's creel. Foundation and sewing of spruce or cedar root. Coiled to the right. Imbricated with cherry bark and grass. Design of vertical stripes. Lid missing. Late nineteenth century. H: 175 mm; L: 240 mm; W: 170 mm. Purchased from J.T. Hooper. 1937.52.18

Fig. 37 **Canada, southern British Columbia, Interior Salish.** Rectangular coiled watertight basket with foundation and sewing of cedar or spruce root. Coiled to the right. Imbricated with chevrons in undyed and dyed cherry bark (red and black) and bleached grass (white). Narrow pedestal at base. Made for sale. H: 125 mm; L: 315 mm; W: 240 mm. Collected by Miss Lilian Hay. H.G. Beasley collection. 1954.8.146.

basket illustrates representational design. These motifs are seen frequently on Chilcotin baskets. The attributed meanings should be taken as suggestive rather than literal, since it is not clear just how much latitude individual basketmakers exercised in naming the designs they used. There is a lively, imaginative sense to Chilcotin design. On the Canadian basket mentioned above, one of the motifs was a flying goose and the bird quill was used to represent the honk (Royal British Columbia Museum n.d.).

There were few, if any, adaptations of Chilcotin basketry for sale. On the other hand Interior Salish basketmakers, living much closer to major centres of transport and settlement on the southern mainland and Vancouver Island, developed a multitude of forms for sale to tourists and non-Native householders: tea sets, end tables, candy dishes, knitting baskets and even suitcases. Although certain of these items are dramatically different in form from the traditional trapezoid-shaped burden baskets, round kettles and rectangular storage baskets, in many cases the adaptation of form was minimal: the addition of loopwork around the rim, the integration of openwork technique into a wall, or the addition of a pedestal at the base. Interior Salish basketmakers also experimented with aniline dyes but found that the traditional decorative materials and colours were more reliable.

The fishing creel (Fig. 36) and the trapezoidal basket (Fig. 37) are very modest examples of basketry made for sale. Fishing creels were not uncommon. The rectangular basket shows a typical Interior Salish design in black, white and red and is much the same shape as a traditional Lillooet burden basket, the shorter walls and the narrow pedestal at the base the only concessions to the tourist market.

The Southern and Central Coast

Of the baskets represented here from this region, the Kwakwaka'wakw burden basket (Fig. 38), the Nuu-Chah-Nulth cradle (Fig. 40)
42

and the dome-shaped hat (Fig. 47) represent three traditional forms within several rich traditions. The small, more flamboyantly decorated wrapped twine baskets (Fig. 41) represent a tradition with a substantial history on the Washington Coast and a much more recent tenure on the west coast of Vancouver Island.

The beautifully formed burden basket, made of spruce root and cedar branch in an open wrap twine technique, was one of the most common household forms among the Coast Salish, Nuu-Chah-Nulth, Kwakwak'wakw and Nuxalk (Bella Coola). The form varied regionally, the fineness of the materials and the open-mesh weave varied with the purpose of the basket. Baskets of this kind were used for gathering firewood, shellfish, and foods ranging from roots to huckleberries. They could be tough and coarse - the equivalent of cardboard boxes - or light and delicate.

The cradle (Fig. 40) woven of the inner bark of the Western Red Cedar (*Thuja plicata*) in a chequerwork technique, was made for a newborn child. Cradles of this type were typically used by the Nuu-Chah-Nulth. A rectangular piece of woven cedar bark, closed along two sides, shielded the child's head from the sun.

The basketmakers of the central and southern coast used cedar bark to make many different fabrics and many different forms of basketry: mats with different, and complementary, geometric designs on obverse and reverse sides; hook bags for tiny bone fish hooks, the hooks kept in a pouch folded over and over into a long flap; large rectangular flat-bottomed storage baskets; and delicate diagonally plaited pouches fitting one inside another.

The kind of basket considered today to be most characteristic of Nuu-Chah-Nulth basketry is the small wrapped twine basket (Fig. 41). It has been made on the coast of the Olympic Peninsula and the west coast of Vancouver Island since the mid-nineteenth century, but the technique has a far longer history in the territory to the south and west. The Nez Perce hat

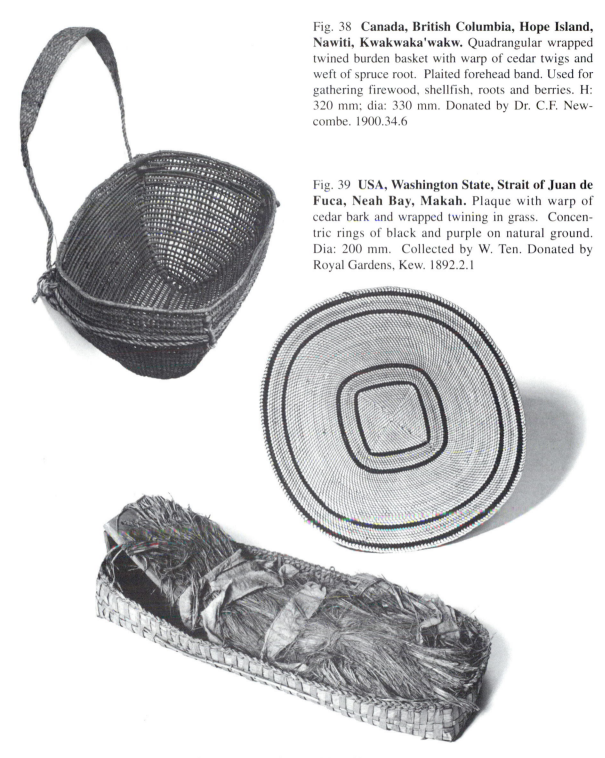

Fig. 38 **Canada, British Columbia, Hope Island, Nawiti, Kwakwaka'wakw.** Quadrangular wrapped twined burden basket with warp of cedar twigs and weft of spruce root. Plaited forehead band. Used for gathering firewood, shellfish, roots and berries. H: 320 mm; dia: 330 mm. Donated by Dr. C.F. Newcombe. 1900.34.6

Fig. 39 **USA, Washington State, Strait of Juan de Fuca, Neah Bay, Makah.** Plaque with warp of cedar bark and wrapped twining in grass. Concentric rings of black and purple on natural ground. Dia: 200 mm. Collected by W. Ten. Donated by Royal Gardens, Kew. 1892.2.1

Fig. 40 **Canada, British Columbia, Vancouver Island, Nuu-Chah-Nulth.** Cradle of plaited cedar bark with board for flattening the child's head. Contains bundles of shredded cedar bark and strips of trade cloth for binding the child to the cradle. H: 150 mm; L: 530 mm; W: 230 mm. Franz Boas collection. 1890.39.6

Fig. 41 **Canada, British Columbia, Vancouver Island, Nuu-Chah-Nulth.** Small basket with chequer plaited base. Warp of cedar bark, wrapped twining in grass. Design of ducks in black, concentric rings in purple and yellow. H: 45 mm; dia: 71 mm. Collected by Beatrice Blackwood, 1925. 1938.36.1930.

Fig. 42 **USA, Washington or Idaho, Nez Perce.** Woman's wrapped twined hat with warp of cedar bark and weft of cotton (at the start) and bleached grass. Design in purple (aniline dye). H: 85 mm; dia: 210 mm. From Denver Art Museum by exchange (Irene L. Secord collection). 1948.12.69.

(Fig. 42) is made with a wrapped twining fabric, although the stitch slant may be different. The British explorer, Belcher, collected small wrapped twine baskets showing European influence on the Oregon coast in the 1840s and these are now in the British Museum.

Although these baskets appear to have almost always been made for sale outside Nuu-Chah-Nulth homes, the development during the latter part of the nineteenth and the early twentieth century can be seen in a series of documented collections in museums in the United States and Canada.

The principal changes from one period to another have been in the choice of motif. Baskets made in the earlier periods are characterized by the use of geometric motifs and simple bands of colour (Fig. 39). Geometric motifs often have vivid metaphoric meanings, e.g. the waves of heat rising from the sea on a hot, sunny day or fleecy clouds over a mountain range (Field Museum of Natural History n.d.) More obviously representational motifs, such as ducks (Fig. 41) and dragons, became common in the early twentieth century.

Wrapped twine baskets were, and are, often made on wooden forms, but from the initial period bottles and shells were used as forms as well. Small round baskets with lids are very characteristic, but typical forms also include rectangular shopping baskets, tiny thimble-shaped baskets and glass net floats with basketry covers.

The basic materials are cedar bark (the warp) and several kinds of sedge or grass (the passive weft and the outer surface). However, during the nineteenth century raffia was introduced on the coast. Its strength, flexibility and availability, in addition to its resemblance to bleached grass, have commended it to basketmakers and it has long been incorporated as a weaving material, particularly for the outer surface of the base.

Where other basketry traditions have fallen into disuse, wrapped twine basketry has continued to develop and to provide a field for considerable innovation and creativity among Nuu-Chah-Nulth women.

The Northern Coast

The northern coast was home to many different forms of basketry. Some, such as Haida and Tlingit spruce root baskets, are very well known; others, such as Gitksan cedar bark baskets, are hardly known at all.

The similarities between Haida and Tlingit basketry can be seen by comparing a Haida basket (Fig. 44) with its Tlingit counterpart (Fig. 43). Both are cylindrical, both are of spruce root, both are made of twined, watertight fabric, both are decorated. There are differences in decoration: the Tlingit basket is decorated with geometric motifs in false embroidery and the Haida basket with solid bands of colour, and this is a difference that is constant for other examples as well. The fundamental difference between the basketry traditions is, however, in the orientation during the weaving process. Tlingit baskets were made with the base oriented to the ground; Haida baskets were made with the base set on a disk supported above the ground, with the warps hanging down. In making both types of basket, basketmakers worked from left to right, and the evidence of the difference in approach is built into the basket wall in the form of a discontinuity or jog. This can most readily be seen where rows of decoration begin and end. On Haida baskets the higher point of the jog will be on the viewer's right; on Tlingit baskets, it will be on the left.

This kind of strong similarity with a reversal constituting a fundamental point of distinction is characteristic of basketry on both the northern and southern coast, where neighbouring peoples share an essential approach to basketry but affirm their own distinctive style.

The cylindrical basket was a form essential to both the Haida and Tlingit traditions, with berry baskets in several sizes a fundamental traditional form. Basketmakers from both regions made baskets for sale, in the traditional types seen here as well as in somewhat adapted forms, e.g. Fig. 46. Tlingit basketmakers drew upon fifty

Fig. AL43 **USA, Alaska, Tlingit.** Twined basket of spruce root with false embroidery in grass dyed pink, yellow and purple with aniline dyes. This is a small size of berry gathering basket. H: 155mm; dia: 150 mm. Donated by Miss E.C. Bell. 1913.22.7

Fig. 44 **Canada, British Columbia, Queen Charlotte Islands, Haida.** Twined watertight cylindrical basket with warp and weft of spruce root. Horizontal brown stripes: colour obtained by immersing roots in mud. H: 200 mm; dia: 200 mm. Donated by Dr. C.F. Newcombe. 1900.34.7

Fig. 45 **Canada, British Columbia, Upper Skeena River, Gitksan (Tsimshian).** Bag plaited from cedar bark, old at time of collection. L: 380 mm; W: 360 mm. Collected by Beatrice Blackwood, 1925. 1926.12.19

Fig. 46 **Alaska or British Columbia, Tlingit.** "Something inside basket", *too-duh-kuhk*, twined of spruce root with false embroidery in grass. "Fern frond" design in black and brown. Lid contains rattling pellets, probably lead shot. H: 150 mm; max dia: 155 mm. Collected by Dr. Frederick Dally, probably in the 1860s. Pitt Rivers collection. 1884.44.19.

geometric designs to decorate baskets in false embroidery, using dyed or bleached grasses and other materials with strong natural colour such as the stem of maidenhair fern. Some Haida basketmakers experimented with false embroidery around the turn of the century, but it remained a characteristic of Tlingit basketry.

Cedar bark baskets such as the container illustrated in Fig. 45 were made by Haida, southern Tlingit, Coast Tsimshian and Gitksan people, with comparable forms made in maple bark on the Nass and upper Skeena Rivers. Decorative colours are black and red, the red achieved by dyeing cedar bark with an infusion of alder bark, the black with mineralized mud. In the upper Nass and Skeena regions the principal contrast is between black and the naturally pale colour of the maple bark.

The basketmakers of the northern coast shared a general approach to the decoration of plaited basketry with some regional differences in composition, the solid blocks of vertical and horizontal bands of the upper Nass contrasting with the sparer, horizontal compositions of the Coast Tsimshian. Optical illusion was incorporated into the vertical black and cream bands of decoration used on the upper Nass, as well as on the plain cedar bark food dish covers woven by Haida women.

Hats

There are three hats here from the coast of Canada: a painted Haida spruce root hat acquired by Charles Harrison in the 1880s, a typical Nuu-Chah-Nulth dome shaped hat woven of cedar bark and from approximately the same period, and a hat acquired by Frederick Dally on Vancouver Island, with a deceptively northern shape. The Haida hat and the Nuu-Chah-Nulth hat represent the two principal hat-making traditions known in the nineteenth century. Evidence can be adduced to show that a third principal form of hat, distinctive to the central coast, was known during the eighteenth

century (Laforet n.d.). Hats represented both high rank and protection from the weather; they were an essential form of basketry in all regions of the coast. The Haida hat (Plate 1) represents a mid-to-late nineteenth century variation on an essentially northern form: a truncated cone, sometimes topped with cylindrical woven rings designating inherited privilege. The principal point of formal variation of this hat from earlier Haida and Tlingit hats is the relative concavity of the walls.

Northern hats were woven of spruce root, with double warps, each hat incorporating several types of twining. The top and upper portion of the wall were woven in three-strand twining, the lower portion of the wall in a combination of two-strand plain twining and twill twining. The stitch slant of the twining on all Haida hats and baskets is Z, i.e. up to the viewer's left. The twill twining was used to weave one of four geometric motifs into the fabric. The different sections of the hat were marked off from each other by single rows of distinctive twining or braid. Inside the hat was a headband. The painted motifs on hats generally represented animal/supernatural beings which were lineage crests of the owner.

The Nuu-Chah-Nulth hat (Fig. 47), in contrast, is a double fabric, made with two identical hats joined together near the brim. The double fabric provided additional protection from the rain.

Nuu-Chah-Nulth hats of this type are characteristically begun with a section of plaiting or chequerwork in wide strands of cedar bark, which are split to make the warps of the hat itself. The construction technique of the body of the hat is two-strand plain twining, with the stitch slant S, i.e. up to the viewer's right. The top and the point where the inner and outer hats are joined are often demarcated by rows of more elaborate twining or braid. Inside the hat is a headband.

Early examples of dome-shaped cedar bark hats have no woven decoration. Some rare examples are covered in red paint. Hats of this type made in the early decades of the twentieth century often had decorative bands of twill

Fig. 47 **Canada, British Columbia, West coast of Vancouver Island, Clayoquot (Nuu-Chah-Nulth).** Twined dome-shaped hat with warp and weft of cedar bark. Double fabric, with two identical hats joined near the brim. Internal headband. For everyday wear. H: 180 mm; dia: 330 mm. Donated by Dr. C.F. Newcombe. 1900.34.6

Fig. 48(a, b) **Canada, Northwest Coast.** Rare type of hat with warp and weft of spruce root, painted with totemic designs in black, red and blue. There is a dome-shaped inner hat of cedar bark. The shape and twining style are from the northern coast, the style of painted decoration from further south. Obtained by Dr. Frederick Dally, probably in the 1860s. Pitt Rivers Collection. 1884.91.18

weave in cedar bark or wrapped twining in grass and aniline dyes.

This was the hat worn by the Nuu-Chah-Nulth people for everyday. There are other, more dramatically painted hats made in the same form, which are rarer. The most famous type of Nuu-Chah-Nulth hat is the knobbed whaler's hat, also made of a double fabric, with an outer surface of grass, with geometric designs and whaling scenes woven into the fabric. By the late nineteenth century this type of hat, depicted frequently in eighteenth century engravings, was no longer common on the coast, although a modern variation in wrapped twining was established by a Nuu-Chah-Nulth basketmaker working with C.F. Newcombe shortly after the turn of the century.

The third type of hat (Fig. 48) is rare, both on the coast and in museum collections. It incorporates elements of both the northern and southern coast. The truncated cone shape is distinctively northern, as is the use of twill twining in combination with two-strand twining on the brim, and the diagonal zigzag lines created with this combination of techniques is a variation on a northern motif.

The stitch slant of the twining, however, is S, i.e. up to the right, the technique used in the south. The painting incorporates southern elements in a composition more characteristic of late nineteenth century hats from the central coast. An unusual hat, and there are very few like it. On those that do exist in the Canadian Museum of Civilization and the Royal British Columbia Museum there is a small, dome-shaped inner hat in cedar bark constructed in two-strand S twining, indicating that these are probably Nuu-Chah-Nulth hats. Fig. 48, which

has a similar inner hat, was collected by Dally, probably during the 1860s. This was a time when many northern people travelled to Vancouver Island. It was the beginning of a period of profound influence exerted by the northern coast on the south and reflected in architecture and carving styles as well as hats. Hats of this type may represent innovations and experiments in response to these influences.

Conclusion

On the Northwest Coast, as in other regions of the world, baskets are far from being simple things. Maintaining a basketry tradition requires excellent supplies of materials, readily available, along with a style of life that allows for the time to gather and prepare them, an educational system that allows a child to start young and practise for years, and a setting that enables the basketmaker to achieve recognition or achieve economic reward for her work. Over the past fifty years these conditions have been increasingly difficult to maintain. It has been more and more difficult to find roots and cedar bark of the proper quality in many areas; children learn other skills in school; the monetary value of baskets has only recently begun to match that of other creative work and, in view of the labour-intensive quality of basketmaking, may never be fully equivalent.

In several areas of the coast, however, basketry either continues as a strong creative tradition or is being redeveloped. Innovations are being added to the long-established diversity of basketry styles and forms on the coast that will carry the tradition into the next century.

Fig. 49 An early, apparently eighteenth century, image of a south central California basket and user. The woman is picking prickly pear fruit, an important food south of San Francisco Bay. She wears a two-part skirt of tanned deerskin, ornamented with olivella shells, which with her jewellery marks her as a woman of wealth. From an old photograph in the U.S. National Museum of a wash drawing, attributed to Jose Cardero, an artist with the Spanish expedition of exploration led by Alejandro Malaspina. Photograph courtesy of the National Anthropological Archives, Smithsonian Institution, Negative # MNH 443.

California Baskets and Basketmakers

by Sally McLendon

The Native peoples of what is now the state of California lived in over one thousand politically independent small tribes or "city states", each with its own political leader or leaders, name and identity. In each, one or more of over sixty distinct, mutually unintelligible languages was spoken, belonging to one of twenty-two separate language families. Tribes controlled specific geographical areas, but were connected to neighbouring towns by marriages, language and/or religious ceremonies, creating networks through which ideas, technology, people and practice flowed across political boundaries.

Despite several important explorations along the coast by English and Spanish ships in the sixteenth century, permanent contact with European peoples only began in the last quarter of the eighteenth century with the establishment of the first Franciscan missions by the Spanish at what is now San Diego (1769), and Carmel (1770) (Fig. 49). By 1823 a total of 21 missions stretched from San Diego north to Sonoma. The discovery of gold at Sutters Fort in 1847 and the annexation of California by the United States in 1848 brought an enormous influx of settlers and fortune seekers, subjecting even inland groups to the stress of dispossession. By the end of the nineteenth century the Native city states of California were much reduced in population, and some had ceased to exist as separate political entities altogether.

When systematic ethnographic research began, tribes which had spoken the same language were grouped together under a single name and treated as a single cultural unit. Deceptively cohesive-seeming groupings, with names like "Miwok", "Pomo", "Maidu", or "Chumash", were created, which are now used in referring to the Indian people of California (see map, Fig. 50).

Two staples in particular made pre-contact sedentary life possible: acorns and fish. Large crops of acorns could be gathered in a few weeks in the fall and stored for consumption throughout the year. The same trees could be harvested year after year, providing the benefits of an annual crop without the need to cultivate, plant or weed.

Similarly, fish could be harvested in quantity during the few weeks of annual spawning runs, to be eaten fresh or dried and stored for use throughout the year. Tubers, fresh greens, fruits and various wild grains were added in season as they became available, as were both large and small game and waterfowl, but acorns and fish provided nutritious, storable annual harvests in predictable, constant locations, permitting a sedentary lifestyle, the accumulation of wealth and considerable leisure.

Baskets played a central role in the acquisition of these two staples of affluence and sedentarism. Acorns were gathered and transported in baskets, de-shelled using baskets (Fig. 62), stored in baskets, ground into flour in a basket hopper on a stone mortar (Fig. 63), sifted with baskets, cooked in baskets (Fig. 52) and served and eaten from still other baskets (Figs. 71, 76). Several species of fish were caught in basketry traps, and all fish were transported home in baskets, often stored in baskets, and served on baskets (Fig.71).

Baskets were also used to gather and parch wild grains (Fig. 53), to collect fruits, vegetables (Figs. 49, 54) and firewood, to store food, water, clothes and valuables, as cradles for babies (Fig. 74) and, by many groups, as hats for both dress and work occasions (Figs. 71, 72, 75, 77, 79-80).

Basketry Areas

Consistent, pervasive differences in techniques and materials group the baskets pro-

51

Fig. 50 California basketry areas. Map adapted from the *Handbook of North American Indians*, Volume 8.

duced by these distinct tribes into four major areas (see map, Fig. 50):

Two Northern California areas in which baskets are always twined, with a conifer root as weft, hazel (or other) shoots as warp, and creamy white bear grass (*Xerophyllum tenax*) as weft overlay, against which designs can be worked in black maidenhair and/or red *Woodwardia* fern.

1. **Northeastern California** where the weft fibre with its overlay is twisted with each stitch, so that the overlay is the outer surface of the weft stitch on the inside of the basket as well as the outside, the reverse of the design showing on the inside. This is usually called "full-twist" overlay.

2. **Northwestern California** where the overlay is carefully kept in front of the weft fibre when it passes behind the warp, so that it does not show on the inside. Although referred to as "half-twist" overlay, the overlaid weft is in fact not twisted.

3. A **Central California** area in which both coiling and twining (without overlay) are used. Coiling is to the left (with the work surface of the basket facing the weaver), except for a small northwestern area of Yuki, Cahto and Wailaki speakers who coil to the right, as in Southern California. The foundation for coiling is normally three rods, except among the Pomoan and Patwin peoples who used both one and three rod foundations. Materials are primarily sedge rhizome (or willow, redbud or conifer roots in some areas and/or baskets) as weft, with designs usually in bulrush, redbud or bracken fern. Willow shoots were primarily used for warps or as coiling foundation.

4. A **Southern California** area (unfortunately not represented here) in which coiling predominates, the work direction being to the right, on a bundle foundation. Juncus, both dyed and natural, and sumac predominate for sewing material and juncus, either whole or shredded, bunch grass (*Muhlenbergia [Epicampes] rigens*), or a combination of the two, served as foundation.

Each group was extremely selective of the materials used, timing their gathering to the season when the plant's fibres had the desired char-acteristics of strength, colour, and flexibility. Since materials from at least two plants and often three or four were combined in most baskets, it could take several months to assemble the necessary materials, all of which needed to be stored, and many of which needed to be seasoned by aging. Basketmaking thus required a considerable amount of planning and preparation.

Early Nineteenth Century Baskets from the San Francisco Bay area

The Pitt Rivers Museum's California basket collections, acquired between 1826/1827 and 1940, include some of the earliest documented California baskets known.

The most important were acquired by Captain Frederick W. Beechey, RN, who visited San Francisco and Monterey in 1826 and 1827 while in command of H.M.S. "Blossom". The "Blossom" was sent to the Pacific to rendezvous with Captains Parry and Franklin in Bering Straits as part of a renewed search for a Northwest Passage. While awaiting the rendezvous, Captain Beechey and his crew were instructed to chart and explore in the Pacific and along the northwest coast of America and to make natural history collections.

In his journal of the trip, Beechey mentions "closely wove baskets" "capable of containing water, [and] used for cooking their meals" (Beechey 1832:337). In 1832 Beechey deposited in the Ashmolean Museum, Oxford, two "Indian baskets of California, made use of for culinary purposes, by heating the water with hot stones", together with a "Belt and feather ornaments, worn by the chiefs of the Indians in upper California" (Duncan 1836:183). These were transferred to the Pitt Rivers Museum in 1886.

The belt is the oldest dated belt known of this type. The two baskets (Figs. 55, 56) are the second oldest group of baskets from California known. (The baskets collected some thirty years earlier by Hewitt during the course of the visits of Vancouver's ships to California in 1792 and

Fig. 51 Mono women grinding acorns on a bedrock mortar, with close twined meal sifters, a spaced twined winnowing basket, and soaproot brushes. Photograph by Dr. John W. Hudson, circa 1901, courtesy of the Field Museum of Natural History, Negative #10563.

Fig. 52 Konkow woman cooking acorn mush for a feast held at Bidwell's Bar, 1901, in traditional three-rod coiled feast baskets. She is dropping a hot stone into a basket. The stone was heated in the fire smouldering behind her, then dipped quickly in water in the small steaming pan next to the fire to remove the ashes. Photograph by Dr. John W. Hudson, courtesy of the Field Museum of Natural History, Negative #95ll.

Fig. 53 Cecilia Joaquin of the Central Pomo speaking community of Shanel, near Hopland, California, demonstrating how wild grains are beaten into a close twined burden basket, using a wicker seed beater. Photograph by Edward S. Curtis in the 1920s near Ukiah, using a basket and seed beater in the Hudson Collection, The Sun House and Grace Hudson Museum, Ukiah, California. Photograph courtesy of the National Anthropological Archives, Smithsonian Institution, Negative #75-14715.

Fig. 54 Mono woman harvesting with open twined winnowing basket into a close twined pack basket. Photograph circa 1901 by Dr. John W. Hudson, courtesy of the Field Museum of Natural History, Negative #A53202.

1793 and now in the Museum of Mankind of the British Museum, and those probably collected when the ships under the command of Alejandro Malaspina visited California in 1791, now in the Museo de América, are the earliest dated California baskets now known.) No record survives of the tribe or mission from which the baskets and the belt came. Since the two baskets are significantly different in their construction, they must have been made by different groups.

Fig. 55 is a classically beautiful three-rod coiled basket, which formerly had tufts of red woodpecker scalp feathers scattered over the light coloured background, and probably clam shell disc beads on the three dark diagonals, of which a single bead survives. It is started with a bulbous knot, a start not used south of San Francisco Bay, but used north of the Bay by Pomoan language speaking tribes and possibly their neighbours, who also favored this style of basket decoration and design. A basket very similar in start and design in the State Indian Museum at Sacramento, California, # 6081, identified as Pomo, was collected near Cloverdale in Sonoma County.

The stitches on Fig. 55 are somewhat different, however, from what is preferred by Pomoan weavers north of Cloverdale in the twentieth century. Since Wappo, Coast Miwok, and Patwin speaking tribes were located in what is now Sonoma County as well as Southern Pomo speaking ones, and the baskets of all these groups are poorly documented, Fig. 55 could be the work of one of these neighbours of Southern Pomo speakers.

Fig. 56 is a fairly tall, straight-sided bowl in sedge root, with bracken fern design formerly scattered with tufts of red woodpecker head feathers The start resembles that of a Plains Miwok basket in the Lowie Museum, LM 1-211527, suggesting a similar source.

Another type of basket described by Beechey had also captured the attention of Sir Francis Drake's men in 1579:

A number of scarlet feathers of the [acorn woodpecker] are wove in with the wood, and
56

completely screen it from view ... to the rim are affixed small black crests of the California pa[r]tridges [i.e., quail] ... otherwise ornamented with beads and pieces of mother-of-pearl [abalone-shell] (Beechey 1832:337).

Although neither of the two baskets which Beechey gave the Ashmolean match this description, a California basket in the original Pitt Rivers Collection, Fig. 57, without other documentation as to source or collector, was originally of this type. Since it is likely to have been acquired in one of the sales held in the 1870s of ethnographic materials collected on late eighteenth and early nineteenth century voyages, it is not impossible that it was originally collected on one of Beechey's visits. It has unfortunately lost most of its former red feathering, the quail topknots at the rim, and many of the dangles and beads, but a ring of clam shell disc beads circles the rim next to where the quail topknots used to be. The start is a stitched around clockspring coil, used by a number of groups to the south of San Francisco Bay. Stitches are regularly split on the interior non-work surface, and designs are worked in olivella shell beads, arranged in seven short columns, at two levels on the basket's wall.

A few baskets of this sort, most apparently collected before 1850, survive in museums around the world, in Frankfurt, Munich, Berlin, Paris, St. Petersburg, Washington, D.C., and the British Museum in London. None are documented as to the group which produced them. Most, like Fig. 57, have no collection history at all. In design and shape they exhibit several distinct styles which it seems logical to suppose were associated with distinct groups, and there is in fact evidence that speakers of Coast Miwok as well as the eight Costanoan languages made such baskets. The Pitt Rivers example, however, seems unique in the austere simplicity of its vertical bars of design in olivella shell beads, compared with the baroque richness of decoration of the others.

Two other early baskets form part of the Pitt

Fig. 55 **California, San Francisco Bay area.** Three-rod coiled basket, foundation of willow shoots sewn with sedge and bulrush root. Coiled to the left. A single clam shell disc bead stitched to exterior dark design: possibly more originally. Red woodpecker feathers formerly scattered over the sedge background. For serving acorn soup. H: 110 mm; dia: 230 mm. Collected by Captain Frederick W. Beechey, HMS "Blossom", 1826/27. Transferred from the Ashmolean Museum, 1886. 1886.1.823

Fig. 56 **California, San Francisco Bay area.** Three-rod coiled ceremonial basket with foundation of willow shoots sewn with sedge and bracken fern root. Coiled to the left. Formerly decorated with red woodpecker feathers scattered over the design area. Four white glass beads stitched on near base. H: 130 mm; dia: 165 mm. Collected by Captain Frederick W. Beechey, HMS "Blossom", 1826/27. Transferred from the Ashmolean Museum, 1886. 1886.1.824

Fig. 57 **California, San Francisco Bay area.** Three-rod coiled ceremonial basket with foundation of willow shoots sewn with sedge. Coiled to the left. Decorated with clam shell disc beads on rim, olivella shell beads forming designs on sides, and dangles of glass beads combined with clam shell beads, terminating in pendants of abalone shell. Formerly completely covered with red woodpecker feathers with quail topknots around rim (one remaining). H: 100 mm; dia: 240 mm. Original Pitt Rivers Collection. 1884.44.2

Fig. 58 USA, Central California, Sonoma County, near Healdsburg, ?Southern Pomo or Wappo. Three-rod coiled basket, foundation of willow shoots sewn with sedge and dyed bulrush root. Coiled to the left. Said to be used for cooking. H: 130 mm; dia: 245 mm. Collected by Mrs. Stephen Fowler, one of the earliest settlers in the area, c. 1850. Donated by her daughter Mrs. Joseph Burtt Davy (formerly Alice Bolton). 1940.6.1

Fig. 59 USA, Central California, Sonoma County, near Healdsburg, ?Southern Pomo, Coast Miwok or Patwin. One-rod coiled basket, foundation of willow shoots sewn with sedge and redbud. Coiled to the left. Said to have contained acorn meal when collected. H: 103 mm; dia: 310 mm. Collected by Mrs. Stephen Fowler, one of the earliest settlers in the area, c. 1850. Donated by her daughter, Mrs. Joseph Burtt Davy (formerly Alice Bolton). 1940.6.2

Fig. 60 USA, Central California, Pomo. Twined hopper with warp of willow shoots and weft of split willow root with two horizontal bands of design in redbud both of which have a break of *dau*, (Central Pomo "door"). Body reinforced with three bands of lattice twining; rim reinforced with oak sapling lashed on with redbud and willow. Used with a mortar stone and pestle for pounding acorns into flour. H: 180 mm; dia: 550 mm. From Denver Art Museum by exchange (Douglass collection). 1949.3.34

Fig. 61 USA, Central California, Pomo. One rod coiled boat basket, foundation of willow shoots sewn with sedge and bulrush root. Coiled to the left. Design includes legs of a man on each side. Stitched with blue glass beads. Probably made for sale. H: 50 mm; L: 260 mm; W: 125 mm. From Denver Art Museum by exchange (Grace Nicholson collection, 665). 1948.12.57

Rivers Museum's important group of early nineteenth century baskets. These were collected near the present town of Healdsburg, to the south of Cloverdale in Sonoma County, by one of the earliest settlers there, Mrs. Stephen Fowler, who is said to have come to California by ship around 1850.

One, Fig. 58, is a three-rod coiled basket, described as used for cooking. It is quite similar to the Beechey basket (Fig. 55) in design and technique, except for the absence of bead and feather decoration. Like the Beechey basket, Fig. 58 is quite Pomoan in technique and Southern Pomo speaking tribes controlled the Healdsburg area. However, Wappo speaking groups immediately to the west could also have produced it.

The other basket, Fig. 59, is said to have held acorn meal when collected. Although collected in the Healdsburg area, it is unlike Pomo baskets in several details. The work surface (which faces the weaver while she works) is on the interior of the basket, although all documented Pomoan baskets, including those of this shape, show it on the exterior. The start is one not otherwise known in documented Pomoan baskets, and the stitch technique is un-Pomoan, with far more split stitches on the non-work surface than Pomoan weavers have found acceptable for the last one hundred years. It may have been made by Coast Miwok or Patwin speaking tribes who lived nearby and often married Southern Pomo people, particularily after European contact.

The Central California Basket Area: Pomo Baskets

All Central California tribes made beautiful baskets, but perhaps the most famous, and certainly the most extensively collected were Pomo baskets. They were not produced by members of a single tribe or group, however. Rather, members of some 72 or more autonomous, independent tribes (or village-communities), living in valleys in the Coast Range of mountains north of San Francisco, and speaking one or more of seven distinct, mutually unintelligible languages, made a range of stylistically similar baskets which are now identified as Pomo.

The various Pomoan tribes are unique in California, and perhaps in all of North America, in making virtually equal use of both major types of basketweaving - twining and coiling - and employing more than one technique in both.

Twined baskets were produced in: 1) plain twining over single warps; 2) alternate pairs twining over two warps (combined with bird cage or wrapped twining for the areas of design); and 3) lattice twining (incorporating a supplemental horizontal warp element). Plain and lattice twining rows could be placed either close together or spaced apart, depending on the intended function of the basket. In addition, three-strand braiding or twining was often used for re-enforcement at the base of a basket and/or at the rim.

Slender willow shoots were used as warps and as foundation rods for coiling. Sedge rhizomes were predominantly used for twining wefts and sewing thread in coiling. (There is some discrepancy in the published literature as to which species of *Carex* was used, see Peri and Patterson 1976:17-19 for details.) In large twined utilitarian baskets designed for cooking and storage, however, the root of the digger pine, *Pinus sabiniana*, or of willow species was frequently used.

Designs were worked by introducing fibres from dyed bulrush root, *Scirpus maritimus*, or the thin peeled reddish brown bark of the redbud bush, *Cercis occidentalis*. Since bulrush grew chiefly in the mud along the shore of Clear Lake, groups living at a distance from the lake seem to have had limited access to this material and that mainly through trade. A second black material, the root of the bracken fern, *Pteridium aquilinum,* is reported used in areas where bulrush is uncommon, especially along the coast (Barrett 1908:139, Purdy 1901-1902:22), although Purdy notes that "the best basket-making Pomo tribes never employ it." Redbud was particularly common as design

59

material in twined baskets used for cooking and storage, as well as in one-rod coiled baskets. When used in horizontal bands of design on twined baskets the redbud strip was often twisted so that the light-coloured inner surface faced outward when neutral background was needed.

Feathers could be incorporated into the surface of both coiled and close-twined baskets to produce splendid baskets especially appropriate for feasts, weddings, religious ceremonies, gifts, etc. Only three-rod coiled baskets were completely covered with feathers, however. Clam shell disc beads (and after contact with Europeans, glass trade beads) were used on both twined and coiled baskets, either with feathers or alone.

Techniques, materials, shape and designs were differently combined in baskets intended for different functions. At least fourteen were distinguished, in addition to six types of fish and bird traps.

Two distinct types of cone-shaped baskets were used for collecting and transporting.

1) A close twined basket in plain twining or alternate pairs twining (combined with bird cage twining for the designs), with designs in redbud (Figs. 53, 63).

2) A spaced twined basket with unsplit willow (or other) shoots as weft as well as warp (Fig. 63).

3) A seed beater, usually made of wicker-work, was used together with the close-twined pack basket to collect wild grains (Fig. 53).

4) Two or three types of close twined plate-form baskets, were used: for containing the pounded acorn flour produced in the mortar basket (Fig. 63); for sifting the pounded flour to separate out the larger particles which then would be re-pounded; for parching wild grains; for winnowing; and for serving. Inverted, such a basket could also be used as a cover for another basket (Fig. 63). Every household required several of these indispensable baskets.

Ranging in shape from very shallow to a quite deep cone, and in size from small to quite large, the plate-form basket could be made in plain

60

twining, plain twining with several bands of lattice twining, totally in lattice twining, or coiled on a one-rod foundation, all with designs in redbud. Barrett (1908:163) claims this basket could also be made in alternate pairs twining, but none seem ever to have been collected. A large one-rod coiled "guests' platter" is in front of Joseppa Dick in Fig. 70.

5) A spaced twined plate-form basket was used for serving fish, meat and bread, for cleaning acorns, for sifting, and for storing anything which needed air circulation (Fig.62). It could be made in either plain twining or lattice twining. When plain twined, willow shoots were used for weft as well as warp (Figs. 68 and 69 where it holds basket materials).

6) A close twined mortar basket was held down on top of a stone slab to contain acorns, buckeyes and wild grains while they were being pounded into flour (Fig. 63). Mortar baskets were cone-shaped with an open area at the bottom through which the pestle could hit the underlying stone slab. They were made in plain twining, sometimes with reinforcing bands of lattice twining, or entirely in lattice twining, with designs normally worked in redbud.

Fig. 60 is a typical example of a mortar basket, made of split willow root weft over willow shoot warps, with design bands in redbud and three reinforcing bands of lattice twining, which probably dates from at least the turn of the century.

7) Two or three types of large, deep, close-twined spherical baskets were used for cooking acorn mush (also called "acorn soup") or pinole (made with wild grains which had been toasted or parched in a close-woven plate-form basket), or for storing wild grains or other fine or small objects.

These close-woven spherical baskets were made in plain, alternate pairs, or lattice twining, all with designs worked in redbud. Baskets of this size and shape were never coiled. A large alternate pairs twined feast bowl is to the left of Joseppa Dick in Fig. 70.

8) A small, close twined spherical basket was used for serving acorn mush or pinole, or for

Fig. 62 Woman at the Central Pomo speaking self-owned community of Yokeya, with hair cut short in mourning, cracking acorns preparatory to grinding. The acorns to be cracked are visible in the large spaced twined basket in front of her to her left. She cracks each acorn individually by placing it on the stone in front of her and tapping it with a small stone. A pile of discarded shells surrounds the bottom stone. In the foreground to her right is a large spaced twined mat on which the de-shelled acorns have been spread out to dry and a metal pan holding water which will be sprinkled on them. These will then be rubbed back and forth on the spaced twined plate-shape basket partially visible to her left to rub off the brown skin. Photograph by Henry W. Henshaw, 1892, courtesy of the National Anthropological Archives, Smithsonian Institution.

Fig. 63 Woman pounding acorns into meal with stone pestle. She pounds down between her extended legs which hold the open bottomed mortar basket down on the stone slab mortar. In front of her feet are two close woven plate-form baskets holding the cracked and shelled acorns to be pounded. At her right hip is a plate-form basket holding already ground acorn flour, with another plate-form basket serving as cover. A large close twined burden basket is on the ground behind her; two spaced twine burden baskets lean against the house wall in front of her. Photograph by Henry W. Henshaw, 1892 at the Yokeya Rancheria, courtesy of the National Anthropological Archives, Smithsonian Institution, Negative #47,750-A.

Fig. 64 **USA, Central California, Pomo.** Three-rod coiled basket, foundation of willow shoots sewn with sedge and dyed bulrush root, giving a black design of "quail topknots". Coiled to the left. Surface covered with tufts of red (woodpecker) and yellow (meadowlark) feathers and stitched with clear glass beads in the dark design area. Design continues on base of basket. H: 145 mm; dia: 240 mm. From Denver Art Museum by exchange (Douglass collection). 1948.12.58.

Fig. 65 **USA, Central California, Pomo.** Three-rod coiled basket, foundation of willow shoots sewn with sedge and bulrush root, giving design of triangles in black. Coiled to the left. Decorated with white glass beads and tufts of red woodpecker feathers, in a style characteristic of ceremonial baskets: earlier examples were decorated with beads of clam shell. This is a gift or ceremonial basket. H: 65 mm; dia: 152 mm. Collected by Barbara Freire-Marreco, 1911-12. 1950.7.5

Fig. 66 **USA, Central California, Pomo.** Three-rod coiled basket, foundation of willow shoots sewn with sedge and dyed bulrush root. Coiled to the left. Decorated with rows of small clam shell disc beads and black quail topknots at rim and red woodpecker feathers on light part of design. Such baskets were traditionally used for gifts, serving food at feasts or burning at funerals. This small example was made for sale as an art basket. H: 55mm; dia: 130 mm. Purchased by Beatrice Blackwood from the Indian Market at the Golden Gate International Exposition, San Francisco, 1939. 1939.8.1B

Fig. 67 **USA, Central California, Pomo.** Three-rod coiled basket, foundation of willow shoots sewn with sedge. Coiled to the left. Decorated with clam shell disc beads and black quail topknots at rim and covered with feathers on body. Yellow feathers from meadowlark, green from mallard, red from wing of redwing blackbird, blue from bluebird or blue jay. Like Fig. 66, this example was made for sale as an art basket. H: 45 mm; dia: 100 mm. Purchased by Beatrice Blackwood from the Indian Market at the Golden Gate International Exposition, San Francisco, 1939. 1939.8.2B

storage of small objects and was woven in plain or alternate pairs twining. An alternate pairs close twined small spherical basket is on the steps to the left of Joseppa Dick in Fig. 70.

9) A large, deep, spaced-twined spherical basket was used for storage, especially of acorns or other nuts. The open spaces between the rows of twining permitted the free circulation of air, thus helping to reduce the growth of mould on the stored foods. Like the spaced twined plate-form basket, it could be woven in either plain or lattice twining. When plain twined, willow shoots were used for both weft and warp. A spaced lattice twined spherical basket is behind Sarah Joaquin Knight Lama in Fig. 68.

10) A small, spaced twined spherical basket was used, according to Barrett (1908:164, plate 25, Fig. 2), for storage of small objects such as basket materials and awls.

Four types of baskets were only made in one-rod or three-rod coiling. With the development of a strong commercial art market for baskets in the early 1890s, these types of baskets were the ones most often made for sale, and are therefore most frequently represented in collections.

11) An elongated oval basket, called in English a "boat basket", was said by Barrett (1908: Plate 20) to be "used by shamans for the storage of sacred objects" or for gifts (Barrett 1908:165), or to store ceremonial or other important objects, but never for food.

From at least the late 1880s, boat shaped baskets were made for sale. Joseppa Dick is weaving a one-rod coiled boat basket in Fig. 70, as is Mary Benson in Fig. 69.

Fig. 61 is a one-rod coiled boat basket acquired by exchange in 1948 from the Denver Art Museum. It had been bought in 1938 from a major dealer, Grace Nicholson, and still bears her original white cloth tag with her number #665, indicating she acquired it between 1902 and 1904 or 1905 (McLendon 1982:218-220). It is typical of the art baskets which were being made for sale in the late 1890s or early 1900s.

12) A flaring mouth, flat bottomed, truncated cone shaped basket may have been used by some groups to serve food. However, Nicholson claimed that especially beautiful baskets of this form were used to wash babies at birth, saved and given to the child when he or she was grown up. Girls at puberty were secluded in a small structure attached to their house and during this period, according to Nicholson and another authority, John Hudson, they used a basket of this shape for washing. It too was saved and used only during a girl's menses.

Flaring mouth baskets were also made for sale from 1900 and possibly earlier. Fig. 64 is a handsome three-rod coiled example with a somewhat variant shape. It nicely demonstrates the rich three-dimensional surface achieved by the incorporation of small tufts of feathers and trade beads into the fabric of the basket.

13) A round basket, which Barrett (1908:164) described as "for ceremonial and other purposes not strictly governed by utility" was probably used for cups and water jars. The Hudson Collection at the National Museum of Natural History, Smithsonian Institution, Washington, DC, includes 28 one-rod coiled baskets identified as cups, jars, meal jars and, in two cases, condiment dishes.

Fig. 65 is a very elegant example, incorporating trade beads and small tufts of red woodpecker scalp feathers in the pattern traditional for baskets intended for ceremonial purposes or feasts, but later common in art baskets. It was given to the Pitt Rivers Museum by Barbara Freire-Marreco (later Aitken), a member of the first class of anthropology students to graduate from Oxford. She carried out archaeological and ethnographic research in the southwest of the United States beteen 1910 and 1913 with the support of a Somerville Research Fellowship, and it seems probable that she acquired this lovely basket during that period.

Fig. 66 is another example of this type of art basket, again incorporating small tufts of red woodpecker scalp feathers. It was purchased by Beatrice Blackwood in 1939 at the famous Indian Exhibit at the Golden Gate International Exhibition in San Francisco, where for the first time Indian peoples were given a place of honour at an important international exposition (Schroeder 1983:184). The exhibit had been designed by Rene d'Harnoncourt, general manager of the Indian Arts and Crafts Board, to demonstrate the diversity of Indian peoples and their cultures and encourage traditional arts by stimulating the market for them. Particularly high quality work was therefore selected, of which this basket is a fine example.

Two types of totally feather covered baskets were made.

14) Baskets with designs worked in different colours of feathers, which Hudson (1899:18) aptly called "jewels". These often were finished with a ring (or groupings) of clam shell disc beads and/or black quail topknots at the rim, and sometimes had dangles of clamshell disc or trade beads, each ending in abalone shell pendants, all items of wealth. They could be given as gifts, sold, or traded, and were often destroyed as a mark of grief at the death of a close relative.

Fig. 67 is an art basket version of this type of basket, again purchased by Beatrice Blackwood at the Indian Exhibit at the Golden Gate International Exhibition. The designs are worked in yellow meadowlark breast feathers, red woodpecker scalp feathers, and blue bluebird breast feathers on a field of iridescent green male mallard head feathers, with a ring of clamshell disc beads and quail topknots at the rim.

15) Baskets totally feathered with the red head feathers of the acorn woodpecker, similar to that described by Beechey (1833:337), and to Fig. 57, but without designs worked in beads.

Weavers in the 1980s remembered that such baskets could only be woven by a woman when fasting. Therefore women would get up and start weaving in the morning, before eating. "When they couldn't stand it anymore", they would stop for the day and eat or drink. It is not clear whether the several baskets of this sort made for sale were woven observing this requirement or

64

not. Barrett (MS.:39) was told that

in the old days a basketmaker could not eat meat while making tasitol [the totally red feathered basket]. *Must stop meat four days before beginning. She worked a few days, then put it by and ate meat, then worked a few days and then ate again, &c., &c.*

16) A baby basket was made in which vertical rods of dogwood or willow shoots were lashed together with twine. According to Barrett (1908:166) baby baskets were made by men, like fish traps, although in recent years most have been made by women.

Before contact with Europeans presumably all adults, both men and women, wove baskets, men weaving traps in addition to baby baskets and, according to Barrett (1908:146), occasionally spaced twined burden and storage baskets, although women wove these too. Barrett (1908:146) claims that all coiling and most twining was the work of women. However, by the end of the nineteenth century several men are known to have made beautiful coiled and twined baskets, the work of William Benson being especially well documented and remarkable (McLendon 1990).

Contact with European and American peoples gave Pomoan peoples access to new technologies and new kinds of wealth. Photographs show that by the late 1860s, if not earlier, people had adopted European styles of clothing, while continuing to live largely in traditional houses. Baskets were still used for gathering and transporting, for cradles for babies, and for at least some cooking, but one also sees metal pails and other metal containers in use.

By the 1890s photographs show that people were largely living in European style houses in addition to wearing European style clothing, and basketmakers normally used a metal pan to hold the water in which the basket materials were always soaked to make them pliable for weaving (Figs. 68-70). Metal pans seem, in fact, to be universally used for holding water or wet substances by this time (Figs. 62, 63).

Fig. 68 Sarah Joaquin Knight Lama, Mary Benson's mother, weaving a twined basket. A fine spaced lattice twined plate-form basket hold her materials by her hip. A large, beautifully made lattice-twined storage basket is behind her. A modern basket awl and a bundle of willow shoots are just in front of her. Photograph by Dr. John W. Hudson, circa 1901, courtesy of the Field Museum of Natural History, Negative #1876.

Fig. 69 Mary Knight Benson demonstrating basketweaving at the Louisiana Purchase Exposition, St. Louis, 1904. She is making a one-rod coiled boat basket. A fine spaced twined plate-form basket holds her materials, with two smaller coiled baskets in front. Photograph by Charles Carpenter, courtesy of the Field Museum of Natural History, Negative #15111.

Fig. 70 Noted basketmaker Joseppa Dick (also called Joseppa Beatty or Joseppa Jeff), with her husband Jeff Dick and son Billy. She is working on a one-rod coiled boat basket and surrounded by her work: a large one-rod coiled "guest's platter" in front, a large alternate pairs twined feast acorn soup bowl to her left, a small alternate pairs acorn soup bowl on the stairs. Photograph by Henry W. Henshaw, 1892, at the Yokeya Rancheria, courtesy of the National Anthropological Archives, Smithsonian Institution.

Fig. 71 Hupa feast after Deerskin Dance, 1889 or 1890. A row of men faces the camera, with a row of women at right angles. All have been served individually a close twined bowl of acorn mush, a spaced twined salmon plate, and a white china cup and saucer. The women all wear dress hats, as well as one girl in front of them. Two spaced twined burden baskets and the foot of a spaced twined cradle are visible between the girls. Photograph by Dr. Charles E. Woodruff, courtesy National Anthropological Archives, Smithsonian Institution, Negative # 75-16181.

Fig. 72 Mrs. Nettie Rubin, a Karok weaver consulted by Lila O'Neale, peeling willow shoots for her "stick" baskets. She wears a dress hat. Behind her are some of her spaced twined stick baskets and bundles of willow shoots. Vertical warps of an unfinished basket are visible to her left in the foreground. Photograph by Lila O'Neale (1932, Plate 1b), courtesy of the Lowie Museum of Anthropology, Negative #15-9017.

By the 1890s most Pomoan people seem to have been using wood-burning iron stoves with metal pots for cooking, although older people still used burden baskets for collecting wood for their fires and for various gathering activities and of course mortar baskets and plate-shaped baskets were still needed for processing acorns. Various sorts of sacks took the place of most storage baskets formerly needed (Fig. 63 along the house wall).

Thus baskets were gradually replaced by the new objects, with cups and those used for containing water being replaced first, those used for cooking probably next and gathering and processing baskets last.

The new substitutes for traditional baskets, while exceedingly practical, had none of the aesthetic qualities of the baskets they replaced. Baskets were beautiful as well as functional, and to work with them or eat from them offered much the same satisfaction and pleasure that fine china or beautifully designed pots and pans now offer. The new substitutes were almost always visually nondescript, if not ugly.

The technological changes of this period thus unintentionally contributed to a separation of function and aesthetics. By 1900 most baskets produced were not made for practical purposes, but rather as objects of purely aesthetic value, and usually for sale, while the material of everyday life was increasingly without any aesthetic value.

Although much less traditional use of baskets was made in daily life by the turn of the century, new uses were also found for baskets during this period. The Elsie Allen Family collection on display at the Mendocino County Museum in Willits, California, includes a small, round, willow shoots twined basket identified as "grandfather's sock basket". Another family has a handsome spaced twined burden basket which was made as a present on the birth of a baby, to carry the diapers down to the creek to wash.

Still another family remembers serving tortillas in a spaced lattice-twined plate-form basket.

In 1889, the completion of the railroad link between San Francisco and the town of Ukiah in the heart of Central Pomo speaking territory brought tourists and summer vacationers. Pomoan peoples had long traded baskets to local storekeepers for supplies and had sold or given baskets to local White residents, particularly those who were friends or employers. The visitors brought by the railroad found these extremely attractive, and a commercial art market swiftly developed.

Pomoan peoples must have found it profitable to turn into cash the old cooking, storage, and food processing baskets which they increasingly rarely used. Clearly, however, the demand for their baskets also offered an attractive means of participating in the market economy in which they now found themselves living. Basketweavers (men as well as women) responded by creating especially splendid baskets, largely in response to that market. Weavers, freed from the constraints which a practical use placed on the form and weave of a basket, experimented with shapes, designs and trade beads, creating what is best called an art basket. Almost all baskets now in museums or private collections were made for this market.

The Northwestern California Basket Area: Hupa and Yurok Baskets

Yurok and Hupa baskets were made by peoples who were less different from each other culturally than the Pomoan peoples, but who spoke totally different, unrelated languages. Unlike the Pomoan peoples who lived in a variety of rather different environments, the Yurok, Hupa, and Karok speaking peoples, lived in very similar environments along two major salmon spawning rivers, the Klamath and Trini-

Fig. 73 Hupa, Yurok and possibly Karok "fancy baskets" displayed in Foster's store, Ukiah, California, c. 1925-1928. Courtesy of Robert J. Lee Collection, Ukiah, California.

ty, which form a rough Y shape in the extreme northwestern part of California.

The groups now referred to as Yurok lived in approximately 54 permanent towns along the lower Klamath, from its intersection with the Trinity to its mouth, and along the Pacific Coast, while those referred to as Karok lived in some 30 or 40 towns upriver of the Yurok along the Klamath above its intersection with the Trinity. Forming the base of the Y, the groups now referred to as Hupa lived in twelve towns in Hupa Valley, with possibly another nine or ten further up the Trinity River.

Although these three languages are totally unrelated to one another, the cultures of the speakers seem to have been virtually identical, as were and are their baskets. Without documentation it is very difficult to identify which group produced a basket. The Pitt Rivers Museum is extremely fortunate in having firmly documented collections of baskets from two of the three groups: the Yurok and the Hupa.

In 1927, Beatrice Blackwood, accompanied by the American anthropologist Gladys Nomland, spent a week at the Yurok town of Weitchpus at the intersection of the Trinity with the Klamath. There she was fortunate in meeting a fine weaver, Mrs. Maggie Peters, from whom she acquired all of the baskets shown in Fig. 74 except for the large space twined burden basket to Mrs. Peters' right.

In l940, Dr. Joseph Burtt Davy of the Imperial Forestry Institute, Oxford University, and his wife, the former Alice Bolton, presented to the museum the Hupa baskets he had collected in Hupa Valley as a young botanist in l897. It is possible that this collection was made with the assistance and advice of the anthropologist and authority on the Hupa, Pliny Earle Goddard, since Goddard credits Dr. Davy for the plant identification in his classic *The Life and Culture of the Hupa* (1903).

Unlike the Pomoan peoples, Hupa, Karok, and Yurok weavers made only twined baskets, in plain twining over single warps in both spaced

70

and close twined forms, although a few baskets were made in alternate pairs twining (O'Neale l932: Pl. 35a). Additional techniques were used at certain points in the basket: three strand twining could be used at the start of a basket, and single rows of three strand twining or paired rows of lattice twining were added to certain types of baskets at the beginning curve of the wall, or about three-fourths of the way up.

As among the Pomoan peoples, techniques, shapes and design decoration were differently combined in baskets intended for different functions, some twenty-seven types at least being distinguished, in addition to an eel pot.

As among Pomoan peoples, two distinct types of cone-shaped baskets were used for collecting and transporting.

1) a spaced twined basket (Fig. 74 for Yurok, Figs. 71 and 75 for Hupa) and

2) a close twined one. Unlike their Pomoan counterparts, these had a flat bottom.

Close twined burden baskets had a fixed design, worked in conifer root against a background of white grass overlay, without any fern overlay (Goddard 1903:42 and Pl.22, Fig.2, O'Neale 1932:45, Moser 1989:frontispiece).

By the end of the 1920s when O'Neale did her research, the close-twined burden or "seed basket", was used only in making medicine for the Brush Dance (a curing ceremony) or as a cover for a storage basket. Weavers consulted at this time disagreed as to whether covers and carrying baskets were interchangable (O'Neale 1932:39). In Fig. 73 such a basket is shown in the lower left as a cover to a much larger storage basket.

3) Spaced plain twined seed beaters, with hazel sticks for weft as well as warp, were used with the close twined burden basket (Goddard (1903: Pl.23,2).

Three types of flat, close twined plate-form baskets existed:

4) sifters, small, stiff, almost flat baskets, reinforced on the underside with bands of heavy sticks, and decorated only with white grass overlay (Fig. 78);

Fig. 74 Mrs. Maggie Peters at the Yurok town of Weitchpec, weaving a twined basket, and surrounded by other of her baskets: a large spaced twined burden basket to her right, two "fancy baskets" made for sale (PRM 1927.43.8 and PRM 1927.43.9), a spaced twined all "stick" salmon plate (PRM 1927.43.5) amd baby cradle (PRM 1927.43.11). Photograph by Beatrice Blackwood, courtesy of the Pitt Rivers Museum, Negative #BB C1 71N.

Fig. 75 Mrs. Freddie, Hupa, leaching acorn meal in a basin of sand by pouring water through it, using a dipper basket. The decorated basket directly in front of her holds the water. She wears a woman's work hat, with simple design band. Behind her is a spaced twined pack basket. Under her right arm can be seen the vertical warps of a basket in progress. Photograph by Pliny Earle Goddard, 1902, courtesy of Lowie Museum of Anthropology Negative #15-3329.

Fig. 76 "An old-time 'set' for acorn soup: [from top down] girl's basket, boy's basket, man's basket with [salmon] plate, dipper" (O'Neale 1932, Plate 5). "The woman placed before the man his basket of soup, on top of which rested a ten-inch Indian plate with his portion of fish. She then served the children, after which she retired to the fire to eat her share of fish from a larger plate upon which she had prepared it, and her share of soup from the cooking basket" (O'Neale 1932:36). Photograph by Lila O'Neale, courtesy of the Lowie Museum of Anthropology.

Fig. 77 "Basket material of the lower Klamath River tribes in various stages of preparation and manufacture from the wild plant to the finished hat." (1) finished Karok hat, (2) brown, baked, split pine root for weft, (3) white bear grass, *Xerophyllum tenax*, prepared for overlay, (4) an unfinished hat, showing hazel warps constituting the frame, (5) prepared stems of the red-dyed Woodwardia fern, (6) Woodwardia fern frond, (7) bundle of hazel shoots for warps, (8) prepared black outer half of the stem of the five-finger type of maidenhair fern, (9) five-finger maidenhair fern frond. Photograph by Governor John Daggett, 1902, courtesy of the National Anthropological Archives, Smithsonian Institution, Negative #81-8355.

72

5) flour trays, a larger, curved, and more flexible plate form basket, with hazel sticks lashed on to the bottom as reinforcement, also decorated only with white grass overlay (Fig. 73);

6) gambling trays, at least among the Karok, which resembled flour trays but were usually deeper, and were more likely to include maidenhair fern in the overlay design. Gambling trays also had hazel sticks lashed on to the bottom as reinforcement.

Sifters were used with flour trays to separate the finer particles out from the coarser ones when pounding acorns. The sifter was "held lightly between the thumbs and first fingers, tilted sharply, and shaken to allow the larger particles to fall back into the hopper for more pounding. The adhering fine meal [was] emptied with a smart tap on the back from the sifter onto the large tray" (O'Neale 1932:38). The Hupa used a "very obtuse cone" as sifter which did not need tapping (Kroeber 1925:91, Goddard 1903, Plate 25, Fig. 1).

7) Plate-form baskets about eight inches in diameter were used before 1900 to "serve the flour from native seeds" (Goddard (1903:43).

8) Plain, undecorated "close-twined almost flat willow trays about eighteen inches across" were kept "exclusively for serving deer meat", at least by the Karok (O'Neale 1932:33).

Several sizes and shapes of spaced twined plate-form baskets, or "stick plates", were used:

9) larger, flatter ones for drying salmon, acorns, etc. (Fields 1985:41), and

10) smaller, deeper plates for serving salmon (Figs. 71 and 76, middle).

11) Close twined mortar baskets, decorated only with white grass overlay, were used in the same way as among the Pomoan peoples.

12) Close twined cooking baskets with vertical walls, ranged, according to O'Neale (1932:35) from one to three feet across. They were also decorated only with white grass overlay, usually in a single band of design on the upper half of the basket. "Old style" cooking baskets had two rows of lattice twining on the

outside upper middle of the basket for strengthening (O'Neale 1932:35; Goddard 1903:42).

13) A basket was kept only for boiling deer meat (Goddard 1903:23), and O'Neale (1932:36) was told that this basket was undecorated and had to be woven at night.

Smaller, close twined serving or acorn soup baskets came in three sizes, each associated with certain design constraints and users.

14) A girl's soup basket was the smallest and had "an easy" pattern (Fig.76 top).

15) A boy's soup basket was slightly smaller than a man's, but any design was appropriate (Fig. 76, second from top), and 75) a man's was the largest, with the most elaborate design (Fig. 76 middle), although all soup baskets had design only on the wall of the basket and primarily in white grass overlay.

15) Undecorated shallow close twined baskets were used to dip acorn soup out of the cooking basket (Fig. 76, bottom).

16) Water baskets were higher and smaller at the top, and usually undecorated (Fig. 75).

Several types of storage baskets were used. Traditional plank houses consisted of one large sunken room, surrounded with an earth ledge at shoulder height, holding "all sizes of covered baskets storing food supplies, clothing and other belongings" (O'Neale 1932:38).

17) Large "all stick" close twined baskets without designs were used for storing dried fish and cracked acorns (O'Neale 1932:3 8). 18) Large close twined storage baskets with designs and covers were used for storing the different seeds and other belongings. "As many as six closely woven baskets were needed to store the different seeds for a well-provisioned family." (O'Neale 1932:39). Some storage baskets were so large that weavers interviewed by O'Neale expressed "their memory of fright when as children they had leaned too far, to find themselves heels over head in the big cipnuks" (O'Neale 1932:38).

19) Special medium-sized close twined baskets with lids, undecorated or with simple

stripes in white overlay, were made especially for tobacco storage. A man's "year's crop might be divided among four or five to ten or a dozen'" (O'Neale 1932:40).

20) Baskets higher than the acorn soup baskets, with small openings and lids, were used for storing valuable property, such as elkskin dresses.

21) All stick, spaced twined baskets, called locally spoon baskets, were made to hold men's horn spoons and women's mussel shell ones, as well as other "odds and ends".

22) A baby cradle was made entirely of hazel rods in spaced twining.

23) Cylindrical baskets sewn from rectangular sheets were carried by dancers in the Jumping Dance and were of great value.

Two or three kinds of hats were made: work hats for both men and women, and dress hats for women only.

24) Men's work hats were plain "root" hats worn "when they packed in deer from the hunt" (O'Neale 1932:42) and sometimes served as a cup or dipper.

25) Women's work caps (Fig. 75) had usually "a design in white grass and one or both ferns" (O'Neale 1932:42). Widows wore undecorated hats, often with holes cut in the top through which their hair cut short in mourning stuck out.

26) Women's dress hats (Figs. 71) were completely covered in overlay with designs in either black maidenhair fern, or red-dyed *Woodwardia*. Women's dress hats were "the technical eminence to which a weaver aspired ... a weaver's ability to make a good one [gave] her a widespread reputation as an expert" (O'Neale 1932:42).

Dr. Davy collected two fine dress hats in 1897 (Figs. 79, 80).

27) A new category of "fancy baskets" evolved from an earlier "trinket" storage basket in response to the commercial market that developed in the nineteenth century. They were made in a variety of shapes, but were normally smaller than traditional storage baskets and more elaborately patterned, with designs and colours formerly typical of dress hats (O'Neale 1932:44, Fig.19).

74

Yurok and Karok weavers had a developed, explicit aesthetic canon which formulated the most pleasingly appropriate combinations of designs, materials and shapes with different functional types of baskets. Hats, for example, had three design zones, each of which required the use of a design conceived of as appropriate to it, which all had to be compatable in size and nature, as well as appropriately distributed and executed (O'Neale 1932 and Fig.20).

In the 1990s baskets continue to be made by many California Indian peoples, although not in as many types as earlier. A major problem for all weavers however is the acquisition of high quality traditional materials. Sedge and willow grow best by creeks in beds which are harvested every year; hazel rods are best from plots which are burned over every year. Neither process is encouraged or understood by the larger White community.

Acknowledgements

Many people have contributed to this paper. First and foremost are the many Pomoan language speakers and basketmakers who have shared their knowledge with me over the years: Bill Graves, Maude Bateman Boggs, Frances Posh Dennison, Ralph Holder, Suzanne Moore Holder, Edna Guerrero Campbell, Elsie Komach Allen, Laura Fish Somersal, Salome Alcantro, Frances Jack, Nathan (Sandy) Boggs and Susan Billy. Nina Cummings, Photo Archivist, Field Museum of Natural History, Chicago, Paula Fleming, Photo Archivist, National Anthropological Archives, Smithsonian Institution, Dr. Ira Jacknis, Senior Research Anthropologist, Lowie Museum of Anthropology, Elizabeth Edwards, Assistant Curator (Archives), Pitt Rivers Museum and Robert J. Lee have all gone out of their way to help in securing good prints of the photographs included here. Eileen Sheerin of Hunter College helped with the printing, while Linda Mowat, Assistant Curator, Pitt Rivers Museum, kindly made the Californian collections available for study. I thank them all.

Fig. 78 **USA, Northwestern California, Weitch-pec, Yurok.** Twined flat tray with warp of hazel shoots and weft of split pine root. Overlay pattern in bear grass. Pairs of reinforcing rods on the underside. This is a model of a larger tray used for sifting acorn meal by shaking or tapping the tray over another basket. Hastily made, probably to order. Dia: 260 mm. Collected by Beatrice Blackwood, 1927. 1927.43.4

Fig. 79 **USA, Northwestern California, Klamath River, Hupa.** Woman's twined dress hat, with warp of hazel shoots and weft of split conifer root or possibly grape vine. Half-twist overlay pattern in bear grass (white), maidenhair fern (black), inner stems of woodwardia fern dyed with alder root (reddish brown) and bear grass dyed with tree-lichen (yellow). H: 70 mm; dia: 175 mm. Collected by Dr. Joseph Burtt Davy, 1897. 1940.6.6

Fig. 80 **USA, Northwestern California, Klamath River, Hupa.** Woman's twined dress hat, with warp of hazel shoots and weft of split conifer root. Half-twist overlay pattern in bear grass (white) and maidenhair fern (black). H: 90 mm; dia: 180 mm. Collected by Dr. Joseph Burtt Davy. 1940.6.7

Those Who Lived Before

'by Claire Farrer

Imagine you live in 1,000 BC in the American Southwest, close to the border of the present-day states of Arizona and New Mexico. It is winter and sunny, but cold.

As you walk into your home, you admire the wisdom of those who lived before, the old ones who are kept alive in your tribe's memory: the same ones who learned that building masonry homes into south-facing cliffs meant they would be cool in summer and warm in winter. You are grateful for that warmth now for, despite the cosiness of your woven feather cloak, the cold seeps through, working its way up from your grass-lined moccasins, past the skin coverings for your lower body, finding the gaps in your cloak, and thoroughly chilling you. The warmth inside your lovely masonry apartment high up the cliff face is appreciated.

As you enter your family's apartment, one of the younger girls passes you a round basketry tray (Fig. 82) filled with piñon nuts - tiny, sweet, oily, delicious piñon nuts. Normally, this tray is used for gruel or other liquid foods, as the pitch coating attests; today, however, it contains the delicious piñon nuts. You have no way of knowing that almost 3,000 years later a similar tray (Fig. 86), will find its way into a museum. What is commonplace to you will also be commonplace to those who come after you in this desert region - there is no reason to change that which works well.

From a rectangular tray you take a piece of piki bread: a tissue-paper thin wrapped and folded rolled wafer of corn meal, ashes and water. As you eat, your glance slides around the room, admiring your family's skills at making baskets, and you know that life is indeed good. There are baskets for cooking, winnowing, sieving, storing, wearing, beating, parching, admiring, carrying and more for music and ceremony. There are huge baskets for storing supplies and for carrying babies. Everywhere your eye lands, there is a finely wrought basket.

This fictitious person might be surprised to learn that the entirety of a cultural florescence was named, and the people remembered, primarily for their skill at basketry. Baskets were so ubiquitous and well-made among the prehistoric Indians of the American Southwest that, early in this century, archaeologists characterized cultural horizons from about 7,000 BC onwards as Basketmaker, further dividing them into Basketmaker I (roughly, BC times), Basketmaker II (about AD 1-400), and Basketmaker III (from AD 400-700). The Pueblo period is generally dated to times after AD 700; however, baskets continued into that time and are present today as well.

Even earlier in time than Basketmaker I there were foragers in the American Southwest who made exquisite stone tools but left us little else of their material culture. Then came the basketmakers who added an amazing variety of woven containers to their cultural inventory. The Anasazi, those who are today considered the ancient ones, produced exquisite pottery between approximately 700 and 1300 AD. Despite the 19th century introduction of metal utensils and then the 20th century invasion of plastic ware, basketry is still made today. Basketmakers and their products follow in a long tradition stretching further back in time than memory can plumb but the tradition is memorialized in myth and story, as with the Hopi Spider Grandmother who is known to have spun her web as she created parts of our earth and

Fig. 81 **USA, Arizona, Western Apache.** Coiled jar with willow or cottonwood rod foundation, sewn with willow or cottonwood and martynia (black). Coiled to the left. H: 310 mm. From Denver Art Museum by exchange (Douglass collection). 1948.12.39

some of the people who inhabit it.

Those Who Work Today

Regardless of how process and product are linked and remembered, basketry is still practised in the contemporary Southwestern United States, albeit in reduced fashion. Myth, legend, and story - as well as personal vision and experience or creativity - still find their way into basketry. In addition, there is a thriving market of basketry divorced from context and intended primarily for the tourist trade.

Tourists and collectors are often interested in whether or not particular items have specific names or symbolic associations, in whether or not the form is a consistent one through time, and in authenticity in general. To assure buyers their purchases are made by Indians, there are co-operative marketing groups as well as associations with galleries and shops as members whose word guarantees a product was indeed manufactured by an Indian person. But that word bond does not speak to meaning, an elusive problem, since many Indian individuals and groups prefer not to discuss meaning with outsiders.

Sometimes those with long experience with an Indian tribe - such as anthropologists or missionaries or traders - are able to discuss meaning woven and stitched into baskets. Often they caution that one be chary in attributing meaning, for an ethnographic report of meaning or symbol may well be idiosyncratic or there may be competing meaning and symbolic systems in operation at any one time. Then, too, scholars and others note that some Indians hire or commission other Indians to make baskets for them with the maker being asked to adhere to the cultural canon of the buyer.

It is usually easier to assess where an item originates than what that item's design means. However, this, too, can be a trap for the unwary. An item purchased or collected at a known place may well have been produced elsewhere. For example, what is Navajo in design, con-
78

struction, and use may well have been made by a Paiute for a Navajo patron, as with basket Fig. 99. Or, as has happened in my own experience with the Mescalero Apache, a basket consecrated for ritual use only was actually produced by a Jicarilla Apache, given as a gift to a Mescalero religious specialist, and subsequently used in several public and private ceremonials where it assumed the status of a "Mescalero" basket through association (see also Farrer 1991). How, then, *are* Southwestern baskets attributed to particular people, time, and place - let alone how is meaning or symbolism ascribed?

Ethnologists, curators, careful collectors, and savvy tourists ask lots of questions and fill their notes with many question marks. Unless one knows the maker of a particular basket, one must rely on provenance - where it was found or purchased and under what circumstances. If possible, the date is established from other associated items, or from information that comes from consultants - whether scholarly or native. One also relies on features of technique of manufacture, as well as design characteristics, to assign a particular piece to a specific tribal and temporal origin. Nonetheless, much guesswork is inevitable. Disregarding problems of accuracy of attribution, the variety in design and construction demand admiration as does the persistence of human endeavour through vast periods of time.

The following discussion provides a guide to the distinctive features of Southwestern baskets, based upon both construction and style.

Anasazi

Although the Southwest is arid and thus provides an excellent environment for stability of cultural materials, the disposal practices of the Anasazi as well as the antiquity of the material mitigate against there being vast quantities of items. Seldom are entire pieces found intact. However, materials that did survive to the present argue for an advanced culture, well-adapted to its environment, as can be seen in frag-

Fig. 82 USA, NE Arizona, Cañon de Chelly, Anasazi. Base of resin-coated coiled basket with three rod foundation. Stitching across several coils suggests an ancient repair. Dia: 105 mm. Collected by Beatrice Blackwood, 1927. 1928.9.27

Fig. 83 USA, Texas, Brewster County, Ber Cave Canyon, Anasazi. Fragments of two sandals, plaited from yucca fibre. L: 210, 200 mm. Donated by L.C.G. Clarke. 1937.44.1-2

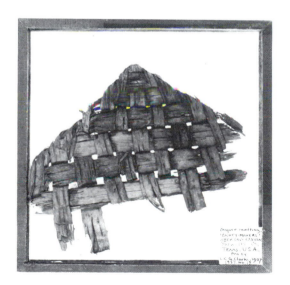

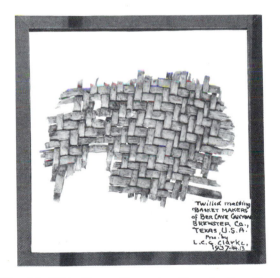

Fig. 84 USA, Texas, Brewster County, Ber Cave Canyon, Anasazi. Corner fragment of chequer plaited matting. 145 x 110 mm. Donated by L.C.G. Clarke. 1937.44.17

Fig. 85 USA, Texas, Brewster County, Ber Cave Canyon, Anasazi. Fragment of twill plaited basketry or matting. 100 x 70 mm. Donated by L.C.G. Clarke. 1937.44.13

mentary material (Figs. 82, 83-85). It is difficult to appreciate craftsmanship in some items, such as cordage or plaited sandals (Fig. 83). However, household items, even when fragmentary, such as mats (Fig. 84) or baskets (Fig. 85) attest to Anasazi control of their materials and techniques.

Unfortunately, with such limited material combined with the far reaches of time involved, it is not sensible to try to speculate on any possible meaning the weavers may have intended when crafting these pieces.

Apaches

There are several different groups of Apaches living in present-day Arizona and New Mexico. In prehistoric and early historic times they were transhumant, if not nomadic; this lifestyle of frequent moves dictated a need for easily portable goods. Thus, they produced baskets for general use far beyond the time when most Pueblos (or sedentary people) had switched to ceramic manufacture. In general, women are the basketmakers.

While Apaches are distinguishable from each other on the basis of several cultural features, they nonetheless speak mutually intelligible languages and consider themselves to be more closely related to each other than to other Southwestern Indians or Indians in general. Most scholars separate them into Western (generally the Arizona Apaches and those who used to live west of the Rio Grande) and Eastern groups (primarily those in New Mexico). As can be seen in the basketry, this seems to be a sensible division. Wherever their location, Apache basketmakers shared in common a reliance on coiled and twined basketry made on a foundation of stick rods and grass bundles.

Eastern Apaches, those on the Mescalero and Jicarilla Apache reservations, do still produce baskets, although there are very few who are skilled and active today (Fig. 87). Jicarilla Apaches are particularly associated with deep bowls and cylindrical jars, often with lids and carrying handles. Their basketry skill was once legendary in the Southwest; for that reason, Jicarilla baskets are particularly prized and are used until they are past mending, as Fig. 86 indicates. This basket, while collected in Santa Clara Pueblo, was Jicarilla-made, again warning one to be chary in attributing source of collection to source of manufacture.

It is difficult to misattribute Mescalero Apache baskets for they are characterized by muted colours of cream, yellow, green, and brown-black, fashioned from wide, flat, coils with symmetrical, and usually even-numbered, motifs that often depict four-pointed stars or circles repeated four times on the design field. Designs are symbolic and named on Mescalero basketry. Mescaleros also used to produce, both for themselves and for trade, rather large numbers of jars that were pitch-covered to allow them to be watertight (Fig. 88).

Western Apache baskets - whether from San Carlos, Whiteriver, Cibique, or one of the other areas - present the most numerous examples and are arguably (with Hopi and Tohono O'Odham) the most widely dispersed of Southwestern Indian basketry. While Western Apache basketmakers produce a variety of shapes (for example, see Figs. 81, 89), they are best known today for their storage and burden baskets. Storage baskets typically have flat bottoms and may or may not be fitted with tops. Burden baskets, highly prized today for ceremonial uses, usually have bottoms that are conical and come to a point while the tops are wide and flaring; rims are usually fitted with leather fringes culminating in tin-cone jingles. The shape of burden baskets dictates that they cannot stand alone; they usually have a tump-line attached.

Western Apaches also produce a rather large variety of trays: shallow, bowl-shaped baskets (Figs. 89-92).

Often Western Apache baskets have figures of either people or animals worked into them as can be seen in Fig. 91. Such baskets are said to tell stories, although one must be thoroughly familiar

Fig. 86 USA, New Mexico, Santa Clara Pueblo, Jicarilla Apache. Coiled tray with foundation and sewing of sumac or willow rods. Coiled to the left. Base reinforced with cloth. This is a well-used domestic basket, encrusted with the food that was prepared and served in it. Collector noted: *The Santa Clara people buy them from the Jicarilla Apaches, who bring a few when they come to Santa Clara feast on August 12. Also, Basillo Naranjo of Santa Clara is married to a Jicarilla Apache woman, and when he comes to visit his mother he brings a basket.* H: 105 mm; dia: 340 mm. Collected by Barbara Freire-Marreco from Filomena Baca de Naranjo, 1910-1911. 1911.86.54

Fig. 87 USA, New Mexico, Dulce, Jicarilla Apache. Coiled basket with three-rod foundation of sumac sewn with sumac (natural white and red dyed with mountain mahogany root) and willow (natural brown). Openwork "lace pattern" around rim, which is finished with false braid. Design has break or "spirit path". H: 70 mm; dia: 360 mm. Made by Mrs. Lydia Pesata and collected by Linda Mowat, 1991. 1991.35.7

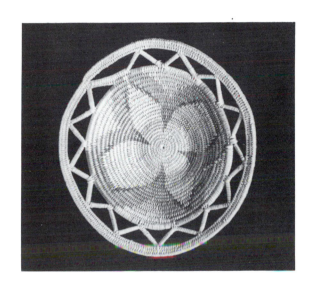

Fig. 88 USA, Arizona, Zuñi Pueblo, ?Mescalero Apache. Twined double-lobed jar of sumac or squawberry with length of rope and loop of hide attached for carrying. Coated with pitch to make it watertight. Obtained at Zuñi Pueblo but probably of Apache origin. H: 240 mm; dia: 130 mm. Collected for the US National Museum. Donated by the Royal Gardens, Kew. 1892.2.5

Fig. 89 **USA, Arizona, Western Apache.** Coiled tray with willow or cottonwood rod foundation, sewn with willow or cottonwood and martynia (black). Coiled to the left. Design of five-pointed "star" or "flower", meaders and lozenges. Used for preparing or serving food, or for holding water. H:63 mm; dia: 285 mm. From Denver Art Museum by exchange (Jeancon collection). 1948.12.41

Fig. 90 **USA, Arizona, Western Apache.** Coiled tray with willow or cottonwood rod foundation, sewn with willow or cottonwood and martynia (black). Coiled to the left. Design of six-pointed "star" or "flower". Used for preparing or serving food, or for holding water. Dia: 300 mm. From Denver Art Museum by exchange(Bretlinger collection). 1948.12.43

Fig. 91 **USA, Arizona, Western Apache.** Coiled tray with willow or cottonwood rod foundation, sewn with willow or cottonwood and martynia (black). Coiled to the left. Design includes human and animal figures. Used for preparing or serving food, or for holding water. H: 80 mm; dia: 270 mm. From Denver Art Museum by exchange (Jeancon collection). 1948.12.42

Fig. 92 **USA, Arizona, Western Apache.** Coiled tray with willow or cottonwood foundation, sewn with willow or cottonwood and martynia (black). Coiled to the left. The design on this basket is sometimes described as referring to a narrative of the Twin War Gods as they sought out their Creator Father; the triangles at the intersections of the lines are conceived of as specific mythical adventures. H: 100mm; dia: 335 mm. From Denver Art Museum by exchange (Mrs. J. D. Whitmore coll.). 1948.12.44

with the culture to "read" the intended narrative.

Western Apache basketmakers seldom share the names of designs, although contemporary basketmakers will comment on the meaning both of their own and other practising weavers" designs while also noting similarities with ancient basketry. Fig. 92, for example, is sometimes described as referring to a narrative of the Twin War Gods (symbolized by the linked triangles) paying a visit to their progenitor, Father Sun (symbolized by the central circle). The dotted lines are then interpreted as referring to various migrations of the Twin War Gods as they sought out their Creator Father; the triangles at the intersections of lines are conceived of as specific, momentous adventures well known in mythic narrative. These adventures sometimes refer to particular places in the contemporary landscape.

Hopi Pueblos

The Hopi people of Arizona live on, or very close to, three mesas stretching like slender fingers into the arid land just west of the New Mexico border and east of the Grand Canyon. The mesas were named by the Spanish as they encountered them in their forays of exploration; they are still referred to by their Spanish designations, albeit in English, as First Mesa (that closest to New Mexico), Second Mesa (the one in the middle), and Third Mesa (that closest to the Grand Canyon). Today's Hopi say they are the descendants of the Anasazi, having arrived on their mesas after a very long period of migrations throughout the Southwest. Regardless of their antecedents, they represent an ancient and continuing Southwestern tradition.

In addition to their exquisite pottery industry, revitalized in the late 19th and early 20th centuries, Hopi people produce basketry that is easily recognizable. In their division of labour, basket making is women's work (Plates 5, 7).

On Second Mesa, Hopi basketmakers employ thick coils primarily to make flat trays (Fig. 93),

frequently with representations of kachinas (Fig. 94). Third Mesa is known for its trays with raised centres, such as Fig. 96. While plaiting is more common on Third Mesa, there are Second Mesa examples of it as well, see Figs. 95, 98.

On Third Mesa, the more popular styles of basket making are plaiting and wickerwork, sometimes in combination. Plaiting is usually done in diagonal patterns. Wickerwork is especially used on plaque trays (for example Figs. 96, 97, front cover) and shallow baskets with a raised centre section, sometimes also with a slightly raised rim. As can be seen from the captions, Hopis are not reticent to share the names and meanings of their designs.

Navajo

The Navajo are the most numerous tribe of Native Americans with a population of over 200,000. Their land is exquisitely beautiful, but mostly barren desert or high plateau and mountains. Those unfamiliar with the Southwest, or desert environments in general, often use the word "desolate" to describe the Navajo area that encompasses parts of three states: Arizona, New Mexico, and Utah.

Most people are familiar with Navajo weaving: tightly woven blankets, rugs, and wall hangings in arresting patterns. Many also are familiar with Navajo silversmithing and the resulting jewellery. Few, however, know Navajo basketry. And that is not surprising, since few Navajo baskets are made today and many of those labelled Navajo were actually made by Ute or Paiute Indians for their Navajo patrons.

Navajo-style basketry, a term that leaves one on safer grounds, like other Athabaskan (Apachean) basketry, is constructed over rods and bundles and usually takes the form of shallow bowls with geometric patterns. In older (pre-20th century) pieces one can also see wickerwork burden baskets, although I know of no one producing them today.

Fig. 99 is an excellent example of the most

Fig. 93 **USA, Arizona, Second Mesa, ?Mishong-novi, Hopi.** Coiled plaque with bundle foundation of galleta grass sewn with yucca. Coiled to the left. "Sunflower" design in black and brown (natural dyes). Used as a bread tray. Collector noted that this specimen was transitional between the deeper old trays and the flat plaques made for the European market. Dia: 360 mm. Collected by Barbara Freire-Marreco, 1912-13. 1913.87.76

Fig. 94 **USA, Arizona, Second Mesa, Hopi.** Coiled plaque with bundle foundation of galleta grass sewn with yucca. Coiled to the left. Design in natural dyes (black and brown) of a female kachina spirit. Collector's original labels indicate details of costume. Used as a bread tray. Dia: 300 mm. Collected by Barbara-Freire-Marreco, 1912-13. 1913.87.60

Fig. 95 **USA, Arizona, Second Mesa, Shipaulovi, Hopi.** Unfinished twill plaited basket of yucca leaf. This plaited mat would be sewn into a wooden ring to complete the basket. L: 590 mm; W: 580 mm. Collected by Barbara Freire-Marreco, 1912-13. 1913.87.78

Fig. 96 **USA, Arizona, Third Mesa, Hopi.** Wicker plaque with warp of sumac and weft of rabbit brush with yucca edging. Butterfly design in aniline dyes (red, green, orange and black). Dia: 400 mm. R.B. Townshend collection. 1931.60.20.

Fig. 97 **USA, Arizona, Third Mesa, Hotevilla, Hopi.** Wicker plaque with warp of sumac and weft of rabbit brush, the edge finished with a strip of yucca. Design in aniline dyes (red, green and purple) of a Havasupai kachina spirit in mask and featgher headdress. Collector's original labels indicate details of costume. She noted: *These ... baskets ... are bought by the Hopi and Tewa of First Mesa, who use them to carry wafer bread when they present it to each other. They also serve wafer bread on them at meals. When a basket is shabby, it descends to the rougher household uses. A woman who has acquired a pretty basket keeps it hanging on the wall, partly as a decoration to the house, partly to keep it clean. It is her individual property.* Dia: 350 mm. Collected by Barbara Freire-Marreco, 1912-13. 1913.87.75

Fig. 98 **USA, Arizona, Second Mesa, Mishongnovi, Hopi.** Twill plaited basket, *pajo*, of yucca leaf. Collector noted: *Used for sifting corn or beans, carrying out rubbish and for rough kitchen use generally. Though, like other baskets,* pajo *are usually made by women, a few men amuse themselves by making them.* This example was one of many thrown to spectators during the women's Basket Dance. H: 70 mm; dia: 300 mm. Collected by Barbara Freire-Marreco, 1913. 1913.87.77

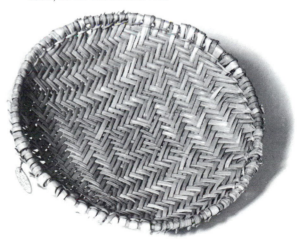

common Navajo-style basket. Termed a wedding basket, and indeed often used in traditional weddings where the bride and groom consume gruel from such a basket, this item exemplifies Navajo-style basketry. The break, or spirit line, is intentional and has many purposes. Among them are orienting the basket properly (with the opening to the east) and purposefully not creating perfection. In Navajo belief, perfection is the province of the Creator - people's arms are too short to box with God so why risk the potential insult by creating perfection oneself? This spirit line can also be seen on traditional weaving and even on the commercial sand paintings produced on hardboard (masonite) for the tourist trade. During ceremonials among the Navajos and among certain Pueblos, baskets such as this are sometimes inverted and laid over the ground where they are struck, as if they were drums, or rubbed, as if they were rasps.

Pima and Papago (Tohono O'Odham)

These two closely related tribes live in southern Arizona on the Sonoran desert, a particularly inhospitable environment unless one knows the ways of the desert very well indeed. In recent years, the Papago have requested that they be referred to by their own name for themselves, Tohono O'Odham.

Both groups formerly used diagonal plaiting as well as coiling techniques in constructing their baskets. Traditionally, coil baskets were sewn with willow and martynia. The Pima sometimes used anthropomorphic or zoomorphic figures in their designs, but are better known for their fine geometric work, some of which has symbolic significance. The Pima variation on a theme through time can be observed in Figs. 102-103, with other variations present such as Fig. 104. But not all is repetition on a theme, as is clear in observing Fig. 100, an unusual form that undoubtedly was intended for a specific use, as were the storage jars of which Fig. 101 is an example.

86

The Tohono O'Odham responded to the demands of tourism by largely abandoning willow and martynia sewing material in favour of the more readily available yucca (Figs. 107, 108). They frequently use a variation of the person-in-a-maze design, having one central anthropomorphic figure, just inside the rim, facing a labyrinth. Almost every shop that deals in Indian material culture will have examples of Tohono O'Odham basketry; their work has been extremely popular in the past decade, allowing the basketmakers to be compensated adequately for their work. Not only are they making baskets for the tourist trade, but also there is a large local market for basketry in everyday use. Making head rings (the bases on which pots are placed to carry them on the head), mats, cylindrical carrying baskets, bowl baskets, trays and horsehair miniatures, the Tohono O'Odham are producing the greatest variety of baskets being made in the Southwest today.

In an unusual division of labour, women generally make the fibre baskets while some Tohono O'Odham men make metal ones that are becoming increasingly popular as fruit, flower or egg bowls (Fig. 106). The metal baskets are made in the style of the old "lacework" baskets that were constructed with string or cordage of agave fibre. The rim of Fig. 105 illustrates the openwork, or lacework, style of the metal baskets. Sometimes made of coat hangers and sometimes of other kinds of thin wire, these metal baskets are assuming an increased place in Southwestern markets, although they do not appeal to every taste.

Pueblos

Those Native Americans generally referred to as the Pueblos today live either near the Rio Grande River (the Eastern Pueblos) or on the deserts to the west in both New Mexico and Arizona (the Western Pueblos). At one time, each Pueblo had a thriving basketry tradition. Now, however, most Pueblos concentrate on con-

Fig. 99 **USA, Arizona, Navajo (Paiute).** Coiled bowl with rod foundation and sewing of sumac. Coiled to the left. Plaited rim. Two horizontal bands of black triangles separated by a plain red band (natural dyes) with characteristic opening in the design. Used to hold the cornmeal eaten by bride and groom in the Navajo wedding ceremony; also in other ceremonies, sometimes turned upside down and used as a drum. Navajo women ceased making baskets in the late nineteenth century; at this time the southern Paiute and Ute took over the manufacture of ritual baskets for sale to the Navajo. This example was probably made by a Paiute. In the last few decades Navajo women have gradually began to take up basketry again. H: 100 mm; dia: 338 mm. Collected by Beatrice Blackwood, 1939. 1946.3.9B

Fig. 100 **USA, Southern Arizona, Pima.** Coiled bowl with jar incorporated. Foundation of cattail sewn with willow and martynia. Coiled to the left. Meander design on bowl. Border of plaited martynia and willow. Used to hold two kinds of food. H: 130 mm; dia: 360 mm. Collected by W.A. Bolton, c. 1890. Donated by his sister Mrs. Joseph Burtt-Davy. 1940.6.4

Fig. 101 **USA, Southwest, Pima.** Coiled jar with foundation of cattail sewn with willow and martynia. Coiled to the left. H: 330 mm; dia: 325 mm. From Denver Art Museum by exchange (Mrs. Percy Jackson collection). 1949.3.30.

Fig. 102 **USA, Southern Arizona, Pima.** Small coiled tray with foundation of cattail sewn with willow and martynia. Coiled to the left. Border of oversewing in martynia. Old at time of collection. H: 25 mm; dia: 127 mm. Collected by Beatrice Blackwood, 1927. 1928.9.28

Fig. 103 **USA, Southern Arizona, Pima.** Coiled tray with foundation of cattail sewn with willow and martynia. Coiled to the left. Border of oversewing in martynia. H: 95 mm; dia: 380 mm. From Denver Art Museum by exchange (J.A. Jeancon collection). 1948.12.47

Fig. 104 **USA, Southern Arizona, Pima.** Coiled tray with foundation of cattail sewn with willow and martynia. Coiled to the left. Border of plaited martynia. H: 60 mm; dia: 300 mm. From Denver Art Museum by exchange (James Harlow collection). 1948.12.48

Fig. 105 **USA, Southern Arizona, Tohono O'Od-ham.** Coiled plaque with foundation of bear grass or cattail, sewn with yucca and martynia. Coiled to the left. Dia: 328 mm. From Denver Art Museum by exchange. 1948.12.51

Fig. 106 **USA, Southern Arizona, Tohono O'Od-ham.** Basket of copper wire, made by Norman Mike. H: 43 mm; dia: 290 mm. Collected by Linda Mowat, 1991. 1991.35.2

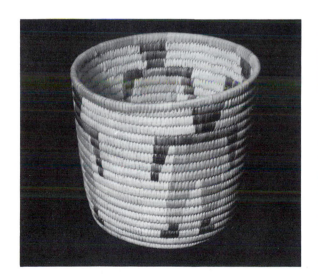

Fig. 107 **USA, Southern Arizona, Tohono O'Od-ham.** Coiled wastepaper basket with foundation of bear grass sewn with yucca. Made for sale. H: 180 mm; dia: 195 mm. Collected by Beatrice Black-wood, 1926. 1927.1.2

Fig. 108 **USA, Southern Arizona, Tohono O'Od-ham.** Open coiled tray with foundation of bear grass sewn with yucca. Made for sale. H: 40 mm; dia: 290 mm. Collected by Linda Mowat, 1991. 1991.35.1

tainers of pottery. There are, however, old pieces in many museum collections that represent industries now quiescent and a few baskets are still made by both men and women. Jemez Pueblo in New Mexico is represented by a few coiled baskets, twill plaited winnowing baskets and mats or rings for jar carrying. Open wicker-work baskets (Fig. 109) have been produced in the Eastern Pueblos of San Juan and Santo Domingo, as well as in San Ildefonso where twill plaited ring baskets and trays have also been made. Rare examples of wicker basketry come from Zuñi Pueblo, in the desert between Albu-querque and Gallup, New Mexico. One of these, Fig. 110, is said to be for the collection of locusts (a protein resource).

Fig. 109 **USA, New Mexico, Rio Grande Pueblos.** Wicker basket of willow with scalloped rim. Old specimen. Donated by Joe Becker. 1991.35.12

Epilogue

Each time I have the opportunity to view an exhibition of basketry such as this one, I am struck by the amazing diversity of human ingenuity. Using only simple tools and materials, ancient and contemporary people, from a variety of cultural traditions, produce not only useful basketry items but also ones that are aesthetically pleasing. Per-haps even more amazing is that despite the relatively limited design potential, dictated by palette and construction techniques, there is no duplication of design. Motifs and color combinations are frequently duplicated, but they provide only a basic grammar to which is appended a unique representation in each item. Not just in the Southwest but through-out the Americas the diversity in basketry is truly astounding.

Fig. 110 **USA, New Mexico, Zuñi Pueblo.** Small wicker basket with strip of cloth attached to rim for carrying. Used for collecting locusts. Collected by James Stevenson, 1884. Donated by the US National Museum. 1896.79.114

Plate 1 **Canada, British Columbia, Queen Charlotte Islands, Haida.** Twined hat with warp and weft of spruce root, painted with totemic design of the Raven in black and red. H: 155 mm; dia: 410 mm. Rev. Charles Harrison collection. 1891.49.36

Plate 2 **USA, Maine, Pleasant Point, Passamaquoddy.** Contemporary ash splint baskets with overlay decoration and sweetgrass trim. Strawberry basket by Clara Keezer, 1991. H: 120 mm. Miniature basket by Clara's son, Rocky Keezer, 1991. L: 22 mm. Collected by Linda Mowat, 1991. 1991.35.25, 28. Wall pocket by Rocky Keezer, 1989. H: 155 mm; L: 190 mm. Collected by Ann McMullen, 1991. 1992.1.9

Plate 3 **Brazil, Para State, Wai Wai.** Twill plaited rattle of reed with pattern in black, decorated with coloured feathers. L: 360 mm. Collected by Zeina El-Khouri Klink, 1990. 1990.47.9

91

Plate 4 **USA, Maine, Pleasant Point.** Clara Keezer, Passamaquoddy, finishing the rim of a woven basket with warp of ash splints and weft of braided sweetgrass. Photograph by Linda Mowat, 1991.

Plate 5 **USA, Arizona, Second Mesa, Mishongnovi.** Pauline Quiyo, Hopi, making a coiled plaque with foundation of galleta grass sewn with yucca leaf. Photograph by Linda Mowat, 1991.

Plate 6 **USA, North Carolina, Cherokee.** Rowena Bradley, Eastern Cherokee, plaiting a doubleweave basket of rivercane. Photograph by Linda Mowat, 1991.

Plate 7 **USA, Arizona, Third Mesa, Oraibi.** Bessie Monongye, Hopi, starting to weave a wicker plaque with warp of sumac and weft of rabbit brush. Photograph by Linda Mowat, 1991.

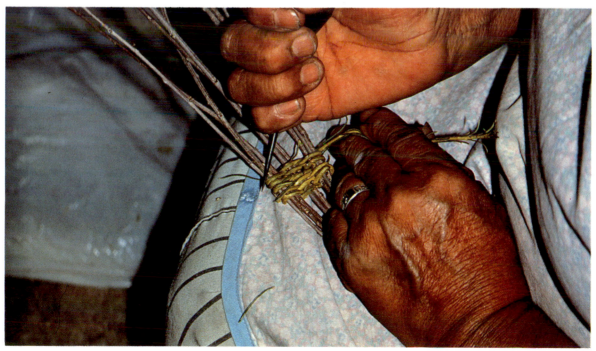

Plate 8 **Peruvian coast.** Rectangular work basket with hinged lid. Twill plaiting over flat ribs. The basket contains 104 spindles, some decorated with painted or pyro-engraved lines. It also contains balls of camelid fibre and cotton yarn, as well as raw cotton. L: 345 mm; W: 155 mm; H: 63 mm. Donated by the Wellcome Historical Medical Museum, 1952. 1952.7.89

Plate 9 **Colombia, Chocó, Waunana.** Two coiled watertight baskets with single rod foundation sewn with palm-leaf. Designs in black and orange (natural dyes). Left: H: 210 mm; right: H: 240 mm. Collected by María Margarita Uricoechea in Cali, Colombia, 1991. 1991.7.1-2

Plate 10 **Mexico, Toluca area, Otomí.** Space coiled basket with grass bundle foundation sewn with palm leaf in aniline dyes and natural colour. Design of human and animal figures. Plaited handle and fastening of string with cane toggle. H: 55 mm; dia: 140 mm. Collected by Beatrice Blackwood, 1939. 1938.36.1825

Basketry in Mexico and Guatemala

by Stuart Carter

Basketry has been practised in Guatemala and Mexico - particularly the region of common ethnic and cultural characteristics known to archaeologists and historians as Mesoamerica - for over 8000 years. The earliest known examples of Mesoamerican basketry, from the Guila Naquitz cave site in Oaxaca, Southern Mexico, predate the development of ceramics in the region: a piece of knotted netting and a miniature coiled basketry plaque have been dated by radiocarbon techniques to between 7000 and 6500 BC. Similar Preceramic Period coiled basketry has been found in Tehuacán, in the neighbouring state of Puebla. Other archaeological investigations have provided evidence that the techniques of twining and looping were also part of the Preceramic repertoire and that such techniques were in use much earlier than the appearance of loom weaving some time between 1500 and 900 BC. The dates for these early Mesoamerican remains are comparable with those from sites in the United States and Peru, which - together with the similarity of the techniques exemplified by the archaeological remains - has led some scholars to propose that "certain non-loom techniques came to the Americas with some of the early migrants across the Bering Strait" (King 1979: 265-266). Techniques of oblique interlacing characteristic of the *petate*, or sleeping mat, are indicated in clay impressions from a later Oaxaca site, and remains from contemporary Tehuacán sites indicate the production of twilled basketry as well as the use of twining in the manufacture of sandals.

Climatic conditions in Guatemala and Mexico have not favoured the preservation of perishable materials, so the total number of textile fragments, both of basketry and loomed textiles, is relatively small. Additionally, the capricious nature of this preservation and the danger that the archaeological record may distort the picture of pre-conquest basketry production must be constantly borne in mind. On the other hand, surviving prehispanic codices, as well as accounts from the period immediately following the conquest such as those of the Spanish chronicler Fray Bernardino de Sahagún, or ethnohistories such as the *Popol Vuh,* recorded in Spanish by the Quiché of the Western Highlands of Guatemala, attest to the wide variety of objects produced by the non-loom weaving of vegetable fibres and semi-rigid materials and their importance in both domestic and ceremonial contexts.

Under colonial domination new technologies were developed, new materials introduced and existing forms and modes of production adapted to meet the changing demand. The establishment of craft guilds in major population centres enabled the Spaniards to exercize control over artisans and the supply of raw materials and to direct production towards the needs of Europeans and Mestizos (in Guatemala, Ladinos: those of mixed or Indian blood who adopted European cultural practices). The European use of hats, for example, gave impetus to the plaiting of palm and the production of hats of all kinds. These ranged from the most simple to the elegant and flexible panama made from a very fine leaf of the palm known as *jipi* (*Carludovica palmata* Ruiz and Pav.). In addition to new forms, the Spaniards brought novel decorative styles. From exposure to endogenous influences, not only European but also, later, Oriental and African, emerged an enriched basketry tradition. Parallel to the art and craft production directed towards the demands of their colonial masters, the majority of the indigenous population maintained their traditional craft practices. Over time, the coexistence of these two forms of production has led, through their mutual influence, to the development of genuinely popular "Mestizo" arts and crafts, the proportions of the contributions from European and prehispanic sources varying with the nature of the craft and the geographical location and ethnic identity of the artisans.

Today, the art and craft of basketry continues to be of importance throughout Mexico and Guatemala and is practised alike in Indian and Mestizo/Ladino communities. (The distinction is today less racial than cultural: Indian groups are those with strong cultural links to a pre-conquest identity, who speak an indigenous language and who accept the appellation, whereas Mestizo/Ladino communities identify with national and international culture and speak Spanish.)While there are probably few regions from which the craft is totally absent, in common with other arts and crafts, basketmaking has assumed greater importance in areas close to sources of the requisite primary materials. Communities specializing in this work are thus most likely to be found near to lagoons or rivers where rushes, bamboos and reeds such as *Arundo donax* (the *carrizo* reed) and willow are found, or in arid regions in which the *maguey* (agave) and other cacti grow, as well as shrubs and trees whose branches and roots also provide materials suitable for the weaver's craft. Various communities in the state of Mexico produce furniture from *tule* reed (*Cyperaceae* family) and toys and religious ornaments from reed or palm. From Morelos come baskets in palm and rattan. In Oaxaca, on Mexico's Pacific coast, a great number of communities are involved in basketry and allied crafts, of which the most outstanding is perhaps the weaving of fine palm hats in the Mixtec region, a speciality too of the Mayan communities of Chamula and Zinacantan in neighbouring Chiapas. The panama hat is produced primarily in the states of Campeche and Yucatán on the Gulf of Mexico; the leaf of the *jipi* palm used in its manufacture is so fine that it can be folded and rolled up without breaking, and even articles as delicate as earrings are made with this material. A local availability of *bejuco* (rattan) has led to the production of fine baskets in parts of Guatemala's Central Highlands, and *carricillo* - a variety of *carrizo*, or bamboo - is woven particularly in Sololá, near Lake Atitlán. In the arid Valle del Mezquital, to the north of Mexico City, *ixtle*, a fibre from the leaf of the *maguey* (agave) and henequen were until recently used in the manufacture of a great variety of domestic products: ropes and nets, mats and carpets, even clothing. The Tarahumara of Chihuahua in northern Mexico plait single- and doubleweave baskets from beargrass (*Nolina microcarpa*), sotol (*Dasylirion wheeleri*) and pine needles. Moreover, the basketmaker's skill is not always confined to vegetable fibres: the hair from the tail and mane of the horse is among other materials exploited in this way. In order to weave larger baskets, four thicknesses may be twined together. Unfortunately, this material appears to have been almost completely superseded by nylon cord.

Of course, the artisans of certain communities may develop expertise over time in the weaving of particular articles that, in addition to their appropriateness to the locally available primary materials, become especially valued for the technical skill exhibited in their execution or for their formal aesthetic qualities. Such objects may become intimately associated with their community of origin and function as symbols of identity. Tzintzuntzan, in the Mexican state of Michoacán, which lies to the west of Mexico City, is famous for decorative straw figures called *pánicua*, as well as for the production of mats and other objects. The Guatemalan village of Rabinal is known for the production of the *colero*, a small and closely woven basket used to sieve corn, and the area around Patzún produces small, rectangular nested baskets, each with its own lid, called *coles*. When woven of wheat straw, the smaller ones are called *coles de seda* (Fig. 111), but larger ones are made of rushes. In common with fishing communities all over the world, a woven fish trap, called *xucubíl* (*garlito* in Spanish) is used in Santa Catarina Palopó, a village on the shores of Lake Atitlán.

96

Fig. 111 **Guatemala, Maya.** Two examples from a nest of three miniature rectangular straw and grass lidded baskets with chequer plaited bases and lids and twined sides. Coloured horizontal bands (aniline dyes). Baskets of this shape are called *coles* and fine examples like these, *coles de seda,* "silken baskets". Larger H: 40 mm; L: 65 mm. Collected by Lt. Col. E.L. & Miss M. Harrison, 1880 - 1903. 1951.11.151-152

Fig. 112 **Guatemala, Maya.** Twill plaited pouches of palm leaf, with overlapping lids. Patterns in aniline dyes. L: 100 mm. Collected by Lt. Col. E.L. & Miss M. Harrison, 1880 - 1903. 1951.11.147-148

Fig. 113 **Guatemala, Maya.** Two miniature cylindrical wicker baskets of split carrizo reed with coloured weft stripes (aniline dyes). Bases and centres of lids begun by chequer plaiting. These were probably children's toys: larger versions are used as storage baskets. Larger H: 60 mm; dia: 57 mm. Collected by Lt. Col. E.L. & Miss M. Harrison, 1880 - 1903. 1951.11.156-157

97

Fig. 114 **Mexico, Toluca area, Otomí.** Twill plaited fire fan of *tule* reed. L: 320 mm; W: 180 mm. Collected by Beatrice Blackwood, 1939. 1938.36.1821

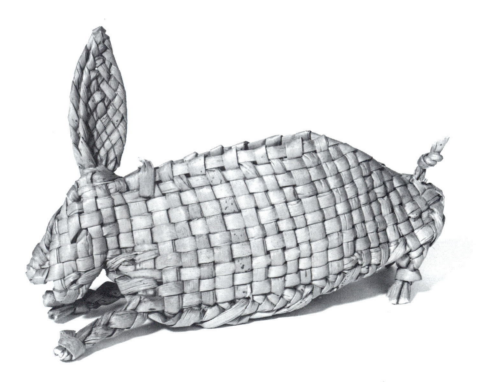

Fig. 115 **Mexico, Toluca area, Otomí.** Chequer plaited basket of *tule* reed in the shape of a rabbit. H: 200 mm; L: 320 mm. Collected by Beatrice Blackwood, 1939. 1938.36.1822

As baskets and other woven articles are so frequently intended for the daily utilitarian purposes of storage, transport and as utensils, the design of much of the basketry of the region has been largely determined by functional considerations and lacks a specific decorative aspect (with the clear exception of those objects intended for ceremonial or festive use). This has tended to limit the artistic or expressive potential of the craft to formal qualities alone. At the same time, both the consequences of the techniques employed and the textural and physical properties of the materials themselves dictate the possibility of achievement of both decorative and formal aesthetic goals. The elaboration of geometric designs in plaited matting and the absence of visible defects in the material testifies at once to the weaver's discerning eye and technical command. Twilled plaiting is employed, for example, in the Otomí fire fan (Fig. 114). In the production of basketry, delicacy and regularity as well as the overall formal qualities of the finished product, are admired characteristics of all work from the finest of palm hats to the largest baskets of *carrizo*, as well as - arguably - a conscious correspondence between form and function. At the same time, ornamentation is often added to the most simple baskets through the basic strategy of colour variation: by alternating the visibility of obverse and reverse of the weft, by weaving materials of distinct natural colours, or by the use of dyes. Simple decorative embellishments of this kind are shown in Figs. 112, 113, 116.

Coiled basketry favours radiating designs, but Mexican and Guatemalan weavers have not in general pursued the decorative possibilities of this form as far as have, for example, the Indians of the American Southwest. Notable exceptions are the Seri Indians of Sonora in northern Mexico, whose territory borders the basket-producing areas of the Southwest, and whose work their fine baskets so much resemble; and the Otomí of Puebla and the state of Mexico. In the 1930s Beatrice Blackwood collected a number of fine examples of coiled Otomí work (Figs. 119-120). Fig. 120 is a particularly fine piece of delicate and elegant lines which both satisfies the formal requirements of its intended use - such baskets are still employed today for carrying eggs and other fragile objects - and displays the basket-maker's fine aesthetic sense of both the formal and decorative possibilities of the medium. Furthermore, the human and zoomorphic figures as well as the geometric designs incorporated into the decorative field of this and other Otomí pieces speak of a rich symbolic tradition and a strong sense of identity. That few investigators to date seem to have turned their attention to these aspects of, particularly, Mexican basketry, seems at least partially due to the greater emphasis placed on loomed textiles as a medium through which to express identity and symbolic values. (Osborne has, however, noted that baskets from the village of Chiquibul may be identified by the distinctive border twined with double weft strands [Osborne 1965:200]).

In fact, in symbolic terms, the attention of investigators has predominantly been directed on a macroscopic level at the basket itself rather than at details of the decorative field. In common with other commentators, La Farge and Byers (1931) noted that weaving baskets and palm hats in Jacaltenango, Guatemala, was at that time an exclusively male occupation, women being engaged in backstrap loom weaving and pottery; but contemporary evidence indicates that women as well as men make basketry, except where the properties of the material require greater physical strength. Another approach has eschewed a gender-based system of differentiation in favour of an ethnic distinction. On a first examination it might appear that, despite the different techniques employed in their elaboration and the variations in the formal and decorative qualities of individual designs, baskets can be conveniently divided into two basic categories: (a) *canastas*, which have a (rigid) handle and (b) *canastos*, which do not (Figs. 116, 117). The Spanish name for

99

the first kind is feminine and for the second masculine and it is also tempting to emphasize the *canasta* as an endogenous, "introduced" form in contrast to the "native" *canasto*, as a number of commentators have done. Indeed, the *canasta* - predominantly produced by the wicker technique - reminds us of nothing so much as a genteel, though obsolete "shopping basket" (Fig. 116), and is certainly of post-conquest introduction, while *canasto* refers to a class of baskets used to carry much heavier burdens on the head. Furthermore, a number of ethnographies, particularly from the Guatemalan Highlands, indicate an indigenous perception of superiority of the male element over the female, and the high value placed upon physical labour. Adding these elements together seems to give a great deal of support to the position of theorists who favour an oppositional two culture model of the complex relations between the Indian and Ladino communities, and who would represent the basket as both a symbol and a metonymic enactment of cultural opposition; but the situation is more complicated in practical terms.

Kelsey and Osborne (1961) report that in Guatemala *canastas* may be of any size and may be brightly coloured and highly decorated, and in Mexico too *canastas* have the same basic form, though they are often naturally coloured. *Canastos*, however, are produced in a variety of forms: in Mexico they frequently have a lid and are used for storage, while in Guatemala they are "shallow and without a handle" (Osborne 1965:198). Larger baskets for carrying produce to and from market are *cestos* in Mexico, but remain *canastos* in Guatemala, acquiring special names which indicate their uses in specific contexts: the *canasto panadero*, large and wide with strong sides, is a bread basket; the *cajero* may hold over 10 kg of fruit or vegetables; while the *cafetero*, or *medio canasto*, is used in coffee picking (Kelsey and Osborne 1961). The Mexican *canasto* and its larger cousin the *cesto* also appear in a great number of guises, from small coiled baskets for fruit (Fig. 119) through

winnowing trays used in the harvesting of grain, to the *huacal*, a large rectangular open-weave wicker basket used for carrying produce to market and which, because of its size and the weight of its contents, is most likely to be carried by men by means of the *mecapal*, or tumpline. *Canastos* also appear in present-day Mexico as nesting boxes for canaries and even cat boxes for transporting reluctant felines; the *canasto* may also have handles (Plate 10). Perhaps the most curious of all these forms is the *canastón*, a remarkable hybrid of basket and hat in which itinerant bread vendors carried loaves and cakes, often while weaving through city traffic on a bicycle! Of course, it was carried on the head. In response to changing needs, baskets have not only assumed new forms which defy simple classification, but these forms are produced and used to a varying extent by both Mestizo and Indian communities: a unity of practice which can be interpreted as indicative of the many understandings shared between the communities, rather than of their contrasts.

Furthermore, it is not at all certain from whose point of view the convenient linguistic differentiation between the two forms is made, many indigenous languages lacking such clear gender distinctions. The complex variety of forms which baskets have adopted in response to the continuously evolving systems of cultural practice renders the simple structural analogy between masculine and feminine, native and introduced forms, merely an analytic tool that cannot be said - without careful research - to reflect the perception of the indigenous producers and consumers of these articles. The fine palm hats of the Maya of Chiapas and Guatemala (e.g. Fig. 118) are perceived by the Indians who wear them as an integral and essential part of the costume (male and female) that proclaims their ethnic identity with respect to both Ladinos and other indigenous groups, rather than as a symbol of cultural imposition. Basketry forms, their continuity and evolution, are a subtle parameter of cultural process, and

Fig. 116 **Mexico, Queretaro, San Juan del Rio.** Child's oval wicker basket of willow, with handle. This is the European style of market basket, *canasta*. H: 110 mm; L: 160 mm; W: 135 mm. Collected by Beatrice Blackwood, 1939. 1946.3.28

Fig. 117 **Guatemala, San Francisco el Alto, Maya.** Woman's circular wicker basket, *canasto*, for carrying on the head. Woven of *carrizo* reed with bound rim. H: 145 mm; dia: 650 mm. Collected by Linda Gelens, 1991. 1991.37.2

Fig. 118 **Guatemala, Huehuetenango State, Todos Santos Cuchumatán, Mam Maya.** Woman's hat of plaited palm leaf strips coiled and machine stitched to shape. Decorative band of red leather with metal-bound eyelet holes and wrapping of blue bias binding. H: 80 mm; dia: 300 mm. Collected by Stuart Carter, 1990. 1990.46.2

we should look more closely at the contexts of their use and production for a perspective that will articulate the values and world view expemplified by this craft.

The practice of basketmaking and the uses of the finished article are part of all aspects of the individual's life, not only economic but also religious and secular. The infant's first experience of the world is gained from a wicker bassinet called a *moisés* (a "Moses", with clear reference to its biblical precedent), and the child's first toys may be animal and other figures of plaited palm (Fig. 115) or miniature baskets such as the early items in the Pitt Rivers Museum's collection. Almost certainly the rather fanciful miniature in Fig. 113 was produced for a child; depending on the viewer's predilection it can be regarded either as a *canasto* with a handle, or as a *canasta* with a lid! Some observers suggest that the proliferation of zoomorphic themes in toys, not only woven but also of wood and clay, reflects an indigenous belief in the *nagual*, a person's spirit double, usually taking the form of an animal. A more prosaic explanation might be sought in the choice of themes from daily life and environment. The *pánicua* figures of Tzintzuntzan model everyday scenes and events in the individual's life, ranging from small animal or human figurines to railways, plane figures to hang on the wall and entire houses - but in all cases human figures intervene, the child sees his own place in this depicted world of experience. From either perspective these delightful works, from the simplest animal figurine to the most splendid cathedral sculpted in *carrizo*, resplendent with its towers and cupolas, describe and through their construction enact a particular view of the world, assisting in the child's socialization into this view.

That these figures are not exclusively regarded as "toys" is further attested by their role in religious observance and in festival. In Mexico, mules woven in *tule* carrying *huacales* filled with apricots, cherries and carnations are offered in thanks at the feast of Corpus Christi; at Christmas, figures of shepherds and kings in straw, reed or wicker pay homage to the Christ Child in the *nacimiento* (crib) both in the church and in the home; and the plaited palm decorations of Palm Sunday symbolize resurrection and renewal. In Guatemala, the Dance of the Baskets is performed annually in Chajul and *canastas* are a special feature of the festival held in connection with the pilgrimage to Esquipulas, where a black Christ hangs on a crucifix above the altar (Osborne 1965, Kelsey and Osborne 1961). As Osborne notes, basketry is present at every stage in the individual's life: in Indian communities in Guatemala small baskets of food accompany the individual on his journey into the afterlife (Osborne 1965:197).

The articles illustrated here, though predominantly smaller pieces and in some cases over a century old (Figs. 111-113), amply demonstrate the techniques found in the contemporary basketmaking repertoire of the region. They illustrate the remarkable resilience of basketry traditions despite the availability of inexpensive industrial goods and the advent of mass tourism. Many forms have indeed been superseded by commercial products - the plaited *tule* rain cape of central Mexico, for example, has been replaced by cheap (and much more efficient) plastic sheeting - but others have evolved to take their place, which is indicative less of a decline in basketry than of its vitality. In fact, some observers have argued that tourist demand has in certain cases invigorated a basketry tradition declining under the impact of mass produced items. Moser (1973) reports that the Seri have fourteen named types of basket, of which eight are considered solely for the tourist trade.

Basketry in Mexico and Guatemala today is a living art, evolving with time and adapting to new conditions even as it did in the Colonial period. It expresses the aesthetic aspirations and the proud technical skills - poorly remunerated and rarely acknowledged - of the artisans who weave its many forms; it embodies a history and a view of the present. An unbroken continuity of practice stretching back over thousands of years, it remains at once a mirror of traditional values and a parameter of social change, a vital and continuing cultural process, an understanding of the self and of its relation to the world.

Fig. 119 **Mexico, Toluca area, Otomí.** Space-coiled dish with grass bundle foundation sewn with palm leaf in red, purple, green, orange (aniline dyes) and natural colour. Butterfly design. H: 55 mm; dia: 210 mm. Collected by Beatrice Blackwood, 1939. 1938.36.1824

Fuegia Basket
or the Life of a Basketmaker in Tierra del Fuego
by Penny Dransart

The storm-washed shores of Tierra del Fuego, or Fireland, and the numerous adjacent islands present a rugged archipelago intersected with channels and indented with fjords. This complicated geography is, in fact, the southernmost limit of the Andean chain and it is distinguished as being the most southerly inhabited land in the world.

Yet the fires and the smoke from which this land received its name have been extinguished. The peoples of the south are known to anthropologists as the foot hunters and the canoe hunters. The former were the Selk'nam (Ona) and the Haush, who both lived on the main island of Tierra del Fuego, and the latter were the Kaweshkar (Alakaluf) and the Yámana (Yahgan), who inhabited the many islands to the southwest of Tierra del Fuego proper. Tragically, they belong to the ethnographic past. The Selk'nam, the Haush and another foot people, the Aonikenk (Tehuelche) who lived on the plains of southern Patagonia, northern neighbours of the Selk'nam, no longer walk the landscape which was their homeland for thousands of years. In 1987, the last remaining Kaweshkar and Yámana descendants were reported as living in communities in Puerto Edén and Ukika in southern Chile (Massone 1987:13).

Although the peoples of the south came into contact with outsiders on an intermittent basis after the voyage of Hernando de Magallanes in 1520, it was not until the nineteenth century that regular contact was made by European settlers, missionaries, sheep and cattle ranchers, miners and convicts. The outsiders introduced infectious diseases such as measles to which the people had no resistance. They also introduced alcohol which resulted in alcoholism among peoples unaccustomed to its use.

Worst of all were the forced removals by the incoming settlers of the peoples from their homelands and the massacres organized by the "hunters of Indians". One of the most notorious assassins was Julius Popper who organized a campaign of ethnocide among the Selk'nam in 1886 (Massone 1987:33). Another scourge of the Selk'nam, Alexander MacLennan, otherwise known as the Red Pig, is denounced by the travel writer Bruce Chatwin (1979:111-112) for slaughtering at least fourteen men, women and children while they were hunting seals at Cape Peñas. The murder of the peoples of the south, their removal to Christian missions, and the peoples' resistance to such attacks on their way of life are recorded by E. Lucas Bridges (1948:265-269). Through the pages of Lucas Bridges' remarkable autobiography, they speak to us with individual voices which are lacking in the anonymous accounts published in scientific journals.

One of the Yámana people known to us through the writings of visiting Europeans is Fuegia Basket. Charles Darwin wrote in his *Journal* that she was "a nice, modest, reserved young girl, with a rather pleasing but sometimes sullen expression, and very quick in learning anything, especially languages" (Darwin 1845:208). Although Fuegia Basket's experiences overseas were hardly typical of other Yámana women, her personal history has been recorded. Hence we are able to understand something of the lifestyle of Yámana women, for whom making baskets was an important activity.

In 1826, the British Admiralty sent the *Beagle* and three other ships to chart the southernmost coasts of South America under the command of Captain Robert Fitzroy. While in Fuegian waters they captured four young Yámana peo-

Fig. 120 **Tierra del Fuego.** Yámana basketmaker. Photograph by De Agostini, 1929.

ple and took them back to Britain as hostages. The story is recounted by Bridges, who tells of the "christening" of the four people with the strangest of names because the crew were unable to ask them their names in their own language (Bridges 1948:30). The three young men were named Boat Memory, York Minster (apparently after a rugged islet near Cape Horn) and Jimmy Button. A small girl of about nine years of age received the name of Fuegia Basket. Boat Memory died of smallpox, but the three survivors were introduced to William IV and Queen Adelaide, who gave Fuegia Basket a lace cap, a ring and a sum of money for her trousseau. These gifts were to prove singularly inappropriate for the young woman. When the *Beagle* returned to Tierra del Fuego, its passengers included the three Yámana survivors and Charles Darwin. Fuegia Basket and York Minster were married on arrival at Wulaia on Navarino Island, and a Christian ceremony was performed by a catechist sent on the voyage by the Church Missionary Society (Bridges 1948:32). The couple quickly reverted to their old life style when the Europeans left.

Many years later, the father of Lucas Bridges met Fuegia Basket. Thomas Bridges had helped to establish the Ushuaia mission in Argentina on behalf of the Patagonian Missionary Society and he was a fluent speaker of the Yámana language. In the account given by his son, a party of Yámana from the outer coast between the Southwest Arm and Brecknock Peninsula went to Ushuaia to visit the missionaries. Among this "wild-looking" group of people from Alisimoonoala, the Yámana name by which their region was known, was Fuegia Basket. She still remembered odd words in English, and Captain Fitzroy and the *Beagle*, but she now preferred to squat on the floor rather than sit on the chair offered her. While in Britain, she had received religious training, but this too she had forgotten. Thomas Bridges spoke with her in her own language, and she said that her husband York Minster had been killed in retaliation for the murder

106

of another man, and that the young man in her company was her present husband. She was over fifty years of age, but he was only about eighteen. This was not an irregular situation among the Yámana, who practised polygamy. This enabled older men to add young, active women to their family, and young men were able to marry older women who possessed considerable knowledge and experience in handling canoes and fishing. Fuegia Basket had spent much time among the Kaweshkar and she also spoke their language well. Her party spent about a week in Ushuaia, but she pined for her two grown up children and her group returned to Alisimoonoala.

Thomas Bridges met Fuegia Basket on another occasion, ten years later in 1883, on London Island, near the Brecknock Peninsula. She was about 62 years old, and nearing the end of her life. According to the missionary, she was in a very weak condition and in an unhappy state of mind. However, she was looked after by her daughter and she had two brothers of her own age whose families would be able to provide for her (Bridges 1948:83-84).

As a name, Basket would probably be unappealing to most. Yet the making of baskets among the Yámana was a skill at which women excelled. Basketry was especially important among the Yámana and Kaweshkar peoples since it contradicts notions held by some people that Fuegian culture "ranks among the most primitive that has been known within the limits of recorded history" (Lothrop 1928:35). Baskets were also made by the Haush and the southern Selk'nam peoples, but not by the northern Selk'nam, nor by the Aonikenk. As a Yámana, Fuegia Basket must have made many baskets throughout her lifetime.

According to S.K. Lothrop, four types of basket were made by the Yámana (Lothrop 1928:133-129, 160). Three of them are based on coiled and looped structures, while the fourth is a crossed-stick basket. These types are all related to basketry structures encountered in the south central Andean area. A native rush called *mápi* by the Yámana (*Juncus magellanicus*) was used for making the baskets. Lothrop describes it as a coarse, round-stemmed grass about 18 inches in height. The women picked long bundles of it to carry back to their encampment. Lothrop considered that the most handsome baskets were made in autumn when the green changed to red, but he says that this brilliant colour faded after a few weeks (Lothrop 1928:134). The women chewed each grass stem before using it to flatten it and to give it more pliability.

The most commonly made basket is called *tawel'a* in Lothrop (1928:134-135). There are three such baskets in the Pitt Rivers Museum, as well as some miniature versions in model boats. The one illustrated in Fig 121 is from the Wollaston Islands, and it was presented by the South American Missionary Society (originally known as the Patagonian Missionary Society). It is formed of two single element simple looping (Fig 125). After making a coiled and looped base two or three inches in diameter, the maker suspended the basket from the middle of the base from a pole so that she was able to continue her work using both hands (Fig 120). The rim was formed by simple wrapping stitches worked from left to right. This particular basket was provided with a plaited handle (a five-strand flat braid) which was simply stitched at both ends to the rim with several cross stitches. However, most baskets of this type were provided with two small loops on the rim, to which the ends of the plaited handle were tied.

Lothrop's second type of basket is named *uloánastába*. The two single element looping employed is more complicated than the first type in that the looped stitch makes a half turn around itself before forming the next loop. Lothrop says that this type was very rare (Lothrop 1928:136-137), and the Pitt Rivers Museum does not possess an example of it.

The third type described by Lothrop is also said not to have been commonly made. It is called *gaiíchim* (or *kaïdjime*) (Fig 122). This type of basket is made of a two single element knotted looping (Fig 126), which produces a more open texture than the closely spaced simple looping. The body of the basket is hung from a circle of split wood, and held firmly in place by wrapping stitches where the ends of the strip of wood overlap. In the Pitt Rivers Museum example, the handle was made from two lengths of three-strand plaiting, tied in four places to the rim. According to Lothrop (1928:138), the outline of the completed *gaiíchim* is often irregular, so the interior was well packed with small pebbles or sand and the contents were kept damp until the basket took on a symmetrical shape.

Finally, the fourth type of basket is known as *chiwanúsh* in Lothrop (1928:138, 160). Structurally, it is the same as the crossed-stick basket of the south central Andes. The Yámana version is made by bending four sticks (according to Lothrop, Winter's Bark or barberry was used) which were secured to a circular rim of the same material. The walls were filled by wrapping *juncus magellanicus* round each spoke. This type is represented here by a miniature version (Fig 123) which belongs to a model bark canoe, also equipped with three stacked baskets of the first type (Fig 124). The *chiwanúsh* was used lashed to a pole as a dip-net for catching small sardine-like fish (Lothrop 1928:160).

These, then were the baskets that Fuegia Basket might well have made. The baskets were important possessions for people who lived by fishing, hunting and gathering. When the baskets became worn out and no longer serviceable, Yámana boys used them in play. Lucas Bridges recalls how he, as a boy, joined in the playtime pursuits of the Yámana children. An evening activity for the boys involved one of them setting off at a run, dragging behind him a tattered basket on a string. The other boys had spears, and they used the moving basket as a practice target (Bridges 1948:97). Bridges was full of admiration for the skill of Yámana men in using bone-tipped spears for catching fish;

Fig. 121 **Chile, Tierra del Fuego, Wollaston Island.** Coiled basket with plaited handle. Bundle foundation closely sewn with buttonhole stitches or simple loops which cross right-over-left. H: 220 mm; dia: 246 mm. Donated by the South American Missionary Society. 1892.50.9

Fig. 122 **Tierra del Fuego, Indian Reach, Patagonian Channels.** Coiled basket with plaited handle. Coiled foundation and stitching are both of the same material, said to be *Juncus Magellanicus*. The stitching is executed in open-worked knotted looping and the rim is formed by a ring of rigid split cane. H: 96 mm; dia: 180 mm. W. Scoresby Routledge collection. 1916.36.2

Fig. 123 **Argentina, Tierra del Fuego, Yamaná.** Miniature crossed-stick fish basket. H: 70 mm; dia: 55 mm. Inside model boat donated by R. Whaits. 1893.39.5 (Fig. 124)

Fig. 124 **Argentina, Tierra del Fuego, Yamaná.** Model of a bark canoe with two harpoons, two paddles, a bark baler, three stacked baskets and a crossed-stick fish basket. L: 770 mm. Donated by R. Whaits. 1893.39.5

despite the refraction of the water, the men were unerring in their aim of spearing fish under the water (Bridges 1948:77).

The Yámana have entered the annals of history as scantily clad people who lived in a cold climate. Unlike the Selk'nam, who were primarily hunters of guanaco, and who wrapped themselves in guanaco hides, the majority of the Yámana lived on the shores of islands where there were no guanaco. They went about their daily business at best partially clad in otter skins and shell necklaces.

According to Bridges, there was a fair division of labour between the sexes. The men gathered the fuel and edible fungus, they tended the fires, made and repaired bark canoes, and hunted otter, seal, foxes, birds and guanaco (if they lived in guanaco territory), and speared large fish. The women cooked, fetched water, fished and paddled the canoes; sometimes they were helped by their menfolk in this last mentioned task. They were, as indicated above, responsible for making baskets. Yámana families spent much time in their canoes and they often ventured into places where there were no beaches on which to haul their canoes. The

women, however, were excellent swimmers and anchored the canoe to thick kelp (a large type of seaweed) which grew along the rocks of the shoreline. After tying the canoe using the rope-like branches of kelp, a woman would slip into the water, swim ashore and dry herself at the fire prepared by her husband. Bridges reports that swimming through kelp was extremely dangerous but the women were accustomed to it because they learned to swim while still infants. He even saw women swimming in winter when the kelp was coated with a film of frost, and a baby girl accompanying her mother would start off the mother's back, but then would crawl onto her head to try and escape from the cold water (Bridges 1948:63-64).

From the ethnographic accounts, it would seem that there was a far greater degree of equality between the sexes than among the Selk'nam. Yámana society was based on the family, and related families often paddled their canoes in twos (Lothrop 1928:160). There were no recognized leaders, and families tended to stay within a limited area, although there would have been much movement within that area. Certain women and men were recognized as

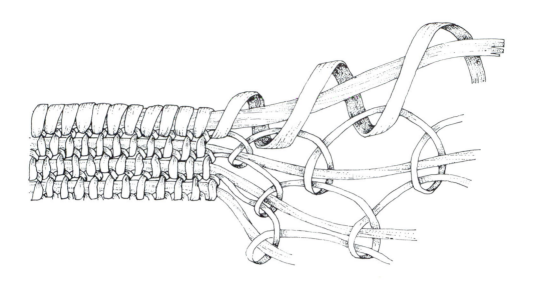

Fig. 125 Looped structure used for the basket in Fig. 121.

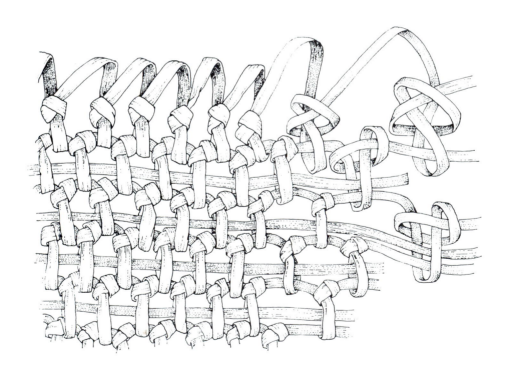

Fig. 126 Looped structure used for the basket in Fig. 122.

possessing occult powers, but female witch doctors were very rare among the Selk'nam.

From time to time, the Yámana gathered together in order to celebrate lengthy *shieháus* ceremonies, or the rites of initiation by which boys and girls were formally educated in the Yámana way of life. Basket making and baskets had a role in these ceremonies. The Yámana believed that their well-being depended upon the *shieháus*, and that without being initiated, one would have little standing in the community. These events have been described in fuller detail by Lothrop (1928:165-170).

Here, the educative aspects of the ceremonies will be emphasized. Each candidate had three "godparents" or teachers, two of the same sex as the initiate, and one of the opposite sex. Their duty was to ensure that their adopted children did everything correctly. The rest of the community also was present as observers. During the first three days, the initiates maintained a fast. In the daytime, they received instruction in the skill necessary for leading the Yámana way of life. The men taught the boys how to hunt, to make tools and weapons, and to build canoes. The women taught the girls how to fish, to make baskets, birch bark buckets, necklaces and how to rear children. However, singing and dancing constituted the main activities of the ceremonies. They were performed in order to communicate with, and at the same time to keep at a distance, a fearsome spirit known as *Yetaite*. The initiates were also given moral instruction, and a fear of *Yetaite* was inculcated in the young people as a religious sanction. Towards the end of the *shieháus*, they were ceremonially received by their "godparents", by whom they were given gifts. According to Lothrop (1928:169) boys received a finely made *gaiíchim* basket adorned with feathers and two other items, but he does not say what the girls received. Finally, the women took charge of the ceremonies, led by an old woman. They sang in the centre of the *shieháus* lodge, and a mock battle between the sexes took place.

This is the lifestyle to which Fuegia Basket was initiated. As we have seen, her life history is unusual because she was taken to a foreign land and she survived to tell her family about her experiences. Sadly, her descendants have not lived to pass on her own version of her life history. In his travels in Tierra del Fuego, Bruce Chatwin interviewed the last pure-blooded Yámana man from Ushuaia, whom the travel writer met at Puerto Williams on Navarino Island. Granpa Felipe told the writer how his people succumbed to epidemics and how he saw all his children, apart from one daughter, die. He had also seen his wife die in her sleep, with her arms folded (Chatwin 1979:125-126). Thus all that remains are a few fragments of life histories of the peoples of the south and some of the material objects they made. The beautiful baskets in museum collections encapsulate a whole realm of human experience and bear witness to the skills of the women who made them.

Basketry in the Northern Andes and Intermontane Valleys of Colombia

by Marianne Cardale Schrimpff

The Colombian Andes, divided into three great ranges or *cordilleras* by the broad valleys of the Cauca and Magdalena rivers, rise in places to an altitude of more than 5,000 m. The highest peaks are capped with perpetual snow and bounded by the cold *páramo* belt where a specialized vegetation resistant to night frosts has developed. Below this one descends through the cool to temperate zone (3,000 - 2,000 m) and the sub-tropical zone (to about 1,000 m), before reaching the tropical lowlands.

This article attempts to give a very general view of the basketry traditions of an area characterized by its diversity. Criteria such as climate and relief would divide the area into many sub-regions, some of which have basketry traditions on which little or nothing has been published. Although there are a number of excellent studies dealing with a particular group or region (Solano 1974, Reichel-Dolmatoff 1985 and Vasco 1987), there is no general survey of the basketry of Andean Colombia. The information is scattered and there are undoubtedly interesting and useful publications of which I am ignorant or which I have been unable to consult. For northern Colombia I have relied heavily on my own work (1985) although basketry was not the main subject of this survey.

When we compare the basketry of the Colombian Andes with that of the Amazon, we are immediately struck by the decrease in the range of items and, to some extent, in quality. Virtuosity flourished in other fields such as woven textiles. As we shall see, a case can even be made for suggesting that the greater part of the indigenous population of the highlands lacked a strong basketry tradition, the place of baskets being taken by bags of various kinds. Baskets do retain their importance, however, among the Indians of the neighbouring lowlands.

This relative paucity can be explained by a number of factors, one of the most important of which is a fundamental difference in the diet. Whereas sweet manioc is grown and eaten wherever the climate permits, bitter manioc is not processed today in the northern Andean area and so the whole range of associated basketry such as cassava squeezers and sieves is likewise absent. When Rivière mentions elsewhere in this volume that no less than ten of the eighteen types of basket used by the Yekuana of Venezuela are devoted to processing cassava, we form an idea of just how important its influence on basketry can be. Maize is an important crop throughout most of the Colombian Andes but while baskets are useful for storing cobs or the grains of cereals, they are not essential. In some parts of the country such as the uplands of Cundinamarca and Boyacá, baskets are used for sieving ground maize either when dry (to separate the flour from the chaff) or as a wet mass when the strained liquid is used in soups or for chicha. Although these areas are now inhabited by Mestizo peasants, it seems probable that this tradition comes from the Muisca Indians who once lived in this region.

Another important factor is the availability of raw material. Although a rather wide range of different kinds of canes, vines, palm midribs and other materials is used, much of the finest basketry is made from strips split from smooth stemmed plants such as the *bihao (Helicania biahi L.)* or the palm-like *iraca (Carludovica palmata Ruiz and Pav.)* which only grows at relatively low altitudes. In the highland areas where there is a strong peasant tradition of bas-

Fig. 127 **Colombia, Arquía, Cuna.** Making an *imiatali* (storage basket). Photograph by Marianne Cardale Schrimpff, 1968.

113

Fig. 128 **Colombia, Nariño, Sandona.** Unfinished hat of *iraca (Carludovica palmata* Ruiz & Pav.) in chequer and hexagonal plaiting. Dia: 315 mm. Collected by Marianne Cardale Schrimpff. 1984.15.22

Fig. 129 **Colombia, Boyacá.** Woman's hat of plaited fibre, coiled and machine stitched to shape. H: 100 mm; dia: 350 mm. Collected by Marianne Cardale Schrimpff, 1965. 1984.15.2

Fig. 130 **Colombia, Cordoba, Tuchin, Katio.** The much sought-after *sombrero voltiao* is made in the coastal lowlands of northern Colombia at centres such as Tuchin and San Andres de Sotovento. The best of these hats are so flexible that they can be rolled up and carried in the owner's pocket without coming to any harm. Made of plaited palm-leaf strips, coiled and machine stitched to shape. H: 110 mm; dia: 350 mm. Collected by Marianne Cardale Schrimpff from the maker, Señora Rujenciz Ortíz, 1966. 1984.15.1

Fig. 131 **Colombia, Sierra de Macuira, Nazarel area, Guajiro.** Twill plaited hat of *muluh* straw with pattern in black. Hatband of woollen braid. This kind of hat is usually worn by women. H: 120 mm; dia: 390 mm. Collected by Marianne Cardale Schrimpff, 1965. 1984.15.3

114

ketry today, much of the raw material has been introduced from temperate climates along with the range of baskets made.

Southern Colombia

Although a number of Indian groups still live in the Andean region of southern Colombia - the Sibundoy, Inga, Kwaiker, Guambiano and Paez - I know of no studies of their basketry. Bags are important among all these groups and baskets appear either to be absent or to play a secondary role, with relatively little time and energy being invested in their production.

Some basketry traditions from highland Nariño have been summarized briefly by Cortés (1989) and appear to be largely non-indigenous in origin or at least associated with non-indigenous uses. Nariño is well known for its "panama" hats made in the small towns of Sandoná, Ancuya, Linares and Florida from the leaves of the palm-like *iraca* (Fig. 128). Although Colombian Indians used a wide range of caps and other types of headdress, there is no evidence that they used hats with brims. According to Cortés, the panama hat industry was introduced to the area during the middle of the nineteenth century.

Nariño is one of the few regions of Colombia where textiles are preserved in graves with any frequency and the remains of mats appear to have been found on a number of occasions (Ortiz 1937:148, Cardale Schrimpff 1979:265-269). However since they usually disintegrated on contact with the air, few details are known. An impression of a mat is preserved on the base of a later period (Piartal-Tusa) figurine in the Museo de Oro in Bogotá (CN5583): this was made in 2:2 balanced twill with between 6 and 8 strips every 50 mm Some of the "mats" were in fact made of the gold/copper alloy *tumbaga* (Plazas 1979:208). Among many Indian groups mats were used as much for partitions or wall hangings as for the floor and in a society such as Piartal-Tusa which made such exquisite textiles, it would not be surprising to find spectacular

wall hangings as well. Another remarkable find from the same area is a basket (MO25613) made from strips of gilded *tumbaga*.

Central Colombia

The central part of Andean Colombia is inhabited by a large urban population and by peasants of predominantly hispanic stock. As the population expanded, new lands were settled and the ancestors of many of these peasant farmers only moved into these areas relatively recently, usually at some time during the last 200 years. A visit to local markets reveals a wide range of baskets, largely of European inspiration.

The central part of the Eastern Cordillera is rather different in that the peasant population is descended from two large and important Indian groups, the Muisca and the Guane, who occupied this territory when the first Spanish expeditions arrived. In the 450 years or so which have elapsed since this event, there has been a thorough mixing of genes and traditions and today it is often difficult to say when any particular trait originated. A number of studies of basketry have been made, some of which, such as Solano's (1974) review of handicrafts in Boyacá or the recent study by NENCATACOA, cover a relatively large part of the region. Others, such as Ortiz (1990) on the basketry of the Tenza region, provide detailed analyses of a particular centre (Fig. 134).

"Traditional" items include those associated with milk products and also with markets and have probably been made since early in the colonial period. The first group are often made of fine reeds (*Spartina patens* or *juncae*) and include small hemispherical, rounded strainer baskets which, although put to many uses, are intended for holding the curd while the whey drains off (Fig. 133). The curd is then transferred to the centre of a plaited band made of the same material which is curled round to form a ring: weighted above with a flat stone, this acts as a cheese press (Solano 1974: fig. 108).

115

These items are made in a number of different centres, among which some of the better known are Raquirá, Cerinza and Belen.

Among the items associated with markets are the sturdy shopping baskets with a strong handle, similar to those used fairly universally in Europe from where the prototype almost certainly came. (The indigenous way of carrying a basket is with a tump-line or band, supported from the forehead.) The rather shallow, round baskets, about a metre in diameter, used for displaying produce in the market place, could perhaps be indigenous in inspiration since the Muisca Indians also had markets. Both types of basket are usually wicker and often made of *chin* or *cañabrava de Castilla* as it is also called *(Arundo donax L.)*. *Chin* is one of the principal materials used in the important centre at Tenza (Ortiz 1991) where it is used for a wide range of baskets. Hats are made in a number of centres such as Velez, Socorro, Utica, Zetaquira, Chinavita, Cerina, Villa de Leiva, Arcabuco (NENCATACOA) and have been an important industry for 200 years or more. Side by side with these items are some simple baskets made from creepers like the oval containers made in the Tenza region and used as cages or, nowadays, for transporting eggs (Fig. 132). Some of these may, too, be indigenous in inspiration. The craftsmen in many of the basket-making centres are very open to change and to new market openings: today we find items such as laundry baskets, bread baskets, place mats and trays (Solano 1974; Ortiz 1991).

This part of the Eastern Cordillera is well known for its archaeological textiles. Muisca and Guane mantles and other items were deservedly famous during the early years of the colonial period and, thanks to a number of dry caves in the region, a relatively large sample has been preserved. However archaeological baskets are virtually unknown. The only description I have come across is of two examples, formerly in the collection of Martin Carvajal and now lost (Carvajal 1940:317; Schottelius 116

1946:220). One of these was a rectangular work box with a lid, closely constructed from strips of cane of contrasting colours, white and brown. It contained lengths of spun cotton and a pan pipe; since it was found on the Mesa de los Santos, it was almost certainly Guane. Sixteenth century documents include occasional mentions of basketry boxes with lids for storing special or sacred items (Londoño 1990:100).

The Chocó

That part of the Pacific lowlands which is drained by the rivers San Juan and Atrato is inhabited by two groups of Indians, the Noanama and the Emberá-Chamí, speaking related but mutually unintelligible languages. The former live in scattered settlements focused on the river San Juan, the northern part of their territory overlapping with the Emberá. The latter inhabit the headwaters of the river San Juan, the river Baudó area and the mountains bordering the river Garrapatas. Basketry is a very important part of the material culture of these two groups and fortunately it has been exceptionally well documented. The fullest accounts are those of Henry Wassén, who visited the Chocó in 1935, of G. & R. Reichel-Dolmatoff who spent four months in the area in 1968 and, most recently, of Luis Guillermo Vasco. The latter, after carrying out fieldwork among the Emberá-Chamí for a number of years, devoted eight months to a special study of the pottery and basketry made by the groups on the upper San Juan and river Garrapatas (1987). The following summary is based on these accounts.

These groups are relatively unusual in northern Colombia in that the baskets are generally made by women although the men may co-operate in obtaining and preparing the raw material. Interestingly enough, they were taught by a female culture hero, Betata (Vasco 1987:87, 145). Nevertheless men may make the *e* carrying baskets and the *inpurr* used for fishing and for sowing maize. Techniques include

Fig. 132 **Colombia, Boyacá, Garagoa.** Baskets in the market at Garagoa. Note the wicker "shopping baskets" with handles, of European inspiration and, in the foreground, the oval containers made from creepers, which may be indigenous in origin. Photograph by María Mercedes Ortíz.

Fig. 133 **Colombia, Boyacá.** Twined strainer basket of reeds with horizontal stripes in pink and green (aniline dyes). Used in cheese-making, for holding the curd while the whey drains off. H: 100 mm; dia: 145 mm. Collected by Linda Mowat, 1985. 1985.31.3

Fig. 134 Making the base of a wicker basket, Valle de Tenza. Photograph by William Paredes.

"plain weave", plain and pattern twill, some rather complex variants on lattice weave, and coiled basketry. When Wassén and the Reichel-Dolmatoffs visited these groups, a rather limited number of materials was in use. An interesting development in recent years is documented by Vasco who found that when a group of Emberá-Chamí moved from the upper river San Juan to the Garrapatas area, their traditional materials were more difficult to obtain and so they began to experiment with other plants, especially creepers, and now use some seventeen different plants as opposed to two (Vasco 1987:98).

Patterns of various types are an important part of Chocó basketry. Simple designs are occasionally found on the *e* carrying baskets but are much more common on the twill baskets, particularly the type of storage baskets known as *jahara* and *peta*. These handsome baskets often have quite complex designs with motifs taken from animals (deer, armadillo, different species of snake, butterfly, firefly, snail, crab, fish, caterpillar) and inanimate objects such as fish hook, hammer, etc. (Vasco 1987:129-35). Although the designs may once have had a deeper significance this appears to have been forgotten and people usually insisted that they were simply decorative.

The following types of baskets are documented:

Carrying baskets

1. Simple cylindrical baskets in hexagonal plaiting and variants are used by both groups for transporting garden produce such as maize cobs, cocoa beans and fruits of the *chontaduro* palm (Wassén 1988:53; Reichel-Dolmatoff 1961: Pl. XVIII).
2. For transporting smaller items such as maize kernels, cocoa beans or wild fruits, similar shaped baskets are made in twill (Reichel-Dolmatoff 1961:99, Pl. XVIII, no. 8).
3. Vasco describes and illustrates carrying baskets known in Chamí-Emberá as *e* and made in a wider range of techniques and materials than those seen by Wassén and Reichel-Dolmatoff.

118

The techniques include wicker, twill and more than one type of lattice technique (Vasco 1987: 111-112, figs. 77, 90-97).
4. Among the Emberá-Chamí special baskets known as *inpurr* and *inpurru* are made usually from strong creepers, using a wicker technique though twill versions are also found. The bottle-shaped *inpurru* is considered feminine. Specially designed as fishing baskets, their roomy interiors and narrow necks prevent the catch from escaping on the journey home (the most common fish in the area, the *corroncho*, continues to give great leaps even when dead and gutted). The version with rather straighter walls, the *inpurr*, is considered masculine: both forms may be used for carrying seed for broadcasting (Vasco 1987:114-116, figs. 108-119). Reichel-Dolmatoff (1961: Pl. VII) illustrates an Emberá Indian with a basket of this type hanging from his shoulder.

Storage baskets

1. Small, cylindrical twill baskets used for storing personal items, nearly always with patterns worked in two colours (Reichel-Dolmatoff 1961:99, Pl. XIX, nos. 5, 8).
2. Similar baskets known as *jahara* are closely associated, among the Emberá-Chamí, with processing maize. They hold first the grains, then the popped corn and finally the flour (Vasco 1987:113-114).
3. *Kora* baskets, similar in form and technique (hexagonal plaiting) to the large carrying baskets described by Reichel-Dolmatoff, are used among the Emberá-Chamí for storage. Emergency disposable versions are also made for carrying, for instance, a present of a few eggs (Vasco 1987:116-118, figs. 120-123).
4. Small, coiled bottle-shaped baskets with lids are used for holding money and jewellery. In the examples illustrated by Wassén and Reichel-Dolmatoff, the foundation element is totally covered by the stitching. Vasco illustrates a coarser variety in which both the foundation and stitching elements are visible (Wassén 1988 54-55, fig. 22; Reichel-Dol-

matoff 1961: fig. 8, L; Vasco 1987:105, fig. 83).

The closely constructed variety may be the ancestor of the larger and very fine coiled baskets illustrated here (Plate 9). These must surely be a recent development since they are not mentioned by any of the three authorities consulted, unless they are the *neenderde* referred to by Vasco (1987:118) as a recent, non-indigenous introduction.

Rectangular boxes with lids

1. Worked in pattern twill, these are used for storing personal items such as clothes or sewing things and probably (by analogy with other groups) ritual paraphernalia. Curiously enough, the Emberá-Chamí term for them is *peta*, presumably derived from the Spanish *petaca* used for basketry or hide boxes of the same form (Reichel Dolmatoff 1961:99, Pl. XIX, Nos. 6, 9 (Noanama); Vasco 1987:113-114).

2. The closely woven twill *borosukas* also have lids but are flat, rather like some spectacle cases. Traditionally used for fish hooks, they are tied to the baskets called *inpurr* (Vasco 1987:114, fig. 107).

Hexagonally plaited **openwork basket cages** are used as temporary containers for chickens and small mammals (Vasco 1987:122).

Fish traps, funnel or bell shaped, are documented for the Noanama, worked in hexagonal plaiting with an additional horizontal element filling what would otherwise be the hexagonal-shaped openings.

The Noanama also make wicker crab traps, cylindrical in shape. They are closed at one end with the entrance at the other. The ends of the slivers forming the long axis of the trap are bent inwards round the aperture so that the crab can push his way in quite easily but finds it almost impossible to get out again (Reichel-Dolmatioff 1961:100, Pl. XVIII, no. 9, Pl.LVII no. 5).

Small rectangular **mats** plaited from palm leaves in 2:1 twill are mentioned by Reichel-Dolmatoff (1961:100) as being used in the chicha ritual. Large twill mats measuring as much as 2 x 1 m. are also found.

Both groups make two different types of **fire fan**, each in varieties of twill weave. One type is an approximately triangular fan with a tubular handle and the other a lozenge shaped fan with a slender handle made of bunched slivers (Wassén 1988:56, fig. 23; Reichel-Dolmatoff 1961: Pl. XIX, nos. 1, 2, 4; Vasco 1987: figs 132, 133).

Vasco illustrates (1987:126, figs. 139, 140) two bases for **crowns.** The first of these is to carry a woollen upper part, the second is a plain weave strip for a feather crown. The same author found three types of hat in use, one of which (125-126, fig. 138), with a square crown made in twill from strips of (?) *bihao* stem, he considers is probably traditional.

Miscellaneous

Vasco describes (1987:124) several rather enigmatic items which he thinks may once have had a deeper significance. One of these, called in Spanish the *robamuchachas*, means literally, in Emberá, "for stealing girls with the little finger". This narrow tubular item is worked in such a way that, like manioc squeezing tubes (Rivière this volume), it becomes longer and narrower when stretched, so squeezing or trapping a finger. Although some people told Vasco that it was merely a toy, others said that it was formerly used in marriage ceremonies. If a young man liked a girl he would visit her and show her the *robamuchachas*. If she loved him she would insert her finger and he would pull it until it tightened. After three such visits they were considered man and wife. These items are occasionally sold as curiosities in ethnographic handicraft shops in Bogotá.

Additional items known as "jaguar paw" and "crab" are illustrated in Vasco's figs. 136-137.

Urabá and the Isthmus of Panama

Much of the lower part of the Isthmus of Panama was inhabited by the Cueva Indians when the Spaniards first reached the area and who, according to early sixteenth century accounts summarized in Romoli (1987:150), were justly famed for their baskets. They made several different kinds, of which the finest, called *habas*, were made for preference from the midrib of the banana-like *bihao* leaf and used to transport or store delicate objects. They were so closely woven that, placed one inside the other and separated by a *bihao* leaf, they were completely waterproof.

The Cuna have traditionally had settlements on both sides of the Gulf of Urabá as well as in Panama, especially the San Blas Islands. These Indians are considered by some to be descendants of the Cueva while others, especially Romoli (1987) consider that the Cuna moved up from the Chocó to fill vacant territory left by the Cueva who were extinct before the end of the sixteenth century. Cuna basketry certainly seems to have more in common with that just described for the Chocó Indians than it does with any other Indian groups considered here. However one important difference is that the baskets are made by men rather than women, taught by the male culture hero Iberogun (Cardale Schrimpff 1985:102). Whereas they use a rather wide range of baskets, only one type of bag is made and this is almost certainly a relatively recent introduction.

The materials generally used are long strips from the stems of *naiwal* (iraca - *Carludovica palmata* Ruiz and Pav.) and *silel* (?*Oencarpus panamenus* Bailey). The former is easily obtainable since it is one of the first plants to colonize abandoned gardens when they are left to go fallow. In Arquía (a Colombian settlement on the west side of the Gulf of Urabá) it is used for all the baskets except the uprights of the *carrpas*. A third type of cane, *masarrwal*, is used for the supports running the length of the fish traps.

Patterns are found only on the large-carrying baskets (Fig. 136) and on the fire fans (Cardale Schrimpff 1985: figs. II, XI). The motifs chiefly represent plants, household or other implements (particularly those used by the men) and, occasionally, animals. It is interesting that this category of pattern is found on a number of other

120

items such as the bead ligatures and the more traditional *molas* blouses but never on such items as hammocks, which have their own range of designs. Although superficially similar to the designs on Chocó baskets, when compared in detail it is difficult to find identical examples. In addition, the Chocó patterns are usually arranged along a vertical axis while the Cuna patterns (with the exception of the fire fans) are along a diagonal axis.

Unless specified, the following types of baskets were being made in Arquía on the west side of the Gulf of Urabá during the 1960s and are described and illustrated in greater detail in Cardale Schrimpff (1985).

Carrying baskets

1. The *carrpa* is a large, patterned basket with a slightly flaring rim. They are used by the women to bring produce home from their gardens, carried on their backs by means of a palm fibre tump-line. They are made in 3:3 and pattern twill, using the sturdy strips of *silel* for the uprights and strips of the more flexible *naiwal* for the horizontals. Each household has at least one *carrpa* for every female member (usually more) and although they are strong, the heavy use to which they are subjected means that they have a working life of little more than two months. A basket of this type will take about five hours to make, excluding the preparation of the fibre (Fig. 135). These patterned baskets are particularly characteristic of the western side of the Gulf of Urabá. In other Cuna settlements the term *karpa* is used as a general term for baskets (Holmer 1952:142).

2. The *silemudit* is similar in shape and size to the *carrpa* but undecorated and made in wicker rather than twill. These baskets are said to be characteristic of the eastern side of the Gulf of Urabá (Caiman Nuevo).

Storage baskets

1. The *imiatali* (from the word *imia* = hole) are openwork baskets in hexagonal plaiting. Hung from the roof or walls, these are used to store household items (Fig. 127). There is usually

Fig. 135 **Colombia, Arquía, Cuna.** Making a *carrpa.* Photograph by Marianne Cardale Schrimpff, 1968.

Fig. 136 **Colombia, Arquía, Cuna.** Two *carrpas* with the *moroka* turtle or tortoise shell pattern (left) and *aleman bander,* "German flag" (right). Photograph by Marianne Cardale Schrimpff, 1968.

Fig. 137 **Colombia, Arquía, Cuna.** Making a fire fan of *naba* palm. Photograph by Marianne Cardale Schrimpff, 1968.

one suspended above the fire to hold kitchen utensils and leaf-wrapped packets of meat or fish to be preserved by the smoke. Some have a small, triangular tongue protruding from the rim so that the basket can be attached to the wall more easily. A smallish one can be made in a little over an hour (not counting the time spent in the preparation of the fibre).

2. *Pilacaki*, flattish, pouch-shaped baskets some 150 mm square, are sometimes hung from the wall to keep small items in. They are made in 3:3 twill and have no lid.

3. The *pirka(t)* is a small cup-shaped basket with a double wall, the outer one forming a ring base so that the basket can be stood on the floor, a stool, or other flat surface and used to hold half finished items such as beadwork and associated tools. They are made in 3:3 twill.

4. Square based 3:3 twill baskets with a herringbone pattern are also made.

Openwork basketry cages made in hexagonal plaiting are used to hold birds and small mammals.

Long tubular basketry **fish traps**, *aglue*, measuring some 2 m. in length, are placed with their funnel-shaped mouth at the apex of a V-shaped dam to trap small fish driven downstream. The technique is basically a type of openwork lattice like that found on the *imiatali* with the difference that the slivers running the length of the tube are placed close together.

The Cuna believe that if someone once looks down the mouth of a fish trap, no fish will ever enter. For this reason they prefer to be alone when making a trap, in case anyone should look down accidentally. A leaf plug is kept permanently in the mouth of a finished trap for the same reason (Cardale Schrimpff 1985:115-116).

A fish trap takes roughly three hours to make, excluding the time spent preparing the materials.

Mats do not appear to be used. Both men and women sit on low wooden stools or relax and sleep in hammocks.

Fire fans

1. The most common type, made of *naiwal*

(iraca) slivers, is an approximately triangular fan with a tubular handle, very similar to those found in the Chocó. Worked in 3:3 and patterned twill, they have geometric designs similar to those on the *carrpas*.

2. A second type is made by the river Paia Cuna from the undyed leaflets of the *naba* palm (*Astrocaryum Standleyanum*, L.B. Bailey). Worked in 2:2 twill, it has a round "fan" while the handle is a bound bundle round a plaited foundation (Fig. 137). Slightly larger than the *naiwal* examples, it is considered more efficient and more durable.

In the past the Cuna made various types of feather **headdresses** with basketry supports (Heye 1924:195-196, fig. 57; Holmer 1951:23; Wassén 1949:57, fig. 26) but none were seen in Arquía.

A rather different range of baskets is made by the Cuna living in the **San Blas Islands** of Panama (Holmer 1952:41, 49, figs. 18, 142; Krieger 1926: Pl.23). In addition, coiled basketry is or was made occasionally (Stout 1948:254).

Lionel Wafer, the Scottish surgeon who was marooned among the Cuna for several months during the seventeenth century, was particularly impressed by the range and quality of their baskets at that time (1934:95). The finest were sufficiently closely woven to be watertight; even basketry drinking cups were made. At this time the baskets were dyed bright colours, but today when making patterns the Cuna no longer dye the material, relying entirely on the colour contrast between the two faces of the slivers.

The Coastal Lowlands

The Chimila

Today a diminished group whose lands have been appropriated by white settlers, these people once occupied a large part of the lowlands bordering the southern limits of the Sierra Nevada de Santa Marta. Accounts dating from the earlier years of this century and the end of the previous one indicate that baskets were once much more important than they are today.

122

Carrying baskets, although replaced in more recent years by coarse string bags (Reichel-Dolmatoff 1946; Cardale Schrimpff 1985:172, 180) were formerly important (Brettes 1898:464). Bolinder (1926:Pl.1) illustrates a Chimila boy carrying a huge twill basket more than a third of his own height which was supported on his back with the aid of a tump-line.

Storage baskets

1. Rather large plaited baskets made of creepers and used for storing food inside the house were in use when Reichel-Dolmatoff visited the Chimila (1946:118).

2. Small twill baskets with rectangular bases and wicker mouths, made of the outer wall of a creeper, were in use in the 1960s (Cardale Schrimpff 1985:188). According to a Chimila, the "whites" (non-indigenous settlers) had taught them to make this type of basket which in shape and size is very similar to the "plain weave" baskets used by peasants in the Sierra de Perija for gathering coffee. On the other hand, similar sounding baskets made of *espartos* (reeds) were seen by Reichel-Dolmatoff in the 1940s (1946:118). They were always made in contrasting colours, natural and black.

The Chimila make **fire fans** of feathers rather than basketry.

Potstands, curious but useful items are quite common in Chimila houses (Fig. 142). They are roughly made cone-shaped wicker receptacles mounted on a central post. These have a variety of uses as supports for round based pots or gourds but also as nesting boxes for hens (Cardale Schrimpff 1985:182). Similar but possibly larger ones, used as granaries for storing maize and other things, were seen by Reichel Dolmatoff (1946:103, fig. 2).

The Sierra Nevada of Santa Marta

The next Indian groups, moving from west to east, inhabit the middle slopes of these impressive mountains whose isolated mass rises abruptly in the middle of the lowlands and ends at the coast. The three surviving Indian groups, the Ika, the Saha and the Kogi, are skilled spinners and weavers but today make almost no baskets. This is another area where, both for carrying and for storage, they are supplanted by bags which are of enormous significance not only in practical terms but also in these Indians' cosmology. Although the three groups have similar material cultures, there are some important differences. I have not come across references to basketry items among the Saha but it seems probably that they once had items similar to those of the Ika and the Kogi.

Crudely rectangular **carrying baskets** for harvesting coffee were made in "plain weave" when Bolinder visited the Ika in the early years of this century (1925: Taf.16, 5). These may well have been adopted with the coffee bean.

For the Ika Bolinder illustrates (1925:Taf. 16, 6) rectangular **storage baskets**.

A lidded **storage box** for more valuable or delicate items is illustrated by the same author (Taf. 26, 3). Formerly similar baskets were in use among the Kogi (Reichel-Dolmatoff 1949-50, vol. 1:65) for storing ceremonial paraphernalia but already by the 1940s they appear to have lost the art of making them.

Mats no longer appear to be made by the Ika but in Bolinder's time, coarse examples called *güii* were laid on platform beds or used as partition walls in the houses (1925:65 and Taf. 15,1). Mats are not used among the Kogi: the men sit on stools and sleep in hammocks while the women sit and sleep on skins or pieces of palm bark. Among this group the walls of the houses were traditionally twill weave (Reichel-Dolmatoff 1949-50, vol. 1:65).

Fire fans are made both by the Ika in extremely coarse 2:2 twill (Cardale Schrimpff 1985:263), and the Kogi (Cardale Schrimpff 1985:243; Reichel-Dolmatoff 1949-50, vol. 1:65).

The elaborate feather **headdresses** illustrated by Brettes (1898:449, 450) appear to have had basketwork bases (hexagonal plaiting in one case and 1:1 "plain weave" in another). In the 1940s, the Kogi still made small, rectangular "trays" of *esparto* on which religious offerings were placed.

The Guajiro

The Guajiro Indians who inhabit this semi-desert peninsula in northeastern Colombia also use bags rather than baskets and basketry never seems to have been an important part of the material culture of this group. While this may be partly due to the difficulty of obtaining raw materials in the desert environment, bags are much better suited to carrying relatively small, assorted loads on donkeys, usually at the same time as their riders. Probably the only items made in basketry technique are headgear . Both items are made in the Sierra de la Macuira near the northeastern tip of the peninsula where the rainfall is higher and there is more vegetation. The material used is referred to variously as *muluh* straw, *isi* grass (Simons 1885:793-4) or, by Billegas and Rivera, as *mawisa.*

Basketwork bases for high feather **headdresses** are shaped like a spool or napkin ring and worked in pattern twill. The designs are in black (sap of the *chipirá* leaf) and the natural white or creamy colour of the fibre. Designs include motifs shaped like a bow tie and one that might be described as a rectilineal S or double spiral.

Broad brimmed **hats**, worn by both men and women, are made in the same technique (Fig. 131). The design usually consists of rectangles and cross-shaped elements. (Cardale Schrimpff 1985; Villegas and Rivera 1982:48-51; Simons 1885:793-794).

The Sierra de Perija

The northernmost part of the eastern chain or *cordillera* of the Andes is known as the Sierra de Perija and is inhabited today by two very different Indian groups. Both these groups tend to be referred to coloquially as "Motilones" because of their short hair but this is one of the

few features that the Yuko (who speak a Carib language) and the Bari (Chibchan speaking) have in common. As with the Guajiro Indians, the frontier with Venezuela runs through their territory. A third group, the Japreria, also inhabit this region but there appears to be little information available on their basketry.

The Yuko

This group is rather unusual among those surveyed here in that bags (knotless netting pouches like those made in the Sierra Nevada de Santa Marta and the Guajira) and baskets are of almost equal importance. Both carrying and storage baskets are found and at least four different types of basketry technique have been described with local differences. They are made by the men using two different kinds of material: *pook* cane *(Stromanthea lutea)* and the outer part of the stem of a creeper *(Souroubea sp.)* Cardale Schrimpff 1985:371).

Carrying baskets, although quite adequate for transporting small loads of food, are not nearly so large as those used, for instance, among the Cuna, probably because the precipitous mountain paths would make carrying big baskets with heavy loads extremely difficult.

1, 2. Among the Maraca, La Laguna and Rio Negro Yuko, a lattice technique basket is used. There is both an openwork (hexagonally plaited) and a closed mesh variety, the only difference between them being that for the latter, two horizontal slivers are taken round at a time. The latter appears to be more usually employed as a carrying basket.

3. Another type of basket in wrapped twining is made by the Pishekakao Yuko. There is no information on its use.

4. A plain weave carrying basket is also made by the Maraca Yuko. This is similar to the possibly introduced Chimila baskets and to those used by the peasant farmers for gathering coffee beans and, according to a Yuko, it was they who had taught them the art. On the other hand a

Fig. 138 **Colombia, Sierra de Perija, Bari.** Making a basket. Photograph by Marianne Cardale Schrimpff, 1968.

Fig. 139 **Colombia, Sierra de Peri-ja, Bari.** Making a mat. Photograph by Marianne Cardale Schrimpff, 1968.

Fig. 140 **Colombia, Sierra de Perija, Bari.** The interior of a Bari house with numerous openwork baskets. Photograph by Marianne Cardale Schrimpff, 1968.

Fig. 141 **Colombia, Sierra de Perija, Bari.** A woman finishing one of a pair of circlets worn by the men. Photograph by Marianne Cardale Schrimpff, 1968.

rather similar basket was seen by Reichel-Dolmatoff (1945:32) when there were few settlers in the area.

Storage baskets may be of open or closed lattice. The former is used for storing clothes and large things that will not fall through the holes.

Small rectangular boxes or pouches, flat 2:2 twill baskets with a close-fitting sheath lid like an old-fashioned spectacle case, are made by the Maraca Yuco. They are rather similar to the *borosukas* of the Chocó. According to Reichel-Dolmatoff they are used by the men as tobacco pouches and for storing herb remedies.

Fish traps are probably absent since the Yuko's traditional method of fishing was with bow and arrow where the rivers are larger and quieter at the bottom of the mountains.

Mats, made by women, are an essential part of the furniture of a Yuko house, being used both for sitting and for sleeping. They are rather fine and closely worked, being made of the leaves of a herbaceous plant called *sharuma* (*Eleocharis geniculata* according to Schon, Jam and Cruxent 1953:38) with the weft of (?) agave string. Jahn (1927: facing p. 108) has published a good photograph of a Macoa Yuko woman making a mat.

Small rectangular **fire fans** in plain 2:2 twill may be made either by men or women. The material is the same as that used for the baskets. These fans are neatly made and flexible; although small they are both efficient and durable. One can be made in approximately one and a half hours, including the time spent in the preparation of the material.

Since contacts with white settlers intensified from about the 1940s, straw **hats** have become common. However the traditional headgear among the Manastara Yuko consisted of a woven cotton headband *(pejoua)* long enough to protect the nape of the neck (Cardale Schrimpff 1985: Pl. 186; Jahn 1927:112). A second type of headgear is illustrated by both Jahn (1927: facing p. 112) and Bolinder (1926: Pl. 15, nos. 28, 29). This is a sort of flower pot shaped cap. Not enough detail is visible for the technique to be specified.

The Bari

This group once occupied an extensive tract of the tropical, jungle covered foothills of the southern and western parts of the Sierra de Perija, a region drained by several important waterways such as the rivers de Oro and Catatumbo. The devastating shrinkage of their territory in recent years has been documented by Lizarralde and Beckerman (1982).

The Bari are - or were until recently - basket users *par excellence* and a single family owns some 40 or 50 of them. They festoon the walls of the *maloca* or long house (Fig. 140), holding food, clothing and household items as well as being used for transport. Unlike other groups where baskets have become a major art form, the Bari baskets do not have designs. They are manufactured by the women from *mirdara,* an unidentified creeper. First this is split longitudinally and the outer and inner bark removed.

There does not appear to be a rigid distinction between **carrying and storage baskets.**

1. By far the commonest kind is a simple, U-profiled basket in hexagonal plaiting (Fig. 138). These vary in size. Many have fine strap handles at opposite sides of the rim. A strip of *bakoura* (bast fibre from an unidentified forest tree) about 25 mm wide is tied to the underside of the basket, threaded through the little strap handles and knotted to form a loop for use in carrying or suspending the basket.

Although these baskets appear, at first sight, rather inadequate for carrying loads of garden produce, Lizarralde and Beckerman (1902: photo 2) have an interesting photograph of a woman harvesting sweet manioc which demonstrates how a large load can be carried in a small basket. The tubers are placed vertically in the basket and the topmost layer, only the tips of which fit inside the rim, are kept in place bound together with a length of string.

127

There is some variation in the time that any woman will take to make a basket of this type but the average appears to be about five hours.

2. A wicker basket, *tocashora,* is also made occasionally.

3. A third type, the shape of a deep, narrow cone and made by coiling a plait of fibre round and round and sewing it into place as on many types of hats, has apparently been adopted from white settlers.

4, 5. Two further types of baskets, both rare and apparently made in some sort of "plain weave" technique, are described by Pinton (1965:275). The first, seen in an abandoned house, were small and cylindrical with a flat base. The second kind, from the river Catatumbo region, was conical.

Mats are a very important item among the furnishings of a traditional long house. The Bari make no stools and although, like most Indians, they use their hammocks for reclining in during the day as well as sleeping in at night, these are hung in the darker, more central part of the house. The long house is made with roof and walls in one, so the only light inside is from the hearths or what comes in from the doors at either end. However, the mats can be pushed into the space near where the roof comes down to the floor and where the leaves of the thatch can be parted to let in extra light. Here the women and children spend much of their day, taking advantage of the cool, shady, insect-free environment to spin, make baskets or carry out other domestic tasks, some of which are done in a reclining position so as to be as near the "window" as possible.

The mats are made from slivers of the outer walls of the shoots of an unidentified palm (*kio:bora*) and from two broad strips of bast fibre from the *bakoura* tree. The strips are laid side by side at what is to be the centre of the mat and worked as wefts in opposite directions until the outer edges of the mat are reached (Fig. 139). The mats measure about 1 x 1.2 m and take (excluding fibre preparation) from three to five hours to make, depending on the

128

skill and experience of the individual woman (Cardale Schrimpff 1985:515-518).

Fire fans are made of feathers, preferably of the wild turkey, rather than basketry.

One of the finest basketry-related items made by the Bari is the twill plaited **head circlet** (*okburra* or, according to Pinton (1965:276), *somanera,* used exclusively by the men (women may not put them on). They wear them in pairs, one inside the other, when in the house, eating or reclining in their hammocks. Since they are considerably smaller than the diameter of the head, they are perched on top and kept in place by pulling up the hair within the circumference of the circlet. Since the hair stands up fairly stiffly, it prevents the circlet from slipping.

The circlets are made by the women (Fig. 141) using slivers of the versatile *iraca* here called *agshura dakana.* Whereas the Cuna and many other groups use fairly stout strips of the stem of the plant for making baskets, for the circlets the strips are split repeatedly into ever thinner layers until the slivers are as fine and flexible as cloth. The preparation calls for skill and patience and for sufficient material for just one of a pair of circlets, an experienced woman will need about seven and a half hours.

The making of the circlets (described in detail in Cardale Schrimpff 1985:507-510) may be done by two women at once. Those I watched were a mother and daughter, one of whom made the inner circlet while the other worked on the larger, outer one; at the same time the mother could help the daughter with the more difficult bits. To complete one circlet took the best part of three days.

Concluding Remarks

When looked at as a whole, the Indians of northern and western Colombia have a relatively homogeneous range of techniques with baskets in various kinds of plaiting being the most frequent. Twill is widespread and much used, whereas wicker baskets are much less common and in several instances may be recent introductions. Coiled basketry is reported only for the westernmost groups in the area (Noanama, Emberá and Cuna). As far as forms of use are concerned, the commonest is for carrying and storage. Lidded boxes for storing delicate ceremonial paraphernalia such as feather headdresses were probably once more widespread before tins and plastic containers became available. The presence or absence of mats (relatively uncommon) is interesting as a reflection of a particular Indian community's way of life. In contrast to many other parts of the Americas, and with the partial exception of the Emberá *jahara* and the smoke larders, baskets associated with particular kinds of food preparation are absent. Designs of any complexity are rare (Chocó groups, Cuna and Guajiro) although where they are present, they are varied and skilfully executed.

It is disappointing to find that, in contrast to the complex symbolism of basketry among the Desana, for instance (Reichel-Dolmatoff 1985) there is little or no information on the significance of basketry in the belief systems of the groups covered in this survey. In some cases this may be because no ethnographers spent long enough with them to learn their language and become intimately acquainted with their cosomology before acculturation had broken it down. In other cases such as the Kogi, for which there exist monumental studies made during the first half of the century (Preuss 1926; Reichel-Dolmatoff 1949-50), it seems that baskets never had an important place in their cosmology. Vasco (1987:145) is emphatic that he was unable to trace any significance of this sort among the Emberá, in contast to the important role still played by pottery in the belief system of this group.

Elsewhere we must be content with crumbs which generally add up to little. We mentioned earlier than in Emberá and Cuna belief, they were taught to make baskets by a culture hero (female in the former case and male in the latter). Pinton (1965:275) has pointed out that the Bari use anthropomorphic terms for the different parts of their baskets: "mouth" for the opening, "eyes" for the hexagonal holes in the lattice and "ears" for the small lateral handles. While anthropomorphic terms for containers are rather widespread - we have only to look at our own language - it is possible that for the Bari the significance was deeper. Rivière (1969) records that for the Tiriyo, on the borders of Brazil and Surinam, baskets have a very strong anthropopomorphic significance since those made by a culture hero in the other world are the outer coverings of people into each of which he puts a soul.

Fig. 142 **Colombia, Coastal Lowlands, Chimila.** Potstands. Photograph by Marianne Cardale Schrimpff.

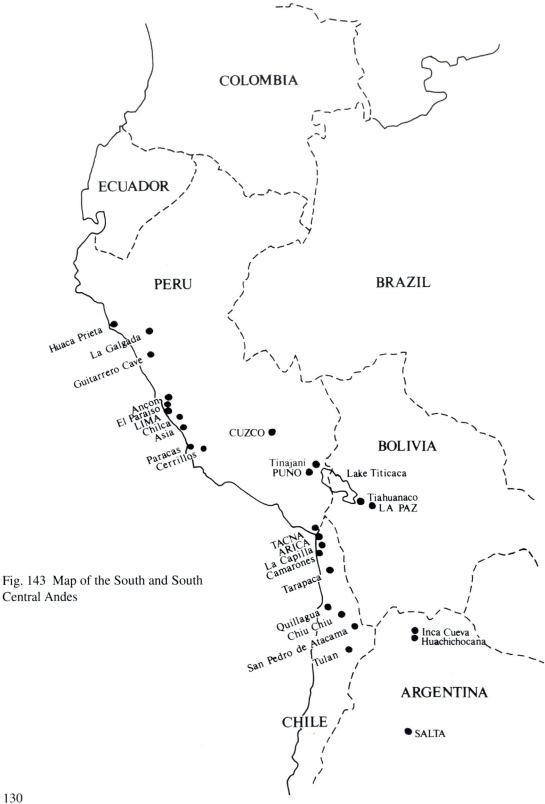

COLOMBIA

ECUADOR

PERU

BRAZIL

Huaca Prieta

La Galgada

Guitarrero Cave

Ancon
El Paraiso
LIMA
Chilca
Asia
Paracas
Cerrillos

CUZCO

BOLIVIA

Tinajani
PUNO

Lake Titicaca

Tiahuanaco
LA PAZ

TACNA
ARICA
La Capilla
Camarones
Tarapaca

Quillagua
Chiu Chiu
San Pedro de Atacama
Tulan

Inca Cueva
Huachichocana

Fig. 143 Map of the South and South
Central Andes

ARGENTINA

CHILE

SALTA

Form and Function
in the Basketry of the Central and South Central Andes:
an overview from Prehispanic times to the present

by Penny Dransart

Long and venerable traditions for making baskets extend back into the mists of time. My aim here is to examine the evidence for basketry through time in the central and south central Andes. In addition, I would like to consider how basketry traditions are connected with other aspects of cultural processes in the evolution of regional cultures.

Basketry from these areas appears in the form of baskets with or without lids, as supports for transporting ceramic vessels, as baby cradles, sandals, headgear, combs and as fans edged with splendid feathers. Baskets most often survive in burials where they occur in all sizes. Small ones sometimes still contain food for the deceased person with whom they were interred, or, in the case of the Paracas cemetery on the Peruvian coast, protect fine ceramic vessels (Carrión Cachot 1949:51). At the other end of the scale, large baskets were made as containers for the flexed corpse of the dead person, a widespread practice observed in many places such as the Paracas Necropolis in Peru (Carrión Cachot 1949) and at the Chilean cemetery site of Tarapacá 40 (Núñez 1970).

We should also take into account the fact that in some places, people lived in houses which may be considered to resemble large upturned baskets, for example at Chilca on the Peruvian coast, 67 km south of Lima (Donnan 1964). Indeed, matting is still an important component in the construction of houses on the coast of Peru and northern Chile. Even boats made by the Uru people, who up until recently have lived from fishing and gathering on the shores of Lake Titicaca, are made from bundles of reeds and may be said to be akin to basketry. Two models of such a *balsa* raft are in the Pitt Rivers Museum (1891.2.1 and 1903.34.1).

Despite the variety of uses to which basketry lent itself in the Andes, the items represented in the Pitt Rivers Museum are mostly small to moderately sized baskets and hats, and this chapter will concentrate on these forms of basketry.

Archaeologists have defined a geographically located series of cultural areas which do not conform to modern political boundaries (Lumbreras 1981:42). According to this scheme, the baskets in the Museum come from the central Andean area, the south central Andes, the southern Andes and Tierra del Fuego (which forms part of Patagonia in the Lumbreras scheme). It should be noted that, of these areas, the south central Andes has produced the greatest number of baskets, and also the hats represented here. This area includes southern Peru, northern Chile, part of Bolivia and north-west Argentina. As it also incorporates the Atacama Desert, which is said to be the driest in the world, the arid conditions favour the preservation of organic materials. Hence Peru and Chile, in particular, have provided items for study which are not available from other parts of South America. In practice, many of the items discussed here came from Arica. Since some of them were collected when Arica formed part of Peruvian national territory, they were entered in the Pitt Rivers Museum's records as coming from Arica, Peru.

It is not known when the making of baskets was first practised in the Andes. A fragment of twined basketry, whether a piece of matting or a wall section of a basket, was found in Guitarrero Cave in Peru, in a level (Complex IIa) dated to *ca* 8600 to 8000 B.C. (Adovasio and Maslowski 1980:265). Basketry has also been reported from the site of Inca Cueva cave 4 in northwest Argentina (Aschero 1984:68), and

CHRONOLOGICAL CHART

CENTRAL ANDES

SOUTH CENTRAL ANDES

Years before present x 1000		Northern Peru	Central Peru	Southern Peru		Tacna - Arica	Peru-Bolivia	San Pedro de Atacama	NW Argentina	
1	INKA EMPIRE / Regional states / WARI EMPIRE / Regional Developmental	CHIMU	Inka Empire / CHANCAY	ICA-CHINCHA		Regional Developments	INKA EMPIRE / Regional Developments		INKA EMPIRE / Regional Developments	
2		MOCHE	Wari Empire / Pachacamac	NASCA • Paracas Necropolis		TIWANAKU / Alto Ramírez • AZ 70	TIWANAKU / PUKARA	TIWANAKU / SAN PEDRO DE ATACAMA CULTURE	AGUADA / TIWANAKU	TIWANAKU PERIOD
3	Formative Period	CHAVIN/ CUPISNIQUE • La Galgada • Huaca Prieta	ANCON Chavinoid? • Asia • El Paraíso	• Cerrillos • Paracas Cavernas		• La Capilla 1		• Tulan 54	• Huachichocana III (preceramic) • Inca Cueva cave 7	Formative Period
4	Archaic Period									Archaic Period
5			• Chilca							
6	Lithic Period									
7						• Camarones 14				
8										
9										
10			• Guitarrero Cave Complex II						• Inca Cueva cave 4	Palaeoindian Period
11										

132

this site has been dated from the ninth to eighth millennium B.C. (Figini, Carbonari and Huarte 1990:205). In addition, these two sites have produced evidence for the making of yarns, and at the former, other fabrics also appear. In Guitarrero Cave, the yarns are all spun from vegetal fibre, whereas the evidence from Inca Cueva cave 4 shows that camelid fibre (that is, fleece from guanaco or vicuña) was the preferred material for spinning yarn. Animal fibre is not a material usually employed in the making of baskets, but some examples from the Andes flout such conventions, as will be seen below.

In a survey of prehispanic art from the Americas, Pal Kelemen saw basketry as the forerunner of weaving and, judging from the omission or exclusion of basketry from later periods in his survey of art objects, the impression given is that basketry has been relegated to an inferior position. In fact, only Anasazi (Basketmaker) baskets from southwestern USA, dating from the first millennium AD, merit inclusion in the plates in Kelemen's book. Otis T. Mason also viewed basketry as the source from which textile art later sprang. The approach to basketry which he adopted in a book originally published in 1904 is in marked contrast to that of Kelemen. "Basketry," Mason declares, "is the mother of all loom work and bead-work .... The first and most versatile shuttles were women's fingers" (Mason 1988:3). Mason speaks with great enthusiasm about the object of his study, and throughout his book he elevates the making of baskets into the apotheosis of fine art (see, for example, Mason 1988:178). However, to claim that basket making predates the making of cloth or *vice versa* is to yield to speculation. Equally, it must be said, we cannot assume that basketry was always the work of women.

Yet the making of baskets and of cloth is clearly related, and it is sometimes difficult to point out where the dividing line between them occurs. This is because the two may employ common structures. Irene Emery admits that there is no clear line of demarcation between basketry and cloth, or even between basketry materials and textile materials. At best, she says, "basketry" may be taken to comprise fabrics which have little or no pliability because of the inflexible character of some or of all of their component materials, while "cloth" may be understood to have been made from materials which are not inherently rigid, and that any inflexibility which may occur in such a fabric is due to the manner in which the flexible elements are combined or constructed (Emery 1966:210).

Two structures are particularly relevant in the context of this chapter. Firstly, weft twining was widely employed in the making of baskets, matting and cloth fabrics in the Archaic periods of both the central and south central Andes. At the site of Huaca Prieta in Peru, twined basketry included an example which bore a design of pairs of birds joined in mirror-image in which the bird design is executed in blue cotton wefts (Bird *et al* 1985:98). Some of the twined fabrics at this site also display elaborate designs executed in a technique which combines weft twining and transposed or crossed warps (Bird *et al* 1985:146-190).

The other structure common to both basketry and fabrics is that of looping. Many varieties of looped structures occur in fabrics (Emery 1966:31-33, 53-54). Coiled basketry resembles simple looping with two single elements in which the looping stitches constitute an active element which passes round an inactive foundation element (Fig. 144). More often than not, in coiled basketry the stitches pierce the foundation rod or bundle of the previous coil, but there are basketry structures which are the exact equivalent of the looped fabric structures. These were used especially in Tierra del Fuego (see the chapter in this volume on Fuegian basketmaking).

Of these two structures, looping (or coiling) proved to be longer lived. In fabrics, weft twining is said to have died out by the end of the Archaic in Peru, and Lumbreras suggests that this structure may be used as a diagnostic element for the Archaic (Lumbreras 1974:45). However, twining does occur in both fabrics

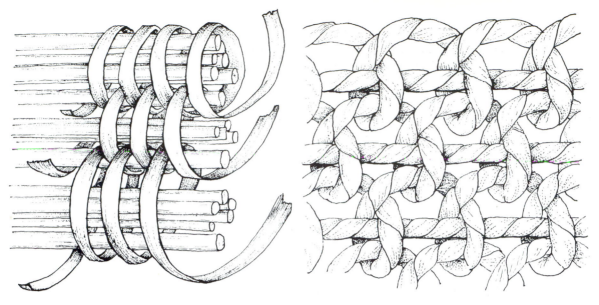

Fig. 144 Coiled basketry compared with looping

and baskets in later periods as a heading in woven textiles and in basketry to strengthen the sides of crossed-stick baskets described below.

The Central Andes

Elizabeth King observed that twined basketry occurs in preceramic and early pottery periods in Peru (King 1965:249). She suggested that it is probably the earliest type of basketry, the use of which persisted through Chavín times and into the subsequent period in the central and south coast regions of Peru. In Wari and later times, it seems to have been replaced largely by twilled basketry, although twilled basketry can be traced back to Archaic period sites such as Huaca Prieta (Bird et al 1985:93) and La Galgada (Grieder et al 1988:153). Crossed warp twining is rather infrequent, but it is reported from Complex IV of Guitarrero Cave (Adovasio and Maslowski 1980:268-9). Unfortunately, this level is heavily disturbed and contains artefacts from different periods, but most of the items probably post date 700 B.C. Crossed warp twining is also reported from the early Paracas period at Cerrillos in the Ica Valley (Wallace 1962:312). According to King (1965:249),

twined basketry does occur on the far south coast of Peru, but in the form of spaced twining which is rare in earlier periods.

Twined basketry is also rare ethnographically (O'Neale 1949:75), and King concluded that twining seems to die out in basketry when other techniques are introduced.

Perhaps the most common type of prehispanic basket mentioned in the literature is the twill interlaced rectangular basket. The Pitt Rivers Museum has four examples in its collections made of oblique twill interlacing over flat ribs which impart some rigidity to the structure (Plate 8). Such baskets were used by spinners and weavers to contain spindles, spun and unspun fibres, and other items such as single or double sided combs. One of the baskets in the Pitt Rivers Museum contains a single sided comb (1895.38.1). This work basket was found in a grave at Ancón, but the combs have been found over a wide geographical area in South America, and they also appear in both earlier and later contexts than the work baskets.

Another type of rectangular basket was made, consisting of panels of vertically arranged canes which were wrapped with coloured yarns that formed a design. The panels were backed by a series of horizontally arranged canes and they were held in place within a rectangular cane framework. An example, possibly from the Huarmey Valley on the north coast of Peru, is illustrated in *Museums of the Andes* (1981:137). Precedents for this type of basket are reported from the richly furnished burial of a "warrior priest" at the site of Huaca de la Cruz in the Virú Valley, dating from the Huancaco period (contemporary with the better known Moche period) (Strong and Evans 1952:160).

Coiled basketry is not frequently reported from the central Andes. A fragment of a type of coiling was excavated from the village area of the late preceramic cotton growing site of Asia on the south central coast of Peru (Engel 1963:52). It is also present in the form of large funerary baskets at the Paracas Necropolis site (Carrión Cachot 1949: plates V and XXIII). Max Uhle collected "two large open-work baskets" from the early part of the extensive site of Ancón, which from Kroeber's description, seem to be a form of space coiling (Kroeber 1944:120).

King pointed out that from an archaeological point of view, coiled basketry is far more common on the extreme south coast of Peru and in Chile (King 1965:250-251). In other words, this is an area which falls within the south central Andes. Significantly, coiled basketry in the more southerly area was accompanied by its analogous fabric structure, looping with two single elements. The preference for simple looped fabric structures and coiled basketry in the south central Andes is in contrast to the situation which applies to the central Andean area where woven fabrics became widespread at an earlier period than in the south, and where elaborate weft twining was used extensively in both baskets and fabrics during the Archaic.

However, a type of looped basketry played a role in what, at first sight, may seem an unusual context. A technique of architectural construction involved the use of baskets at certain imposing sites on the central and north coast of Peru in late preceramic and Chavín times. This is called the *shicra* or bagged-fill technique. At El Paraíso, near the mouth of the Chillón River, excavations in one of the mounds revealed a complex building, resting on platforms, constructed in at least five or six phases. Made of locally available grasses or rush in a loop-and-twist (two element) structure, the *shicra* bags were found containing their fill of rocks (Engel 1966:65-66). The *shicras* were used to block chambers thereby allowing the redevelopment of the site. This construction technique has been seen as demonstrating "the intentional, organized abandonment of a structure prior to rebuilding it in a more prominent, elevated position" (Feldman 1983:300). It has been used to calculate units of work undertaken by individuals collaborating in a communal enterprise (Quilter 1985:294-296).

The fact that most of the basketry mentioned in excavation reports was obtained from funerary sites may mean that we have received a skewed picture regarding the development of basketry in the central Andes. The excavations at Cerrillos in the Ica Valley uncovered a refuse accumulation, the later part of which (the Isla phase) is associated with terraced houses built of adobe. From this phase, fragments of basketry were uncovered, including the crossed warp twining mentioned above. The excavator reported other types of basketry; a fragment of coiling, a twined basket with a simple band of contrasting colour, and a fragment of simple half-hitch looping (Wallace 1962:312). This is an interesting occurrence of a structure which, as we have seen, is more often used in cloth fabrics further south. Given the fact that basketry is said to be rare at this site, the variety of structures encountered is intriguing.

The South Central Andes

As mentioned above, twined basketry (or matting) was reported from Inca Cueva cave 4. However, coiled basketry was by far the preferred method in this cultural area (Fig. 145). As yet, it

135

Fig. 145 **Chile, Arica.** Basket with coiled foundation, sewn with simple, non-interlocking stitches. The colours of the stitching material vary from dull light beige to richer tan colours without forming an obvious design. H: 59 mm; dia: 150 mm. Collected from a grave exposed by an earthquake in 1868 by Lt. M.J. Harrison. Donated by J. Park Harrison to the Ashmolean Museum in 1886 and transferred in 1950. 1886.1.1035.1

Fig. 146 **Chile, Río Loa, Quillagua.** Basket with coiled bundle foundation, sewn with simple non-interlocking stitches. Design in red and black against a natural orange-yellow ground. H: 80 mm; dia: 250 mm. From a prehispanic grave. Donated by Mrs. Jones, 1933. 1933.24.35

Fig. 147 **Northern Chile or Southern Peru.** Basket with coiled bundle foundation sewn with simple non-interlocking stitches. Design on the walls in natural tan (used as an outline), red and very dark brown. H: 88 mm; dia: 380 mm. Purchased from J.T. Hooper, 1930. 1930.73.14

is not clear when it first emerged. The most detailed information comes from the far north of Chile. This overview will consider first the Archaic Period, then Formative and later times.

The Archaic Period
in the South Central Andes

Sophisticated coiled basketry appears at many Archaic period sites in the south central Andes. It is present, for example, at the site of Camarones 14 which dates from the sixth to fifth millennium B.C. This site has given its name to a cultural complex which extended from Arica to Pisagua along the north coast of Chile, and which has been defined as the *Complejo Camarones* by Agustín Llagostera (1989:63). The people had a specialized fishing and gathering economy. However, the presence of basketry is more frequently reported in later cultural complexes of the Archaic. The *Complejo La Capilla*, for example, includes sites such as La Capilla 1 (a cave site), Quiani 7 (a cemetery) and Camarones 15. The cave site provided evidence for cultigens (cotton, sweet potato, gourd and manioc), coiled basketry and looped fabrics among other artefacts. It is of interest to note that the walls of the cave were painted with geometric and zoomorphic designs (Muñoz and Chacama 1982:31-38). The camelid and lizard-like zoomorphic designs resemble motives which appear in some of the coiled baskets which accompanied the burials at Quiani 7 (Dauelsberg 1974:14).

Funerary sites attributed to these cultural complexes (early Camarones, late La Capilla and an intervening one known as Quiani) have yielded evidence for funerary practices which included a spectacular form of mummification. The bodies were arranged in an extended position, and underwent a process of skinning and evisceration. Following this, the body cavities were stuffed and the limbs reinforced with bundles of vegetal matter. The bodies were further elaborated, wrapped, in some cases, with ban-dage-like strips of human skin and provided with modelled masks and wigs. Children's bodies were given the most complicated forms of treatment. These funerary practices constitute the Chinchorro Tradition (Llagostera 1989:63). Later on in this tradition, the bodies were remodelled using a cement-like substance. Camarones 14 provided evidence for the early use of these mortuary practices, and one of the latest and least elaborate manifestations appears at Camarones 15. Thus the tradition lasted for about four thousand years. Of interest are the infant burials at Camarones 15, where the extended bodies of babies were found in place on cradles made of canes lashed together. One of the cradles had narrow woven bands attached, providing an early instance of true weaving in the south central Andes (Rivera et al 1974:84; Santoro and Ulloa 1985:31).

Another example of non-coiled basketry comes from the site of Tiliviche 2, a late preceramic cemetery. The basket is illustrated, but not described, by Standen and Núñez (1984:150, plate 4c). The illustration does not permit identification of the structure, it is possibly a form of wrapped warp twining. Coiled baskets also accompany the burials. Evidently, the people had abandoned the funerary practices of the Chinchorro Tradition. Instead there are several instances of intentional shaping of the skull, a practice which was to become much more widespread in later periods (Standen and Núñez 1984:140).

Coiled basketry is also known from north west Argentina during the Archaic, but the situation is complicated by the presence of another type of coiled basketry. Both Inca Cueva cave 7 (I.C.c.7) and Huachichocana cave III (CH III) are sites from where both types have been reported. In a preceramic level at the latter site, a bowl-shaped basket 60 mm deep and 190 mm in diameter was found. It was coiled, evidently using a bundle foundation of *espuro* grass (*Sporobolus rigens*), sewn with simple stitches (item number 2020, Fernández Distel

1974:114). In the same level, the excavator also reported the occurrence of a fragment described simply as a coiled basket "with an armature" (Fernández Distel 1974:115). There is a slightly more detailed description in the report of the preceramic site of I.C.c.7 of fragments of "coiled basketry with an armature of curved rigid sticks, held together with reddish brown sandy-clay covering" (Aguerre *et al* 1973:211). These fragments were judged to have come from a globular shaped basket due to the curvature of the pieces. It is not clear from the description whether this type is, in fact, similar to the wrapped twined basketry of the Lake Titicaca area, which will be described below.

It would seem that the grasses used in the bundle foundation and stitching of the coiled basketry at these two sites were available locally (Fernández Distel 1978:99). However, other vegetal fibres reported in some of the vegetal fibre yarns came from much further afield. *Agave sisalana* or sisal was identified at I.C.c.7, and a *Bromeliaceae* species, similar to a vegetal fibre known as *cháguar* was identified at CH III. Both of these plants are said to come from the Chaco region to the east of Salta, or from the Chaco Formosa near the Paraguayan border (Fernández Distel 1978:101).

The Formative and Later Times in the South Central Andes

The dominant pattern of coiled basketry continues into the period known as the Formative. This period witnessed changing subsistence economies as the exploitation of resources expanded to include horticultural or even agricultural activities. In particular, these activities were to become dominant in the areas surrounding Lake Titicaca and in fertile valleys such as the Azapa Valley, which crosses the far north of Chile, reaching the Pacific at Arica. Elsewhere, the herding of domesticated camelids was to form the base of the subsistence economy, and llamas and alpacas became an important part of

the Andean landscape. Yet the hunting, fishing and gathering way of life did not disappear, and people obviously combined new activities with the old, or continued in some areas to live without recourse to agriculture or herding.

It is possible that the making of baskets was localized and dependent on locally available raw materials. Such an interpretation is suggested by the early Formative site of Tulan 54, situated in the Tulan Quebrada south east of the Salar de Atacama, at an altitude of approximately 2,900 m above sea level. This site consists of a loosely clustered group of oval structures surrounded by deep, densely packed midden deposits. The people seemed to have lived by herding camelids, hunting rodents and birds, and gathering plant foods. Excavations through part of the midden revealed that the people spent much time spinning camelid fibre into yarn, and in addition, there were fragments of looped fabrics made from these yarns (Dransart 1991:312-3). Amongst the masses of camelid fibre yarns, rodent skins and vegetal fibre, were three fragments of basketry. One was a tiny piece of woven cane, with over one, under one interlacing. The other two pieces had been repaired in ancient times. A section of handle or rim consisting of a rod 59 mm long, wrapped with decorative stitches in a series of X shapes, had been broken. This break was joined using yarn spun and plied from camelid fibre. The third piece consisted of the flat base of a coiled basket (Fig. 148). It had been repaired with long stitches of camelid hide which held the coils together. The repairs to these two items suggest that camelid fibre yarns and leather thongs were more easily available than the materials used to make the basket in the first place.

Coiled basketry with a similar type of stitched repair has been reported from the site of Chiu Chiu 200, located near the confluence of the Loa and Salado rivers (Benavente 1982: plate 1). This site was more or less contemporary with Tulan 54, but differences in locally available resources may be noted. For example, the

138

Fig. 148 **Chile, San Pedro de Atacama, Tulan Quebrada.** Detail of base of coiled basket, sewn with simple non-interlocking stitches, excavated from the site Tulan 54 (TU54), dated c. 3000 BP. The basket was repaired in antiquity by sewing the worn coils together with strips of leather. Museo Gustavo Le Paige S.J., San Pedro de Atacama.

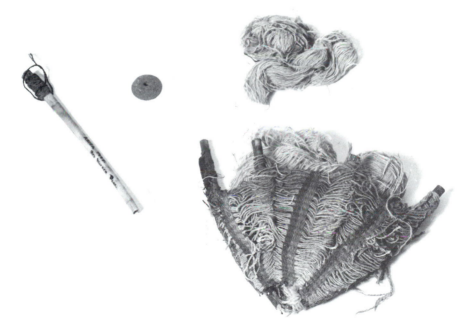

Fig. 149 **Chile, Arica.** Small work basket constructed from three sticks bent into a U shape and lashed together at the base. The walls were formed by wrapped strands of white camelid fibre yarn, held in place by bands of weft twining in dyed camelid fibre yarn. The basket contains seven hanks of white camelid fibre yarn some of which are daubed in red paint, an incised bird bone and a stone spindle whorl. H: 150 mm; L: 186 mm. Collected by Rev. W. Warner Parry and transferred in 1887 from the University Museum, Oxford. 1887.1.633

fabrics at Chiu Chiu 200 are not only of camelid fibre as at Tulan 54. Instead, many of the Chiu Chiu 200 fabrics are made of vegetal fibre yarns. However, it would seem that basketry was not abundant at either of the two sites.

During the Formative, the use of ceramics spread into the area. Yet the use of pottery did not bring about the decline of basketry. In fact, quite the contrary occurred. The cemetery of Tarapacá 40 contained flexed bodies placed inside large coiled baskets. The bodies were first wrapped in tunics and wore "turbans" formed from large amounts of yarn wrapped round the head. In turn, the bodies were covered with more upturned baskets. A few ceramics were included in the grave goods (Núñez 1970:106-8). The baskets from this site are exceptionally well made. For the most part, they are undecorated, but some are said to display geometric, anthropomorphic or serpent-like designs. Two photographs of basketry dishes with geometric designs are reproduced in Núñez (1970: plates B1 and B2).

The first of the two basketry dishes illustrated by Núñez has a design consisting of a double line which steps up and down in the manner of battlements. This simple device appears six times, and all of these up and down lines are concentric. Thus the overall design appears to rotate round the dish. One of the baskets in the Pitt Rivers Museum from Quillagua in Chile displays a related design (Fig. 146). This design incorporates another motif with a jagged edge, and the battlement design has undergone modification. It now consists of single broad lines which have been rotated through ninety degrees so that the battlement outline cuts across the rotations of the coiling instead of moving in the same direction. Yet the overall design does display rotational symmetry if rotated through 180 degrees, in fact, the design is marked by an axis line which cuts across the diameter of the bowl.

Another Pitt Rivers Museum coiled basket (Fig. 147) displays rotational symmetry, also a quadripartite design which repeats when rotated

140

through 180 degrees. However, the design of this basket, with its interlocked key pattern, is more typical of the late pre-Inka period. It is important to note that that none of these designs display mirror-symmetry as in the case of the Huaca Prieta twined basket. In other words, there is a balance between structure and image, which emerges in the course of construction as the worker rotates the basket.

Another type of basket seems to have come into use during the Formative period. In Spanish, it is known as *capacho* (literally, a hamper or a large basket). However, it may occur in all sizes and some are, in fact, very small indeed. In English, Junius B. Bird called it the "crossed-stick pack basket" (Bird 1943:271). This term refers to the structure of the basket since it is made by bending three sticks into a U shape. These sticks are crossed and lashed together at the base of the U, and the walls of the basket are formed by wrapping yarn round each of the sticks in turn. Thus the sticks act as spokes. The strands of the wrapping are sometimes held in place by bands of twining. An example from the cemetery site of Azapa 70 is illustrated in Muñoz (1989:114, figure 3c). This site is considered to belong to the Alto Ramírez Phase in the far north of Chile, one of the most characteristic features of which is the occurrence of tapestry woven textiles which display Pukara style designs from Pukara, north of Lake Titicaca.

Subsequently, the emergent Tiwanaku empire spread its area of influence to the coastal valleys of northern Chile and the far south coast of Peru. Since the central site of Tiahuanaco, with its impressive architectural complexes, is located in the moist Titicaca basin, perishable basketry has not been reported from the Tiwanaku heartland. However, site Azapa 6, a mound cemetery near the village of San Miguel de Azapa approximately 16 km from Arica, was found to contain predominantly Tiwanaku types of pottery. Coiled basketry is also reported from these graves, but some new shapes appear in the repertoire. Not only do the forms represented include traditional dish and bowl shapes, but vase and jar shapes are also featured, and some of the baskets stand on a ring base (Rivera 1977:226). These new shapes in basketry are clearly influenced by ceramic vessels. It would seem that a complex interacting process was occurring. Not only did baskets now mimic ceramic or even metal vessels (the typically Tiwanaku cup-like *keru* shape occurs in pottery, wood, gold and basketry), but the designs born by these vessels also were exchanged. In addition, textiles and sculpture share similar, often more elaborate, iconography which in turn reappears on basketry and pottery. In fact, the Tiwanaku empire is understood to have exported its religious beliefs, expressed in elaborate iconography, to other parts of the Andes. Textiles and ceramics are most often considered to constitute the vehicle by which this visual imagery was introduced to new areas, but perhaps we should also consider basketry in this category of easily transported items.

The San Pedro de Atacama area received prestige goods from Tiwanaku in the form of of textiles, ceramics, gold vessels, basketry and exquisitely carved wooden trays used with tubes for sniffing drugs. However, the arrival of Tiwanaku style goods did not swamp the production of locally made artefacts, and it would seem that the thriving San Pedro de Atacama culture was not fully incorporated into the Tiwanaku empire. Excavations in extensive cemeteries clustered round the modern oasis town of San Pedro de Atacama have revealed some burials which were very rich in grave goods. Typically, these contained well made coiled basketry with stunning designs. The most frequently occurring shapes are cylindrical baskets and flat discs. The multicoloured designs executed in the stitches of the coiling include geometric motives as well as anthropomorphic and camelid designs (Llagostera and Costa 1984:48). These baskets were perhaps made locally, following traditions established in the San Pedro de Atacama Culture, and the better

quality ones tend to be associated with fine polished blackware ceramics. Other baskets, with a more flaring outline, sometimes on a ring base, bear Tiwanaku designs; they may have been imported. These baskets tend to display more colour (Llagostera and Costa 1984:49).

Basketry is virtually always made from vegetal fibres. However, it was mentioned above that Andean basketry sometimes flouts this convention. An example occurs in a twined basket from one of the San Pedro de Atacama cemeteries. It has flaring walls, in which the rigid stakes are of vegetal material and the weft twining yarns which form the walls of the basket are spun and plied camelid yarns. These yarns are dyed in bright colours, and the basket bears a design of four stylized figures, executed against an alternating blue and red ground (Llagostera and Costa 1984:49, figure 54). Although staff-bearing figures constitute a typically Tiwanaku style representation of the human form, these figures carry a spear thrower in one hand and three crossed arrows in the other. They perhaps indicate Aguada influence from Argentina rather than Tiwanaku influence. Aguada pottery and wooden sculpture is also known in San Pedro de Atacama (González 1977:173).

Basketry also appears in the form of headgear during this Middle Period. In the Arica area a phase known as Cabuza, belonging to the early Tiwanaku period, has been distinguished. Some Cabuza burials contained the corpses of warriors, to judge from the protective helmet with which they were equipped. These helmets combine coiled basketry and warp twining; both coiled and vertical vegetal rods are stitched with camelid fibre yarns. They are provided with protective ear flaps, made from canes held together with coloured yarns arranged in horizontal stripes (Santoro and Ulloa 1985:48,65; Museo Chileno de Arte Precolombino 1985:67).

Following the demise of the Tiwanaku empire, the south central Andes saw the development of many regional cultures, hence the name Regional Development Period is applied.

141

Craft workers continued to be as prolific as in the previous period, but new designs and different colour combinations bear witness to changing artistic canons. These new times were also conflict-ridden since fortified villages and towns are common in the south central Andes.

Besides the ubiquitous coiled basketry, other types have been reported from cemetery sites. These tend to be undecorated, and would have been more quickly made than coiled baskets, the making of which is extremely time consuming. Llagostera and Costa (1984:50, figure 56) illustrate a wicker basket from a grave in one of the San Pedro de Atacama cemeteries. Another simply made basket is illustrated by Bird (1943:220, figure 13i). It is a circular basket made from spaced twining, found in a disturbed grave in the Playa de los Gringos cemetery south of Arica. Crossed-stick baskets are common from this period, but their reduced size means that they no longer served as pack baskets. Such a basket was found in another grave at the Playa de los Gringos cemetery; it measured 150 mm deep and 140 mm wide, and it contained a few kernels of corn. It is described as having some of its side panels reinforced. Two sides were strengthened with twill weaving, and another side was reinforced by twined vertical strands (Bird 1943:219, 220, figure 13g).

In the collections of the Pitt Rivers Museum there are four small crossed-stick baskets collected from graves in or near Arica which were exposed by an earthquake in the late nineteenth century. They all have walls made from camelid fibre yarns which were wrapped round the crossed sticks and strengthened with bands of twining. Some of them are equipped with suspension handles. They served as work baskets, and were found to contain unspun and/or spun yarn. The one illustrated here (Fig. 149) also contained a stone spindle whorl and an incised bird bone.

That coiled basketry was used not only in funerary contexts in the late prehispanic period, but also in daily life, is graphically demonstrated by the Chuquicamata miner. This unfortu-
142

nate person was trapped by falling rocks while gathering copper ore in coiled baskets, which are illustrated in Mason (1988:plates 245-7).

Most reports suggest that the coiled basketry of the area was executed in non-interlocking stitches, but Isabel Flores Espinoza indicates that the small coiled baskets of the Tacna area of southern Peru in the late pre-Inka period include interlocking and split stitching (Flores Espinoza 1969: plate IVA and D). A basketry tray with split stitches on the interior surface from Quillagua in Chile was presented to the Pitt Rivers Museum by Mrs Jones (Fig. 150). Also illustrated here is a steep-sided bowl of coiled basketry on a ring base, and the stitches are the more normal non-interlocking type (Fig. 151). The base of the bowl and the star motif are executed in light tan stitches, and the background in dark brown stitches. This design motif, which is repeated three and half times, resembles a design which appears on complementary warp woven textiles of the Regional Development period in the Arica cemeteries.

The Inka empire emerged in the Cusco area in the highlands of Peru, from where it rapidly expanded to cover an extensive territory from northern Ecuador to as far south as the central belt of Chile. Distinctively Inka basketry has not yet been recognized at coastal sites, although double sided combs of the type described above do seem to have been used by the Inkas.

However, the principles of coiled basketry appear in typically Inka style hats which have been found in coastal graves. These hats seem to conform to standardized types, although they have been little studied. Standardization in the production of textiles has been demonstrated by J.H. Rowe in the case of Inka tapestry tunics (Rowe 1979). The Pitt Rivers Museum possesses one fez-shaped cap and another incomplete version which shows how the caps were made (Fig. 153). This second item is said to have been found inside the complete hat (Fig. 152), which retains the remains of a chin strap and is lacking only its fine feather crest. As the com-

Fig. 150 **Chile, Río Loa, Quillagua.** Coiled tray, with a bundle foundation sewn with simple non-interlocking stitches which pierce the stitches of the previous row on the inner surface. The rim is missing. H: 33 mm; dia: 266 mm. From a prehispanic grave. Donated by Mrs. Jones, 1933. 1933.24.34

Fig. 151 **Chile,** possibly from **Arica.** Bowl of coiled basketry on a ring base. Coiled rod foundation, sewn with simple non-interlocking stitches. The design motif, in light tan on a dark brown ground, is repeated three and a half times. The design resembles textile motifs of the Regional Development Period in the north of Chile. H: 114 mm; dia: 162 mm. Purchased from J.T. Hooper, 1929. 1929.89.12

Fig. 152 **Chile, Arica.** Inka style (c. 1470-1535) fez-shaped cap. Coiled foundation of thick camelid fibre yarn, sewn with buttonhole stitches. Design in camelid fibre yarns in dark brown, mid brown, yellow and green, in a hook and step motif which conforms to a standard pattern in this type of cap. Flat top in mottled brown. Remains of a chin strap at the base. H: 96 mm; dia: 165 mm (across base). Collected from a grave by Lt. S.C. Holland RN. Transferred from the University Museum, Oxford, 1887. 1887.1.525.1

Fig. 153 **Chile, Arica.** Unfinished Inka style (c. 1470-1535) fez-shaped cap and attached ball of yarn. Coiled foundation of thick camelid fibre yarn, sewn with buttonhole stitches. Hook and step design in camelid fibre yarns in dark green, blue, red, yellow and white. This item is said to have been found inside Fig 153. H: 22 mm; dia: 123 mm. Collected by Lt. S.C. Holland, RN. Transferred from the University Museum, Oxford, 1887. 1887.1.525.2

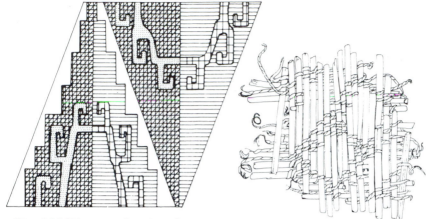

Fig. 154 Diagram showing the repeat motif on Fig. 153.

Fig. 155 **NW Argentina, La Rioja, Sances Village.** Wrapped twined basketry fragment from a prehispanic grave. The two layers of rods were stitched together using vegetal fibre yarn. Worked on the inner face. 68x 66 mm. Collected 1882-1886 by H.D. & C.L. Hoskold. Lent in 1938 by the Cotteswold Naturalists' Field Club. 1947.7.061.6

pleted cap has a basal diameter of of 165 mm, the wearers of this type of hat may have had artificially shaped skulls which required a smaller hat than normally is the case for an adult. The colours have not survived well in this hat, and Fig. 154 shows a reconstruction of the design. Natural brown colours fill the triangles and the inverted ones have a stepped outline executed in white. Both upright and inverted triangles contain a hook motif in dyed green and yellow. Traces of red can be seen at the top of the hat, indicating a missing red border. A similar cap also from Arica with identical colours is illustrated in Santoro and Ulloa (1985:63, figure 79). The incomplete cap shows the thick camelid fibre yarn which was used for coiling and the buttonhole stitches worked in dyed yarns, forming a tightly worked looped structure with two single elements. Because these hats are three dimensional and because the stitches pierce rather than pass round the foundation coil of the previous row as work proceeds, they may be said to be more akin to basketry than cloth, but the distinction is a fine one.

An unusual feature may be observed in the incomplete hat which suggests that it had been unpicked rather than left unfinished. The ball of foundation yarn is pierced by very short lengths of dyed, fine camelid fibre yarn which resem-

bles the yarns of the looped stitching. In its colour combinations, this item is similar to a complete red and blue hat with a feather crest in the Museo San Miguel de Azapa in Arica (Museo Chileno de Arte Precolombino 1985:59). These caps continued to be worn after the Spanish invasion of 1532, for the body of a mature man wearing such a hat was found in a bundle at Caleta Vitor, about thirty kilometres south of Arica. A printed paper was discovered folded against his chest, a Proclamation of Indulgences, signed by the Licentiate Pedro de Valarde and dated 1578. The corpse and its wrappings are now in the American Museum of Natural History and they have been described by Bird (1943:250-251).

Basketry from the highlands is rare, because of the humid conditions. However, a fragmentary small, bowl-shaped basket was found at a pre-Inka burial site called Tinajani, near Ayaviri, Peru. It was constructed of a coiled bundle foundation, stitched with the more typical non-interlocking stitches. The grass used was identified as *Festuca dissitiflora* (Tschopik 1946:48).

Another burial site near Tinajani, the *chullpa* (burial towers) of Arku Punku, contained some pieces of matting. The most complete fragment was made from braided strands of *Festuca dissitiflora*, in a wrapped twined structure

(Tschopik 1946:48, figure 34). However, the diagram published by Marion Tschopik shows every second vertical strand as unsecured to the passive weft. Other variants of wrapped twined weaving do occur, and the Pitt Rivers Museum collections include six fragments from a prehispanic grave found in La Rioja Province, Argentina, in the southern Andes. Two layers of rods, the upper perpendicular to the lower, were stitched together using vegetal fibre yarns, the stitches passing over two or three rods at a time. The work surface was the inner (concave) face. One of these pieces has the stitches arranged in a series of lozenges (Fig. 155). Unfortunately, it is not known to which period these fragments belong.

Stig Rydén suggests that the Arku Punku fragment is perhaps related to a type of basketry which he describes as a variation of coiled basketry and, at the same time, of wrapped twined basketry (Rydén 1955:57). He purchased such a basket from an Aymara person on the island of Taquiri, Lake Titicaca, but the seller said that it had been made in Puno (Rydén 1955:59, figure 1a). In his article, he compares the basket he acquired with baskets from Moho in the Province of Huancané, Peru, and from Chipaya, east of Oruro, Bolivia (Rydén 1955: figures 2a, 4a-c). The Taquiri basket was used for carrying earthenware cooking pots to the fields, but the Chipaya one is said to be used for catching fish when the lakes are flooded, or for holding small items (Rydén 1955:58). This type of basket may be related to the unillustrated coiled baskets "with an armature" of the Archaic period at I.C.c.7 and CH III, and also to the Cabuza helmets of Arica.

In the Andean highlands of today, people tend to use woven sacks and carrying cloths for tasks for which people elsewhere might prefer baskets (gathering harvested potatoes, for example, or for taking produce to market). The beautifully made and decorated coiled baskets belong to the past. However, undecorated stake and strand baskets continue to be used in some areas, and the Titicaca coiled/wrapped twined baskets demonstrate the re-emergence of a type which is known to have occurred intermittently over thousands of years.

Conclusions

Two geographically located cultural areas were considered in this chapter: the central Andes and the south central Andes. In both areas, the making of baskets and of cloth were compared. Because the two crafts may employ common structures, it is sometimes difficult to distinguish basketry from fabric. However, two main patterns were noted in the distribution of the archaeological material. Weft twined fabrics and twined baskets were common in preceramic times in the central Andes. The use of weft twining died out at the end of the Archaic in Peru, to be replaced by a great variety of woven textiles, and plaiting became the dominant technique in twilled basketry.

In contrast, coiled basketry and its analogous fabric structure, simple looping, survived from Archaic times in the south central Andes and continued into later periods, until the arrival of the Spanish. There was a great flowering of coiled basketry in the Middle Period, seen especially in locally made San Pedro de Atacama products and in Tiwanaku baskets.

There are of course exceptions to the backdrop of these main patterns. One of the most intriguing is the occurrence of a loop-and-twist structure in the making of *shicra* baskets in the construction of large buildings on the coast of the central Andes. As the quickly made baskets were fashioned from grasses or rushes, the twisting of the looped structure would have imparted strength to allow for the weight of the stones. If this structure had been used in a fabric, the yarns would have almost certainly been spun and plied in advance.

Nowadays, the most frequently found baskets in this part of the world are of a wicker construction, but a technique which combines coiling and wrapping has been reported from Lake Titicaca and Chipaya. This was seen to have ancient precedents in the south central Andes.

Fig. 156 **Surinam.** Tiriyo man starting to plait a palm leaf burden basket. Photograph by Peter Rivière.

Fig. 157 **Surinam.** Tiriyo women carrying burden baskets. The men carry bows and arrows. Photograph by Peter Rivière.

146

Baskets and Basketmakers of the Amazon

by Peter Rivière

Throughout the Amazon region of Lowland South America, basketwork objects are items of fundamental cultural importance. They are at the same time an essential part of the technology and an artistic form that transcends this world's daily subsistence needs. Unlike elsewhere in the Americas, for many people of Amazonia it is basketry rather than pottery that is the major art form. Often there is a striking contrast between the beautifully woven and decorated baskets and the plain, crudely made pottery. This was not always the case, because numerous pre-Conquest Amazonian groups had well made and decorated pottery and the present dominance of basketry may well be a result, at least partially, of the migrations and decimations that followed on the Conquest. The pre-Conquest pottery belonged to more permanently settled people and baskets are more readily transportable than pots, although few Amerindian groups are so nomadic as to make this an entirely satisfactory explanation. Nor is this to say that basketry was unimportant before the Conquest. It almost certainly has a very long tradition but one which, because of the nature of the materials used, leaves little or no trace in the archaeological record. There are certain technical operations for which there is almost certainly no alternative to a basketwork device, and it is noticeable that whereas pots and other clay objects such as cassava griddles are eagerly replaced by such manufactured items as aluminium pots and cheap bowls, this is rarely the case with basketwork. However this alone can barely account for the continued use of a wide range of basket objects that could be readily replaced, and in many cases are, by a functionally equivalent manufactured object. Basketry, as we will see, is of cultural and aesthetic value that in some cases far outweighs its functional importance.

The native peoples who dwell in the vast lowland region drained by the Amazon and Orinoco Rivers share many cultural features. Their subsistence economies, in varying degrees, all depend on slash-and-burn cultivation, hunting, fishing and collection. Through most of the forested area, the staple crop is cassava, mainly bitter varieties to the east and sweet to the west where an increasing amount of maize is also grown. To the south where the forest gives way to bush, savannah and gallery forest, the Gê peoples have only small cultivated plots and devote more time to other subsistence activities. The division of labour is mainly along sexual lines. There is little formal specialization other than that of the shaman, although as we will see, the roles of certain craftsmen, including that of the basketmaker, attain a status akin to that of the shaman. Men are responsible for the hunting, housebuilding and the early phases of the agricultural cycle. Women look after harvesting the crops, preparing the food and minding the children. Both sexes engage in collecting raw materials from the forest and in the manufacture of articles. The general rule is that it is men who weave the baskets (Fig. 156), and even where both sexes perform this task, it is more likely that men make the higher quality objects. The material culture of all existing groups has been strongly influenced by the introduction of European metal goods, especially cutting tools, firearms and cooking pots. Trade has always played an important part in the Amazonian economy and the relatively easy lines of communication afforded by the main river routes facilitated it. Settlements vary greatly in size and duration, but are virtually everywhere autonomous units within a pattern of shifting alliances with similar neighbouring units. Settlements are formed by one or more communal houses, or a collection of individual family dwellings. Houses are timber framed and thatched with a variety of palm leaves. Despite the degree of contact which most groups have experienced, many of them continue to have an intense ritual life with numerous ceremonies marking both seasonal and life cycles.

II

Baskets and basketwork are used for a very wide range of purposes, but the most important distinguishable group is that concerned with the preparation of food, above all with the staple cassava, the processing of which is particularly elaborate (see Mowat 1989). For example it has been reported that among the Carib-speaking Yekuana of Venezuela ten out of eighteen types of basket identified are wholly or partially devoted to processing cassava (Hames & Hames 1976:4). It is interesting to note that such items are mainly those that have not been replaced by imported manufactured objects. The reason for this is simple. The objects, in particular the cassava squeezer, are highly specialized and there are no manufactured equivalents. Indeed non-Amerindian people who have taken up cassava cultivation often adopted the Amerindian technology that goes with it.

Baskets play an important part in the whole process of cassava production. A woman, when she goes to the field to harvest the crop, takes with her a large, stoutly made carrying basket. These baskets, normally made by men, are used by men and women for carrying heavy loads of all sorts from cassava roots to firewood to game. On journeys household possessions, hammocks, food and other items, are packed in these baskets and usually borne by women leaving the men free to hunt as the opportunity occurs (Figs. 157, 159-160). The basket is normally supported by a tump line round the forehead when loaded, but may be slung across the shoulders when light. As well as these relatively durable carriers, Indians make a whole range of carrying baskets as and when required and of

148

appropriate size. They are made in order to carry fish or game or some other item that has been found in the forest and has to be transported home. One type, plaited from a single leaf, is like a container and is suitable for carrying liquids like honey. All these baskets are made very quickly and like the supermarket plastic bag, are likely to be disposed of as soon as their job is done (Figs. 158, back cover).

When the woman gets back to the village with her heavy load of cassava roots, she grates them and then feeds the resulting wet mush into the cassava squeezer. This is the most complex piece of basketwork made by Amerindians and it is extremely efficient. It is a woven tube with one end open and the other closed and with a loop at both ends. It basically works on the Chinese sleeve principle so that as it is extended so its diameter contracts. The loop at the upper end is hung over a protruding rafter and a lever, secured at one end to a housepost, is passed through the lower loop. The device is operated by an Indian woman sitting on the lever and thus stretching the tube and squeezing the juice from the cassava. This is by far the best known and most effficient form of cassava squeezer and the one best adapted to processing large quantities of cassava flour (Fig. 161). However, other forms of cassava squeezer are also found. For example, the Indians of the Upper Xingu River in Central Brazil use a squeezer made from strips of cane secured together with cotton yarn. The cassava mush is placed on this mat-like device and is squeezed by rolling up the mat with it inside. Another type from Central Brazil is plaited from the inner bark of a tree and the squeezing is achieved by a twisting action. When removed from the cassava squeezer the flour forms hard and compact sausages which are placed on a woven mat awaiting the next stage of preparation (Fig. 162). This is to crumble the flour in the hand and pass it through a basketwork sieve (Fig. 164). Sieves are made with different sized holes and the one used on any occasion will depend

Fig. 158 **Venezuela, Gran Sabana, Eruwaui River area, Taulebang.** Twill plaited basket made from a single palm leaf. H: 210 mm; L: 310 mm. Collected by Audrey Butt Colson, 1957. 1958.3.43

Fig. 159 **Guyana, Rupununi, Macusi.** Burden basket of reed made by four-strand plaiting. Wooden frame, bark forehead band. Small size, probably for a child. L: 340 mm; W: 185 mm. Rev. James Williams collection. 1941.8.241

Fig. 160 **Surinam, Lawa River, Kawemakan Village, Waiyana.** Twill plaited burden basket of reed with wooden frame. Pink trade cotton incorporated in the plaiting. "Tiger", "bat" and "frog" patterns in black. Decorative baskets like this are used for carrying personal possessions rather than garden produce or firewood. L: 700 mm; W: 250 mm. Collected by Audrey Butt Colson, 1963. 1964.2.33

149

Fig. 162 **Surinam.** Tiriyo woman crumbling squeezed cassava and passing it through a basketry sieve into a tray. Photograph by Peter Rivière.

Fig. 161 **Surinam.** Tiriyo woman operating a cassava squeezer. Photograph by Peter Rivière.

Fig. 163 **Surinam.** Tiriyo woman turning a loaf of cassava with the help of a basketry fire fan. Photograph by Peter Rivière.

on the coarseness or fineness of the flour required. The resulting flour may be cooked in a number of ways but commonly it is baked on a large griddle, to produce round, flat loaves (Fig. 163). During the baking the loaf has to be turned like a pancake and to help in this task an all-purpose piece of basketry is used. This is often described as a fan for the fire, and although that tends to be its main use, it has a number of other purposes. For example, it may be used as a plate on which cassava bread is served (Fig. 166). There are also a large number of other round or square flat baskets or baskets with edges. Some of these are quite large and are used for serving food, bread and meat (Fig. 165). Others are used by women on which to keep their cotton and spindles. When these baskets get old and tatty they are often put to use as dustpans. The household waste is swept on to them and carried to the edge of the village to be dumped.

The main basketwork item used by a man in his subsistence activities is the fish trap (Fig. 168) of which a variety of types are found through Amazonia. Another fishing instrument is a plaited scoop, used by women at fish poisonings when large numbers of fish, stunned by the poison, float to the surface and may be easily netted. When hunting with blowguns, men will carry the darts in small quivers. These have a basic basketwork construction but are finished with rubber or other plant resin to seal them. This is important as the darts are tipped with a lethal poison and it is necessary to ensure that there is no accidental extrusion of a point through the wall of the quiver that might cause a wound to the carrier. Along with the quiver is a small woven container that holds cotton or other suitable material that is wound round the end of the dart as wadding, to provide a proper airtight seal in the barrel of the blowgun (Fig. 167). Any additional items that a hunter may wish to have with him are carried in small satchels that are slung over the shoulder.

A whole range of woven boxes or containers of different sorts and sizes are made. A feature of many of these containers is that the lid is of slightly larger dimensions than the base and fits completely over it (Fig. 169). Sometimes a number of containers are made to nest inside one another. Most men and women have one or more containers in which they keep their personal possessions. A man may have a box in which he keeps his cosmetics, a ball of red *urucu* paste wrapped in a palm leaf, a small looking glass, a comb, a pair of scissors and perhaps some tweezers for plucking his facial hair, eyebrows and lashes. In another box there may be more mundane things such as a penknife, a whetstone, a spare bowstring, a pig's jaw used as an adze for shaping bows, some feathers for making arrow flights and any other bits and pieces. In yet another box there may be his ceremonial regalia, mainly consisting of feather ornaments including elaborate headdresses which are dismantled for storage. If the man is a shaman he will have a box which contains his shamanic equipment of which the single most important item is the rattle which contains the material representations of his spirit helpers. The rattles themselves are often decorated with basketry or are of basketwork construction (Plate 3). A woman will also have her own box of personal possessions, but of great importance in her case will be the container holding the balls of cotton yarn, ready to be woven into a hammock. Other baskets, hung from the roof beams, are used for storing a variety of items such as dried peppers.

Items of basketry also enter into ceremonial life. For example, the feathers of headdresses are mounted on basketwork crowns (Figs. 172, 174). Also of a ritual nature are ant or bee frames, usually made in the form of a jaguar and decorated with feathers and other objects. During initiation rites among the Waiyana of Surinam and French Guiana, a frame is filled with stinging ants or bees. This is done by squeezing the creatures into the interstices in the weave so that they are trapped with their

151

Fig. 164 **Brazil, Amazonas State, Satare-Maue.** Twill plaited rectangular cassava sieve of reed with pattern in black. Cane supports. For sieving cassava flour after squeezing and before baking. L: 385 mm; W: 365 mm. Collected by Zeina El-Khouri Klink, 1990. 1990.47.1

Fig. 165 **Guyana, Upper Mazaruni district, Akawaio.** Round twill plaited cassava tray of reed with "pineapple" pattern in black. For holding cassava bread at meals. Dia: 340 mm. Collected by Audrey Butt Colson, 1951-52. 1954.2.12

Fig. 166 **Brazil, Para State, Apalai.** Rectangular fire fan twill plaited of reed with pattern of two caterpillars in black. Cane grip. L: 450 mm; W: 260 mm. Collected by Zeina El-Khouri Klink, 1990. 1990.47.6

152

Fig. 167 **Guyana, Upper Mazaruni district, ?Yekuana.** Wicker quiver of reed with gourd base and rubber lid. The basketry is completely covered with tree resin and the centre is bound with cord to which a plaited carrying strap is attached. Contains poisonous blowpipe darts. The small wicker basket is for silk cotton or ordinary cotton which is wound around the end of each dart before use. Although this was obtained from the Akawaio, they no longer made these quivers at the date of collection. It was probably made by the Yekuana or another group in Venezuela. L: 380 mm. Collected by Audrey Butt Colson, 1951-52. 1954.2.49

Fig. 168 **Guyana, Kamarang River area, Akawaio.** Fish trap of liana made by wrapped twining. Used in conjunction with a fishing dam of saplings and leaves. When the river rises in the wet season, fish swim up small creeks to feed. The Akawaio make dams across the creeks with gaps through which the fish pass. When the river begins to drop and the fish return to the main stream, these traps are thrust through the bottoms of the newly repaired dams, their openings pointing upstream. In their attempt to get through the dams the fish swim into the traps and cannot escape. The end of the trap is unlaced to remove the catch. L: 970 mm; dia: 255 mm. Made by Danny. Collected by Audrey Butt Colson, 1957. 1958.3.35

Fig. 169 **Guyana, Upper Mazaruni district, Akawaio.** Rectangular twill plaited basket of reed with "monkey" pattern on sides of lid. For holding personal belongings. H: 180 mm; L: 280 mm; W: 185 mm. Collected by Audrey Butt Colson, 1951-52. 1954.2.16

Fig. 170 **Southern Venezuela, Yekuana.** Twined burden basket made by women from *heteropsis* vine with reinforcing coils of another vine, *Hubebuia pentaphylla*, lashed to the inside. "Frog" and "toad" designs in black. Used by women for carrying garden produce, firewood, fish, game and household items. H: 210 mm; dia: 250 mm. Collected by Marcus Colchester, 1979-80. 1981.33.12

Fig. 171 **Guyana, Rupununi, Macusi.** Twill plaited basket of reed with pattern in black. Cotton string for suspension. For holding personal belongings. H: 210 mm; W: 150 mm; D: 120 mm. Rev. James Williams collection. 1941.3.75

stings all pointing in the same direction. This is then pressed against the chest of the initiate who may have to undergo this a number of times in a series of rituals. It is not unknown for the initiate to pass out, either from the pain or from the toxic substances injected into him. In simple terms the aim is to strengthen the individual and further evidence of this derives from the fact that without much ritual formality people suffering from various ailments, including the inability to hunt successfully, are treated in a similar manner. The ant frame in Fig. 173 is of this kind and is much smaller and less elaborate than the frames used in ceremonies.

Basketwork may also be used as decoration. Its use in this way on rattles has been mentioned and one finds a similar usage on the handles of clubs. Small pieces of basketwork are also worn, as part of ceremonial dress, hanging down the back. In sum, baskets and basketry are an important part of all aspects of the Amazonian Indian's life.

III

As has been mentioned, the manufacture of basketwork, and especially the more elaborate and better constructed items, is usually in the hands of men, although it might be noted that it is women who are the main users of the objects. An exception to this is the Yekuana, a group famed for the quality of its basketwork, among whom women make their own carrying baskets (Fig. 170), elaborate items which require much time to weave. The Hames reckoned that among the Yekuana "men and women devote more time to basket manufacture than to all other handicraft activities combined' (1976:25). Men may be found engaged in basketmaking at any time of the day, but a favoured hour is around dawn when the material left out overnight is pliant as a result of the night's dampness and thus easier to handle. A number of different techniques are used throughout the area and detailed descriptions of these are available (see, for example, Roth 1924; Guss 1989). A wide range of materials, mainly from varieties of palms and reeds, is used in weaving, although almost everywhere the most favoured are reeds of the *Ischnosiphon* species (*itiriti*). The raw material is cut in the forest as and when needed and brought back to the village. At this stage the outer surface of the reeds is either dyed (red or black) or left in its natural colour. Once the reed has thoroughly dried, the outer covering or bark which is the material used is taken off in long thin strips and then thinned again, as required, in order to achieve the desired thickness.

The motifs on the baskets are many and varied and have even been described as "almost unlimited" (Yde 1965:260). Most obvious are the representational forms that draw their inspiration from the animal world: jaguars, frogs and monkeys being amongst the most common although scorpion and insect patterns are not unknown. There are also vegetable motifs such as the pineapple or seed pattern. Many designs appear to be purely geometrical figures. These designs, as with the representational motifs, are picked out in a different colour, usually black but occasionally red. The referents for these designs are often the markings of animals, but attention has also been drawn to the similarity between these patterns and those used in body painting. This similarity may receive mythic support and the Tiriyo, a Carib group of the Brazil-Surinam border, say that a culture hero created men by weaving and placing a soul inside the finished product, which is the reason why the designs on baskets and body decorations are similar. All baskets carry designs, but many are the result of the weaving technique and are thus part of the construction of the basket. For example, many baskets are covered with little crosses of "eyes", some in the natural colour and some in black. These are an essential part of the construction of the basket and are made more obvious by the use of two colours (Fig. 171). Such designs may or may not be named by the makers and even with representational and geometric designs care has to be taken with the identification. In the case of the Akawaio box Fig. 169 there is likely to be general agreement that the figures are monkeys not only among the Akawaio but more widely through Amazonia. However, this may not be generally true. For example, Reichel-Dolmatoff (1985:39, Fig. 22) reports a great discrepancy between the Desana and Vanano of the Northwest Amazon concerning the interpretation of the same figure: the former claiming that it represents a frog, the latter a tapir. Indeed for many figures there is no clear agreement about what designs represent. This is not merely so from one people to the next but within the same group. Even the same informant may not be consistent from one occasion to another. Henley and Mattéi-Müller, writing about the basketry of the Panare of Venezuela, have stressed this problem of the interpretation of motifs.

Most Panare regard the insistence that the motifs should have meanings as at best amusing and at worst tiresome. Consequently, even at the best of times their interpretations are only half serious. When not in the mood for humouring the authors, the Panare would claim that they didn't know what the motifs meant or would say whatever came into their heads. (1978:95)

These same authors have claimed that the inconsistency of interpretations result from *ad hoc* rationalizations, for the design is there as a requirement of the basket's construction. Furthermore technique and functional necessity severely limit what can be portrayed. Because baskets are functional as well as aesthetic objects and have to have sufficient strength to fulfil their purpose, the freedom of the maker to portray what design he wishes is curtailed by a medium that imposes angular and linear graphic forms. As evidence of this Henley and Mattéi-Müller point to what has happened to the Panare baskets which are made solely as souvenirs for sale to Venezuelans. In order to achieve a much wider repertoire of motifs,

including such things as jeeps and trucks, the strength of the weave is weakened to the point that the basket is no longer functional.

However, Henley and Mattéi-Müller have been reproached by Guss for their claim that by transcending technical limitations the Panare have freed themselves from an art previously confined by functional requiements. Guss, who worked with the Yekuana, who are celebrating for their basketmaking, suggests that the Panare's action would never be contemplated by the Yekuana.

To the Yekuana ... the success of a work of art is in the integration of every aspect, wherein no part dominates and none is wasted. This perfect balance between content and form, technique and image, function and material, is what defines a Yekuana basket ... To disturb these relationships would be to undermine the overall meaning of the work, to create a mutant form halfway between a basket and something else (1989:89-90).

Guss is also far more confident about the identification of designs on Yekuana baskets, although this may be because the basket is such an important item in Yekuana culture. He claims that it was only through his apprenticeship as a weaver that he came to be incorporated in Yekuana society and to appreciate the significance of basketry to them.

IV

Although basketry is an essential component of Amazonian technology and is at the same time an aesthetic object, the act of its creation also has social and cosmological significance. The ability to weave is regarded throughout the area as a competence that signifies a proper man. For the Tiriyo, one of the criteria employed in judging a man's worth is whether he is up well before dawn to weave. Among the Yekuana, an individual's skill as a basketmaker is used as a general indicator of his competence and maturity (Guss 1989:79-80). Among the

156

Fig. 172 **Guyana, Upper Mazaruni district, Akawaio.** Man's ceremonial hat made from a framework of twill plaited reed surrounded with macaw feathers, black powis feathers and a thick band of cotton yarn. Two long protruding macaw feathers are decorated with duck down and worn at the back of the head. Formerly worn for war or celebrations; more recently for the symbolic dance of cassava growing. H: 600 mm. Collected by Audrey Butt Colson, 1951-52. 1954.2.105

Fig. 173 **French Guiana, Litany River, Yakatowgu Village, Waiyana.** Ant frame: a strip of chequer plaited palm leaf. A few ants or bees are placed in the interstices in the plaiting and the strip is applied to the forehead for a headache, or to any other part of the body which is hurting. This is an everyday medicine charm: elaborate feather-decorated frames are used for ceremonial purposes. L: 300 mm; W: 30 mm. Collected by Audrey Butt Colson, 1963. 1964.2.84

Barasana of the Northwest Amazon, an important feature of the male initiation ceremony is that the elders systematically teach the initiates how to make all the different kinds of baskets. These baskets are then given away to the women responsible for feeding the initiates during the ceremony, to those women who paint them and to the presiding shamans; in each case creating a special relationship (Hugh-Jones 1979:85-6, 96-7). The manufacture of basketwork items is frequently mentioned as a typical duty that a young man owes to his parents-in-law in the early days of marriage when his suitability as a son-in-law is still being assessed. The ability to make basketwork objects is widely regarded as a skill that all adult men should have mastered to some degree and in some groups the skill might be said to take on a moral quality. Thus among the Carib-speaking Yupa of northwest Venezuela the quality of an individual's basketry is the test of whether, on death, he will arrive in the Land of the Dead or be devoured by wild beasts (Wilbert 1974:23-5).

Among some peoples, even in this life the truly skilled basketmaker may be regarded as transcending the purely technical ability to make baskets. Thus, among the Warao of the Orinoco Delta, the master craftsman becomes possessed by the Itiriti Spirit and obtains shamanic powers on a par with those of an ordinary shaman (Wilbert 1975). The Yekuana see weaving as a creative act of cosmic significance and equivalent to singing as a means of ordering and maintaining the universe. The basket is a metaphorical representation of the world so that the act of weaving involves a cosmic reproduction. The old man who achieves total mastery of the art of basketmaking is thought to be endowed with qualities that transcend those of simply technical competence. He becomes "the one who knows" and is assumed to have other ritual and practical skills. This idea that basketmaking is more than just the manufacture of baskets is widely found. There are two Tiriyo myths in which the extra-natural powers of weavers are apparent. In one a small child shows himself to be a better weaver than his father and produces a basket with a jaguar design of such excellence that it turns into a jaguar. The myth reveals that this child is a spirit. In the other myth twins who are very skillful weavers make themselves jaguar clothes (i.e., basketwork with a jaguar design) which they put on when they go hunting (Koelewijn 1987:107-9, 118-20).

Thus the basketry of Lowland South America is not just utilitarian, although at the same time it is difficult to identify items that lack a practical purpose and are purely aesthetic. Most basketwork objects are essential tools in everyday activities, but at the same time they carry an important symbolic load. Reichel-Dolmatoff, writing of the Desana of the Northwest Amazon, comments:

"In fact, a simple carrying basket, a fish creel, or a woven mat may contain a body of condensed information that transforms these simple objects into icons recognised by all as embodying ideas that express organizational principles and guidelines to proper individual and collective behaviour (1985:1).

In varying degrees the manufacture of basketwork, its construction, its design and its use are an integral part both of the Amazonian Indians' technology and economy and of their ideas about the world in which they live and which they strive to maintain and recreate.

PRÉPARATIFS DE LA DANSE DU MARAKÉ

Fig. 174 "Preparatifs de la danse du Maraké" from *Voyages dans l'Amerique du sud* by J. Creveaux (1883). Copyright Bodleian Library, Oxford, UK.

The Art of Basketry:
Aesthetics in a Cross-Cultural Perspective
by Howard Morphy

Writing in 1904, Otis T. Mason begins his compendious work on American Indian Basketry with a reflection (or perhaps more truly a lack of reflection!) on the newly awakened interest of that ubiquitous follower of ethnographic fashion, the private collector.

In the past few years a sympathetic spirit has been awakened in the United States to keep alive this charming aboriginal art and to preserve its precious relics. In every State in the Union will be found rich collections, both in public and private museums. People vie with one another in owning them. It is almost a disease, which might be called "canastromania". They resemble the "merchantman seeking goodly pearls, who, when he had found one pearl of great price, went and sold all he had and bought it." The genuine enthusiasm kindled in the search, the pride of success in acquisition, the care bestowed on them, witness that the basket is a worthy object of study. The story is told of a distinguished collector who walked many a weary mile to the shelter of a celebrated old weaver. He spent the day admiring her work, but still asking for something better. He knew she had made finer pieces. At last flattery and gold won. She tore out the back of her hut and there, hid from mortal eyes, was the basket that was to be burned at her death. Nothing could be more beautiful and it will be her monument (Mason 1904: viii-ix).

The paragraph represents an excellent text for a critical sermon on ethnographic museums, the presuppositions of the early twentieth-century collectors of ethnography and primitive art, the post-colonial context of production, the inequalities in the relationship between Native Americans and the colonial admirers of their artefacts, and any number of other themes. The text is so redolent with the assumptions of the time that it

is hard to resist littering the quotation with [sic]s, (!!) and underlinings. One cannot help hoping that as soon as the collector left, the basket maker replaced the missing basket with the next one in line for burning. However, as with any text that presents so clearly the presuppositions of its times, it is too easy to treat it unfairly and ahistorically as if it was written today. The themes that I want to take up in this chapter are as controversial today as they were at the time that Mason was writing. They are: the presentation of objects of other cultures as aesthetic forms or as art, and the extent to which this involves a distortion or appropriation of their value. Underlying these themes is the question of the relationship between the aesthetics of an object as viewed by its Western audience and the aesthetics as viewed by the producer, which in turn has embedded within it the general issue of the usefulness and even the validity of the notion of aesthetics for cross-cultural analysis.

James Clifford (1991:241) has written that "one of the best ways to give cross cultural value (moral commercial) to a cultural production is to treat it as art." Mason's writing is clearly a part of this process and illustrates particularly well the linkage between what Clifford refers to as the moral and commercial dimension of value. The value (as "a worthy object of study") is proved by the interest of the collector who is prepared to risk all in the pursuit of beauty. The basket on the pedestal in the museum becomes the ultimate monument to its creator. On the other hand Russell Handsman (1987:147) notes in his radically titled "Toward an anti-catalogue of woodsplint basketry": "When seen as art artifacts [are] separated from their human, historical and political relations." As they stand the two statements are quite compatible since it could be argued, as Handsman does, that the cross-cultural value created by art is an imposition of a nineteenth-century Western European concept, and that its application incorporates the objects of other cultures within the framework of Western European values and blocks the understanding of their indigenous meaning and cultural context. Moreover the concept masks the process by which the object was acquired: "basket diverted by flattery and gold from funeral pyre" is unlikely to be part of the label. There are certainly these dangers in the aestheticization of the works of other cultures. However I argue that the fault lies not just in the overall context exhibitions in art galleries, but also in the concept of aesthetics employed.

The incorporation of things within a unitary category of "art objects", which are to be viewed together as an exclusive set specifically for their aesthetic effect, is what appropriates their cultural value and history and subordinates them to Western values. If, rather than seeing aesthetics as referring to this unitary category of objects, we see it as a dimension that any object can potentially possess, then the danger of imposing one set of values over others can be avoided. Instead we may be able to enter into a cross-cultural discourse over the aesthetic potential of objects. Russell Handsman is certainly right to say that such a discourse requires more than the display of objects on a pedestal in a particular light, and indeed more than the simple presentation of the objects. Such an impoverished and narrow conception of the way in which the aesthetic dimension of an object can be appreciated is indeed an imposition of taste that narrows rather than opens up the possibilities of cross-cultural appreciation. Handsman and MacMullen (1989:34) go so far as to suggest that "when presented and interpreted as art, splint baskets were not and cannot be, 'read' as artefacts of specific societies." However, they may be falling into a trap in identifying aesthetics and art with nineteenth-century values: by defining art and aesthetics ethnocentrically they deny the possibility of their existence in other

cultures. By creating the category "art" in relation to a particular kind of non-functional aesthetic display valuable, our predecessors appropriated not simply the objects that were put into that category but also the concept of art itself. "Art" became limited for a while to a certain category of objects. This definition is not only subject to an anthropological criticism, but was also subject to critique from Western "art" producers.

Art across cultures

The word "art" defies simple definition; it can be treated as a number of different words whose meaning varies depending on who is using it and when. But it is possible to suggest some core components which seem to be common to most of its usages. The defining characteristics of art objects or the artistic dimension of objects tend to include references to their aesthetic properties, to their effect on the senses, and to their expression of meaning and value. While not all objects labelled as art share every one of these characteristics they tend to form part of a polythetic set with overlapping attributes. The narrow Western definition of art, with its category of "set aside" objects, is misleading because it has appropriated many of the more general ideas that lie behind the concept and because it has added so many irrelevant exclusion clauses. Art objects become objects that have no other function, or are the product of individual creativity, or are defined according to innumerable other criteria that were signs of the myths of a particular period of history and a particular ideology.

Guss (1989) addresses this issue in his rich analysis of the basketry of the Yekuana, a people of the Upper Orinoco River in Venezuela. He argues that while the Yekuana do not have a word for art they do distinguish between works that are manufactured under the guidelines of traditional design (tidi'uma), and the mass of goods that they acquire through trade (mesoma): "Mesoma remains a synonym for

161

any insipid alien object" (p.69). He argues that *tidi'uma*, on the other hand, combine, in their manufacture, raw materials and use, a fusion of symbolic elements and functional values: in making and using them individuals continually recreate the cultural values and physical and metaphysical processes of which they are a part.

To become a Yekuana is not only to develop the physical skills demanded of one's gender, but also to develop the spiritual awareness that the preparation of these goods imparts. In a society that has no special category for a work of 'art', there can be no object that is not one. Or to put it another way, to become a true Yekuana is to become an artist (ibid: 70).

Guss's analysis at first sight seems to contain a paradox: he begins by stating that the Yekuana have no word for art and yet ends up by stating that to become a true Yekuana is to become an artist. Is there simply a lexical gap in Yekuana that is filled by the English term, is Guss writing rhetorically, or is this simply a case of muddled thinking? The answer is most likely none of these. It lies in the problem of the concept of cultural relativism and the limitations of ordinary language, though rhetoric may play a part. From a cultural relativist perspective concepts are defined according to the particular context in which they occur; it is not anticipated that the concept of "art" will be any different from concepts such as "marriage", or a "relative", or "conception" in that they all vary cross-culturally. Yet the very fact that we are applying the terms and seeking the equivalent concepts across cultures implies that we have a more general concept that transcends the particular case and is part of the anthropologist's metalanguage. What Guss is saying then, is that what he understands by or defines as the concept of art is found in something of the activities of every Yekuana. By definition that concept could or should not be identical to the concept of art as used in Western European culture, since that concept in turn will be relative to its cultural context and hence be culture-bound.

162

The metaconcept is related to the Western concept since the anthropologist begins his or her comparative enterprise from his or her own culture, and in its recent origins anthropology is a Western science. The concept should be defined independently but necessarily with reference to the ordinary-language usage of the word "art".

The situation is even more complex than this. The Western concept of art is itself a many-headed monster and people are continually struggling to try and change its definition. Indeed, the "arts" of non-Western peoples, folk art, and Oriental art, have been used by artists as part of their intra-cultural dialogue to inspire Western practice and change Western concepts. Thus the analyses that anthropologists or art historians make of the arts of other cultures can in turn have a consequence for Western art: unlike the Yekuana, Western artists are attuned to seeing the aesthetic value in other peoples' cultural products. The presentation of Yekuana basketry as "art", the assertion that it has an aesthetic dimension, that it is a sculptural form, is both a challenge to the Western category of art and at the same time, if it is successful, something that results in a broadening of the category. The Western category of art, Anaconda-like, responds to criticism by swallowing it whole. The Western category of art is broad in ways that the Yekuana category is narrow. The Yekuana do not recognise any cultural value in objects introduced from outside for functional purposes. Western cultures, on the other hand, consume through aesthetics the objects of other cultures and discard their functions. The basket becomes a "sculptural form", no longer a container for grain or a plate for cassava. This paradox has something to do with economic processes and the articulation of modes of production, but also has much to do with cultural differences. Whatever the cause, one of the consequences has been that while people of the Fourth World stop producing baskets and replace them with plastic containers and recycled products from the industrialized world, the industrialized world will simultaneously be exhibiting Fourth World products as works of art and increasing their "value".

Exhibiting art

When trying to persuade a Western audience of the aesthetic dimension of other peoples' material culture, anthropologists present their arguments not only through their writings but also by organizing exhibitions of other peoples' work as art. And as we have seen, it is in the context of the art gallery that the Western definition of art and the anthropological metaconcept of art have the opportunity to get almost inextricably muddled.

There are two reasons why exhibition as art became an almost inevitable part of the anthropologists' presentation of their case. First, part of the metadefinition of art involves aesthetics, and one of the Western ways of communicating the aesthetic properties of an object is through exhibition. Secondly, part of the cultural relativist agenda is to signify the essential equivalence of world cultures by a metaphysical criterion of equal cultural value. The agenda grew out of opposition to nineteenth-century evolutionary schema which created out of the worlds' cultures a graded series in which those at the top had art, science, and civilization and those at the bottom did not. This imposition of a particularly culture-bound definition of art in association with a colonialist ideology denied art to many cultures and, since art was one of the signs of civilization, devalued the things they produced. George Kubler (1991:84) writes about

the distaste for America in European thought and literature. The distaste was and remains a negative aesthetic expression about America and Americans during the Enlightenment, and it survives in Europe and elsewhere to this day ... the dominant belief in enlightened Europe, from 1750 to 1900, was that America was inferior as to its natural and racial endowment. Buffon as a naturalist in 1759 deprecated the

animal species as inferior and the humans in ancient America as "impotent and savage". Kant's verdict as a philosopher in 1778 - that Amerindians were 'incapable of any culture, still far behind the negroes' - was followed by Hegel's immature and impotent continent..

It is against this background that we should see the work of early museum ethnographers such as Mason and W. H. Holmes and the even more fundamental contribution of Franz Boas. They were concerned to communicate the aesthetic features of Native American material culture through the development of collections and the organization of exhibitions as well as through their writings. In doing so they were involved in a process of asserting the value of Native American culture and way of life, making Native Americans visible again as people and showing them in a positive light.

The initial division between ethnographic museums where Native American arts were shown, and art galleries where art in the European tradition was exhibited, was of course in itself a continuing imposition of the Western concept of art. In one sense, the failure to divide the products of Native American cultures into art and non-art, would have accorded with Yekuana classifications, but in another sense it represented the continued subordination of Native American artefacts to the evolutionary schema. This contradiction cannot easily be resolved, for if only certain works are selected for inclusion within the art gallery, being chosen either on arbitrary aesthetic grounds or by analogy with Western categories of art objects - for example objects with painted designs - then that continues the process of appropriation; the objects are being reclassified without reference to indigenous values. It is here that exhibiting ethnography as art becomes part of a radical critique of art galleries: it provides a challenge to narrowly constructed definitions of art and to the separation of art from artefact that was the product of a particular period of European history. And though it can be argued that this strat-

163

egy also incorporates artefacts within global processes that are essentially part of a Western agenda, it has the advantage of doing so by making people reflect on other peoples' categories and other constructions of the world.

Other peoples' aesthetics

In discussing the exhibition of products of the Fourth World (see Graburn 1976), of "other cultures", as aesthetic objects, it is helpful to make the initial distinction between the aesthetics of the producing culture and the aesthetics of the exhibiting culture (though we will see that the distinction is not an easy one to maintain). To begin with we will assume that the distinction is a strong one and we will accept the cultural relativist position that different cultures have different and relatively autonomous aesthetic traditions. What is beautiful to members of one culture may not be to members of another, or, to phrase it more generally, the aesthetic sensibilities of one culture may differ radically from those of another. The same object may be seen, felt, or appreciated in different ways and on the basis of different attributes, to the extent that it may, arguably, become a different object. To take an apparently extreme and hypothetical example, aesthetics might include how the object smelt in one case and might focus on attributes of shape in the other. If an object from the former culture were exhibited on the basis of its shape and surface form, then it would be treated in terms of the aesthetics of the exhibitor rather than the producer. In the case of basketry it is quite conceivable that matters such as the smell or the feel of the basket as well as its appearance should be part of its aesthetics to the producer. It is worth quoting at length a passage by Trudie Lamb Richmond, a Native American, writing about Schaghticoke basketry:

To understand and appreciate Native American basket-making fully, one must make the transition in thinking from materialism to spiritualism ... I spoke to a Mohawk basket-maker

164

not long ago and asked her how she felt about weaving sweet grass into her baskets. Sweet grass is used by her people in their ceremonies and like tobacco is believed to have great power ... She told me she had thought about this meaning and that was why she always talked to the sweet grass and to her baskets as she made them. She said that she asked forgiveness for having to sell the baskets, but that she needed the money to survive. Using the sweet grass would keep the baskets strong and alive, and she hoped that people who bought them would appreciate their significance. The basket weaver explained that she never picked the grass without making a tobacco offering (1989:127-8).

The particular raw material used will have an impact on the visible form of the object, but this is not necessarily the only impact. Moreover the aesthetic appreciation of that visible form may be enhanced by knowledge of the properties of the raw materials used and their cultural significance. It is sometimes difficult and sometimes even impossible for museums to allow their audience access to the full aesthetic potential of an object, since touching the object may transgress the requirements of conservation and smells, like colour, fade with time. However it should always be possible to draw the audience's attention to the existence of such properties.

Aesthetic relativism thus applies in the case of the non-visible properties of objects and to the intersection of form and cultural meaning. But it also applies in the case of observable form. When considering shape alone there is no reason to suppose that the attributes of observable form that were appreciated by the maker and are part of the object's intended form are going to be the ones seized on by the consuming or exhibiting culture. Mason sets out what he considers to be the basis of the aesthetics of Native American basketry:

Unity in variety, the underlying principle in all aesthetic composition, finds its first step illustrated in the making up of a basket ... The unity is of a very high order for in many exam-

ples, coupled with a monotony of elements absolutely under the control of the artist, there is at the same time a charming variation of width and length in harmony with, and made necessary by, the widening and narrowing of the basket ... Usually the perfection of stitch is the aim of the worker (1904:142).

In the next paragraph he provides a lyrical description of a Washoe basket that efficiently summarizes a whole range of attributes that go into the Western appreciation of a basketry form.

A rare coiled basket made by a Washoe woman named Datsolalee. It is in the collection of A. Cohn, Carson City Nevada. The piece measures 8 1/2 inches high, is 12 inches wide, and 6 inches wide at the opening. The stitches number more than fifty thousand, being thirty to the inch. The body colour is a rich light gold, and the figures are in red and black. It weighs 16 ounces and is valued at many hundreds of dollars. The figures on the basket represent birds migrating or flying away, the motto being, "When the birds leave their nests and fly away we shall move". The shape of the piece and the quality of sentiments in the markings are excelled only by the inimitable quality of the work on the surface. It is difficult to conceive a more perfectly uniform piece of handiwork than this..

It is easy to see how this description comes out of his theoretical framework, with its emphasis on technique and form. The weights and measures, the meticulous countings of stitches and the stress on uniformity, gain meaning through the idea that perfection arises out of the application of technique to functional form. There is nothing wrong with such a perspective and it is one that has in Mason's case resulted in a magnificent examination of the relationship between technique and form that can constitute the basis of much further research. However the description tells us little about the aesthetics of Washoe baskets from the perspective of the Washoe producer. For example although it hints that there may be a dimension of content that articulates with technique and form it leaves

that unexplored. While Washoe aesthetic processes and concepts may share much in common with Mason's interpretations of the aesthetics of their baskets we are not presented with any evidence that this is the case.

A cross-cultural definition of aesthetics

Although it may be perfectly legitimate to see other peoples' works through the eyes of one's own culture, the anthropologist's job is to reconnect aesthetics with the culture that produced the object. I have discussed the issue of cross-cultural aesthetics in detail elsewhere (Morphy 1989). Here I would simply state that if one can teach people to interpret and value the properties of the objects of another culture according to the aesthetics of that culture, then one may provide a powerful insight into that world, and into what it feels to be a member of it.

Guss's (1989) analysis of the cultural context of Yekuana basketry, to which I have referred earlier, provides an excellent basis for the understanding of Yekuana aesthetics. The Yekuana employ a technique that is widespread throughout much of the Amazonian region and many of the designs that are found on their basketry occur throughout the region. Employing a perspective from Western aesthetics, for example that used by Mason, would make it difficult to differentiate between the particular cases. Yet, despite the existence of common cultural themes that cross-cut the region, we know that the meaning of the particular elements and the context of their occurrence and use varies from place to place. Guss's particular focus is on the *waja*, the circular serving trays that are used for the staple food cassava. It is impossible to summarize the full complexity of his analysis, and I will concentrate only on a few aspects of it. In a revealing section he shows how baskets mark stages in the first year of a marriage. A man is expected to make nearly the full complement of baskets that his household requires. The first basket that he weaves for his wife is a version of a plain basket called a *waja tingkuihato*. It is a finely woven basket made from cane. Although woven in a single colour, the mosaic of the weave produces a pattern of radiating lines referred to as *kutto shidiyu* (or "Frog's bottom"). It is from this basket that the couple eat during the first year of their marriage. At the end of the year the husband weaves a *waja tometo* ("painted" basket), whose pattern is marked out by the use of alternating black and white plaits. By changing the sequences of plaiting the technique can be used to produce an almost infinite variety of different designs. The particular design selected is chosen after consultation with his father, and may well be one that was used by his father or grandfather for one of their wives. The use of the painted *waja* is a sign that their marriage is established, "the special images woven into this 'painted' waja will be a clear statement of the strength and uniqueness of their bond" (1989: 83).

In order to explain the opposition between the Frog's bottom baskets and the painted baskets, and the different contexts of their use we must consider both the significance of the materials of which they are made and the significance of the designs themselves. The plain basket is made from *Kana,* a sacred cane that had its origins in "heaven" and was one of the original materials brought down to earth (ibid:141). It is considered both a pure and a safe substance; it is also in some sense considered to be pre-cultural. Plain baskets similar to the "Frog's bottom", but less finely made, are used in the context of fasts and in other situations where people are particularly concerned with purity. The painted *wajas* are made from two varieties of cane that are associated with powerful and dangerous spirit familiars that can be life threatening unless treated with care (ibid:127). People who are in a weak or spiritually dangerous condition or who are responsible for someone in such a condition (for example, the father of a new baby), must avoid contact with the cane and eat from a plain basket. The designs themselves reflect this ambivalent status, since they represent subjects that are both potentially dangerous and of cultural value, for example sources of poisons, and animals such as the jaguar. For people who are in a spiritually strong condition the painted baskets can be a positive force, purifying food by symbolically removing poisonous substances, marking the identity of the person and enabling the maker to reflect on myth and cultural process. The use of the plain basket during the early part of a marriage can thus be seen as precautionary, while a potentially dangerous relationship is being established in which childbirth and anger are never far away. It also serves as a sign of the newness of the relationship and its potential (ibid: 81). The painted basket, on the other hand, is a sign of the strength of a relationship that is well established and marks it with a particular identity. It links the marriage with the history of a family and of a culture.

Thus to the Yekuana the aesthetics of their basketry involves its integration within a cultural context in which the form of a basket and the contexts of its use together provide the framework of the Yekuana world. The value of the plain basket exists in relation to the value of the painted baskets, and a Yekuana appreciation of its form will involve the understanding of its significance as an object of purity, a connotation that can be equally conveyed by its "material technique design and function - coordinated to communicate the same message" (ibid: 146).

Conclusion:
Basketry, aesthetics and colonialism

Even with the information we now have, we do not know how the Yekuana "see" their basketry, how they divide it up into components, how baskets fit in with their world of perception. As Forge (1970: 286) wrote "it is impossible to see through the eyes of another man, let alone perceive with his brain. Yet if we are to consider the place of art in any society ... we

166

must beware of assuming that they see what we see and vice versa." An anthropology of perception, if such existed, might enable us to get closer, but to see as the Yekuana do would require that we were socialized into their world, and that we were used to the light and shade, and the sounds and smells of the rainforest. But the ethnography does give us a greater understanding of what the baskets mean to the Yekuana and provides a perspective on how to view them and how to value them. With this information we certainly do not see the baskets as we saw them before and we may have shifted a little closer to the Yekuana view. We appreciate the baskets on the basis of their form, texture, colour, and even smell just as the Yekuana do; and knowledge of the way these are culturally valued brings us closer to the Yekuana aesthetic system and enables us to reflect on whether the form, texture, colour and smell is the same for them as it is for us.

We have learnt that it is possible to gain insights into other peoples' aesthetic traditions. Using a variety of different sources of information - the objects themselves, written texts and labels, film, photography, dioramas - it would be possible to create a museum exhibition that was specifically designed to evoke and inform about the aesthetics of another culture. Indeed it might be argued that in designing ethnographic exhibitions, anthropologists should be able to help people see the objects in that light, and should always be aware of the dangers inherent in subordination to an alien aesthetic tradition. Once people are attuned to the idea that other aesthetics exist - that there are ways of understanding a set of objects which are separate from the cannons of our own taste and outside the historical tradition of our own art - then it is a lesson that can be applied even in cases where the viewer is ignorant or where information is lacking. The aesthetic contemplation of the objects of other cultures in the light of knowledge of cultural difference encourages people to reflect on the meanings that may be

there and on their cultural value and hopefully will encourage them to look beyond surface form. The aesthetic dimension could provide a source of information about other cultures just as much as any so-called objective abstraction from the object, such as its function, can.

Such is the complex nature of human cultures that any way of exhibiting objects involves selection and simplification. Seeing objects as functional types, or regional types, or frozen in some pastiche of their cultural context in the form of a diorama, can be as misleading as displaying them on pedestals as "art", and is just as likely to confirm cultural stereotypes. Exhibiting as "art" does have benefits. If the historical context is right then the assertion of the value of the objects as art can play a part in the process which results in the acknowledgement of the equal humanity and cultural achievement of the producers, and can have consequences on the recognition of their rights. It can even have economic consequences: products that are no longer used to store grain can be produced for sale to the market, resulting in a form of economic integration that, paradoxically, can help to maintain and perpetuate cultural differences through a process of cultural transformation.

The manufacture of objects for sale inevitably results in an interchange of value and in the migration of aesthetic concepts. However this neither lessens the authenticity of the objects nor makes them into alien products, but merely adds another screen through which to view the complex emergent image of cross-cultural aesthetics. Aesthetic systems have never been neatly packaged into discrete boxes labelled with individual cultures. Although, as a symbolic system, Yekuana baskets seem to fit together in a neat package, they were always being traded with neighbouring groups who shared many of the same designs and symbolic themes and defined themselves in relation to those themes. Coherence is created through the flux. Native American basketry exists as part of a regional network of trade and exchange in which styles change over time and in which aesthetic appreciation of neighbouring styles must always have been a factor. Trade with Europeans added another dimension to basketmaking, albeit one that for most of its duration has been indissolubly linked with colonial process and has had the strands of domination, expropriation, and exploitation woven into its being. But together with these are other strands of more positive origin, consisting of the aspiration of the weaver, the struggle to survive, to engage the other and to define the self. The overall mosaic, as Handsman suggests, was a fusion of colonial process and indigenous struggle. The baskets woven and traded became instruments of survival which in more positive times could become objects of reflection and a basis for the continued assertion of cultural identity. Reflecting on the aesthetics of Native American basketry means reflecting on the aesthetics of particular cultures, on the interchange of aesthetics and values between Native Americans and Europeans. But it also means reflecting on the fear, hostility, appropriation, dispossession and alienation that lies in between.

Fig. 175 **Brazil, Roraima State, Yekuana.** Twill plaited tray of reed with design of two capuchin monkeys in black (*jenipapo* dye). For holding cassava bread at meals. Dia: 323 mm. Collected by Zeina El-Khouri Klink, 1990.

Basketmakers Today and Tomorrow

by Linda Mowat

As the foregoing essays demonstrate, the fortunes of basketry have not followed the same course all over the Americas. In some areas where baskets were once produced they are made no longer. In other places they are still made but have changed their form and meaning to accommodate new demands and pressures placed upon the lives of their makers. Occasionally we still find baskets fulfilling the same role they have held for centuries (Cardale Schrimpff and Rivière, this volume).

What has led to this diversity in the development of baskets? What prospects does the future hold for Native basketmakers in the Americas? How much of the story is told by the baskets in the display cases of our museums? It is worth examining some of the factors that have led to the current basketmaking scene.

The advent of the white man's goods - metal pots and pans, crockery, plastic bowls and buckets - has certainly had its effect on basketry production. These items, cheaply available and costing no time or effort to make, began to replace baskets long ago in many Native American homes. Why not, when a day's wage labour could buy more containers than months of basketmaking might produce? Where baskets were retained for limited use only, it sometimes became preferable to trade them from another group. Among the Navajo, who stopped using baskets except for weddings and curing ceremonies, the complex taboos surrounding basketmaking may have contributed to its demise (Tschopik 1938:259). People of the Rio Grande Pueblos obtained most of their baskets from the Jicarilla Apaches after about 1880 (Ellis & Walpole 1959:197).

The economics of basketmaking have been a powerful factor in its decline in many areas (McMullen, this volume). While the sale of baskets to Europeans has undoubtedly made a significant contribution to the income of many Native American people over the years, it is debatable whether the going rate for the job has ever been fair. Making a fine basket requires time, skill, hard work and physical energy, which is seldom adequately accounted for in the market price of the item. The hidden costs of collecting and preparing materials are not apparent to the buyer. The middleman - trader, gallery or shop - acting between the basketmaker and the buyer will also appropriate a significant proportion of the price of every basket. Abenaki basketmakers from Odenak, Quebec made a far better living before the 1920s, selling direct to white tourists, than they did once dealers began to control the business (Pelletier 1982:5-8).

Many young Native Americans today have no interest in learning the craft skills of their ancestors. While some might enjoy the creative work of actually constructing a basket, they begrudge the time and effort necessary to gather and prepare the materials in order to begin. Basketry splints are hard on hands unaccustomed to manipulating them, and this is an additional deterrent. The prospect of meagre financial reward after so much painstaking work is usually enough to turn a young person's energies in a different direction, usually towards the wider job opportunities offered by the white man's America. Experienced basketmakers agree that young people will only learn to make baskets if they want to.

Another problem faced by many basketmakers today is competition from products made in other parts of the world. Baskets from China, the Philippines and southern Africa are marketed in the United States for a fraction of the price of Native American baskets. We are all accustomed to seeing such anonymous imported baskets sold for pennies in our high street gift shops: what hope is there for a realistically-priced Native American basket placed side by side on the shelf with one of these items? To

169

take but one example, a willow basket made at San Juan Pueblo sells for $50 in the Pueblo's craft centre; in a supermarket a virtually identical basket from the Philippines is available for less than $2. While this raises all kinds of questions regarding the life and rights of the Filipino basketmaker, our concern here is for the Native American, faced on the one hand with the expenses of life in the United States and on the other with the consumer's assumption that baskets are worthless because they can be imported for next to nothing. Until people understand the amount of work that goes into a basket and measure this against their own society's cost of living, this problem will continue.

Traditionally, baskets were made from locally available natural resources. These resources were renewable and basketmaking did not place any great strain upon them. Nevertheless, Native people have always treated the plants they use with care and respect, taking no more material than is needed for the work in hand (Lamb Richmond 1987:127-129).

Since the white man first crossed the Atlantic all natural resources have been threatened due to over-exploitation. The situation is worsening daily and the "Green Revolution" may not be in time to halt the destruction that has taken place, not only in the much-publicized Amazon rainforest but all over the Americas. Basketmakers, in their small way, are gravely affected by these changes.

Many plant resources have been physically removed by the appropriation of land for agriculture, pasture, dams, National Parks or urban development. Basketmakers need to travel further from their homes to find their materials: the Tohono O'Odham may drive 100 miles to collect the yucca and beargrass needed for their baskets (De Wald 1979:31). Some plants, such as the rivercane used by Southeastern basketmakers, are damaged by carbon monoxide emissions from relentlessly increasing numbers of vehicles (Green, this volume). Ash has become more difficult for Northeastern basketmakers to find as landowners tighten up on the

170

fencing and posting of their woodlands.

The destruction of the Amazon rainforest by cattle-ranching, logging, gold prospecting and road construction is removing more than the trees and other plants of the forest: it is depriving indigenous people of their livelihood, infecting them with diseases they cannot resist and effectively destroying them. Some of the most traditional basketmakers in the Americas, the fortunate ones who survived the depradations of the *conquistadores* and the rubber barons, are struggling against tremendous odds to maintain their traditional lifestyle. Others have already disappeared. The Indians of Tierra del Fuego, makers of beautiful and unusual baskets, did not survive their contact with Europeans (Dransart, this volume). Many of the tribes of North America have vanished for ever, leaving only their names as marks on the landscape.

Tourism, although it has often acted as a stimulus for the production of baskets, can by its capricious nature also be responsible for their decline. The Waunana Indians of Colombia, whose fine coiled baskets (Plate 9) had begun to contribute significantly to their income, face the disappearance of this trade as tourists, alarmed by political unrest, delete the country from their itineraries. Tourism can also become a form of enslavement. In 1991 Antonio Cahuachi, a Yagua Indian from the Peruvian Amazon, observed (1991:9):

We have seen how our crafts are exploited to such an extent that in many of our communities our brothers have to spend their whole time on this activity, causing them to abandon the cultivation of land and thus the production of food

Fortunately this situation is not universal among Native Americans. In Hopi society, for example, quantities of baskets still need to be made every time there is a wedding, as repayment by the bride's family for the wedding robes provided by the family of the groom. New baskets are also used in the O'waqölt and Lalkont basket dances performed by the women's societies, as well as other ceremonies (Breunig 1982:9). These regular needs keep the art alive, and many young as well as older Hopi women know how to make baskets. Those not needed for gifts are sold to museums, collectors and tourists, the high prices dictated by the long hours of work that go into them as well as by the vicissitudes of the Southwestern art market. The Hopi Craft Co-op on Second Mesa markets the baskets and ensures fair prices to their makers. Some individual basketmakers have achieved such a reputation that they are able to work to commission most of the time.

Particularly in North America basketry has been actively encouraged in this century, not only by tourists who may be less than discerning but by collectors, specialist dealers and museum curators with an interest in preserving excellence. Many museums have shops which act as outlets for Native American crafts of all kinds. Basketmakers demonstrate their art at exhibitions and fairs, along with potters, weavers and metalsmiths. Prizes are offered for the finest products, increasing their value. Basketry has been taught in schools, and classes for adults are also arranged. On the Jicarilla Apache reservation at Dulce, New Mexico, women learn from an experienced basketmaker and are paid by the hour for the work they produce.

At Cherokee, North Carolina, Qualla Arts and Crafts is a co-operative encouraging and marketing the work of its members, many of whom are basketmakers (Blankenship 1987:viii). High standards of craftsmanship are demanded, fair prices are paid and profits shared. While the more recalcitrant materials, rivercane and white oak, are still worked mainly by older members, younger people have become involved in weaving baskets and mats of honeysuckle vines. Qualla's large retail store and gallery are a popular attraction for the thousands of tourists who flock to the Great Smoky Mountain National Park every summer.

Certain groups have adapted positively to today's problems of scarce materials by selecting alternatives. When the onset of tourism created a higher demand for their baskets, the Tohono O'Odham abandoned their customary willow and martynia in favour of yucca leaves and bear grass (Whiteford 1988:136). These materials, more readily available and easily worked than the traditional plants, resulted in a completely new style of production. The Tohono O'Odham now market their baskets more widely than any other North American tribe.

Tourist items have been introduced into the repertoire of many basketmakers: waste-paper baskets, laundry baskets, fishing creels, wall pockets, sewing baskets, thimble holders, teapots, animals and delicate miniatures. Although not traditional, these are still Native American baskets, finely made to supply an active demand. Experimentation has resulted in the vivid fruit forms made by Passamaquoddy basketmaker Clara Keezer (Plate 2) and the subtle natural dyes reintroduced to Jicarilla Apache baskets by Lydia Pesata (Fig. 87 and Herold 1984:53). Young people are beginning to develop an interest in craft as a means of expressing their ethnic identity and personal creativity. The Navajo, who bought their baskets from neighbouring groups for many years, have since the 1960s been experiencing a basketry revival, producing not only the traditional "Navajo wedding basket", but also innovative and experimental designs (Mauldin 1984:35-36).

In some Native American homes, baskets still fulfil the function they always did. In the Amazon, when people are able to live in peace, dozens of different baskets are in everyday use, many so efficient that nothing the white man has produced can supersede them (Rivière this volume). Elsewhere, baskets may be seen as we have come to see them: primarily as objects of beauty rather than use.

Baskets in museums attract the visitor by their beauty first of all. But once you have been drawn into the complexity of their structure, entwined in their natural elements, wrapped in their coils - then is the time to step back and marvel at the minds that designed them, the hands that fashioned them, their special importance in the lives of their makers. When meaning and form are brought together, Native American baskets come into their own.

A Guide to Plant Materials used in Native American Basketry

This table, while not fully comprehensive, is intended as a guide to materials mentioned in the text.

Abbreviations:

Cfo	Coil foundation	Twp	Twining warp material
Csew	Coil sewing material	Twft	Twining weft material
Ci	Imbrication on coiled baskets	To	Overlay on twined baskets
Wwp	Wicker warp material	Tfe	False embroidery
Wwft	Wicker weft material	P	Plaiting elements

NAME	AREA	PURPOSE	NOTES
Agave	N, M, S America	cordage	
Agave americana			American aloe (maguey)
Agave sisalana			Gives sisal hemp (henequen)
Agave fourcroydes Lem.			Fourcroya
Alder (white)	California	dye	Orange-brown from bark.
Alnus rhombifolia			
Alder (red)	NWC	dye	Infused with water or chewed.
Alnus oregana	California		
Ash	NE	Wwp Wwft P	Splints used.
Fraxinus nigra			
Bear grass (squaw grass)	NWC	Tfe	
Xerophyllum tenax	California	To	
Bear grass	SW, M America	Cfo P	
Nolina microcarpa			
Bihao	Colombia	P	
Helicania biahi L.			
Bitter Cherry	NWC	Ci	Natural red-brown or dyed
Prunus emarginata (Villosa)			black with mud or iron-water.
Bloodroot (puccoon)	SE	dye	Red.
Sanguinaria canadensis			
Bracken fern	California	Csew Twft	Root used for black designs.
Pteridium aquilinum			
Buckbrush	SE	Wwp Wwft	
Symphoricarpos sp.			
Bulrush	California	Csew	Root used for black designs.
Scirpus maritimus			
Bunch grass (saw grass)	California	Cfo	
Muhlenbergia rigens			
Butternut	SE	dye	Black from bark and root.
Juglans cinerea			
Cane	Amazon	P	Yekuana twill baskets.
Guadua latifolia			
Carayuru	Amazon	dye	Red.
Bignonia chica			

NAME	AREA	PURPOSE	NOTES
Carrizo reed *Arundo donax*	M America	Wwp Wwft	
Cattail *Typha angustifolia*	SW	Cfo	
Cedar (Western Red) *Thuja plicata*	NWC	P Cfo Csew Twp Twft	Root, bark and twigs used.
Chin (*Cañabrava de Castilla*) *Arundo donax* L.	Colombia	Wwp Wwft	
Cottonwood *Populus fremontii*	SW	Cfo Csew	
Creeper *Souroubea sp.*	Colombia	P	
Devil's claw *see* Martynia			
Digger Pine *Pinus sabiniana*	California	Twft	
Espuro grass *Sporobolus rigens*	Andes	Cfo Csew	Found in warm valleys on eastern flanks of the Andes.
Fescue grass *Festuca dissitiflora*	Andes	Cfo Csew	Found in Titicaca basin.
Fir (Douglas) *Pseudotsuga*	California	Twft	
Galetta grass *Hilaria jamesii*	SW	Cfo	
Giant Chain Fern *Woodwardia spinulosa*	California	To	Dyed brown with chewed alder bark on Hupa baskets.
Hazel *Corylus cornuta*	California	Twp	
Henequen *Agave sisalana*	N, M, S America	cordage	Sisal hemp.
Hickory *Carya sp.*	SE	P Wwp Wwft	
Honeysuckle *Lonicera sp.*	SE	Wwp Wwft	Japanese honeysuckle introduced in 18th century.
Iraca *Carludovica palmata* Ruiz & Pav.	Colombia	P	
Iris *Iris sp.*	California	Twft	Stem and leaf used.
Itiriti reed *Ischnosiphon sp.*	Amazon	P	
Jenipa *Genipa americana*	Amazon	dye	Black.
Jipi *Carludovica palmata* Ruiz & Pav.	M America	P (hats)	
Liana (bush rope) *Heteropsis jenmani*	Amazon	Twp Twft	
Maguey *Agave americana*	M America S America	cordage	

NAME	AREA	PURPOSE	NOTES
Maple	NWC	P Twp Twft	Bark used.
Acer sp.	SE	Wwp Wwft P	Splints used.
Maidenhair fern	California, NWC	To Twft	Black.
Adiantum pedatum			
Manna grass	NWC	Tfe	
Parricularia nervata			
Martynia (devil's claw)	SW	Csew	
Proboscidea sp.			
Mountain mahogany	SW	dye	Red from root.
Cercocarpus betulifolius			
Naba palm	Colombia/Panama	P	
Astrocaryum Standleyanum L.B. Bailey			
Naiwal	Colombia/Panama	P	
Carludovica palmata Ruiz & Pav.			
Oak (white)	SE	Wwft Wwp P	
Quercus alba			
Palm	Amazon	P	
Mauritia flexuosa	S America		
Astrocaryum sp.			
Pine	California	Twp Twft Csew	Root used.
Pinus sp.	SE, NWC	Cfo	Needles used.
Piñon	SW	pitch for	
Pinus edulis		water jars	
Pook cane	Colombia	P	
Stromanthea lutea			
Rabbit brush	SW	Wwft	
Chrysothamnus sp.			
Raffia	NWC	Twft	Imported. Used on Nuu-Chah-Nulth fancy baskets.
Raphia ruffia or			
R. taedigera			
Redbud	California	Twft Csew	
Cercis occidentalis			
Reed	Colombia	Twp Twft P	
Spartina patens			
River cane	SW	P	Formerly used by Pima.
Phragmites communis			
Rivercane	SE	P Wwp Wft	
Arundinaria sp.			
Rush	Tierra del Fuego	Cfo Csew	
Juncus magellanicus			
Sedge (sough grass)	California	Csew	
Carex sp.			
Sharuma	Colombia	Mats	
Eleocharis geniculata			
Silel	Colombia/Panama	P	
?*Oenocarpus panamenus* Bailey			

NAME	AREA	PURPOSE	NOTES
Sharuma *Eleocharis geniculata*	Colombia	Mats	
Sotol *Dasylirion wheeleri*	SW, M America	P	
Spruce *Picea sitchensis*	NWC, California	Twp Twft	Root used.
Squaw grass *see* Bear grass			
Sumac *Rhus trilobata*	SW	Cfo Csew Wwp	
Sunflower *Helianthus petiolaris*	SW	dye	Black from seeds.
Sweetgrass *Hierochloë odorata*	NE	Wwft rims, handles	Often braided. Fragrant.
Tule reed *Cyperaceae sp.*	M America	P	
Urucu *Bixa orellana*	Amazon	dye	Red.
Vine *Anthurium flexuosum* *Hubebuia pentaphylla*	Amazon	Wwp Wwft Twft	
Walnut *Juglans nigra*	SE	dye	Brown.
Wheat *Triticum vulgare*	M America	P Twp	Straw used.
Willow *Salix sp.*	M America California, SW	Wwp Wwft Twp Twft Cfo Csew	
Wolf moss *Evernia vulpina*	California	dye	Yellow.
Yucca *Yucca sp.*	SW	Csew P	

This table was compiled with reference to Willis, J.C. 1973. *A Dictionary of Flowering Plants and Ferns.* Cambridge: University Press.

Bibliography

Adams, M., with K. Cook and T. Lauzon. 1990. 'Weaving a Life: An Interview with Mohawk Basketmaker Mary Adams'. In Dixon, S.R. (Ed.)'Unbroken Circles: Traditional Arts of Contemporary Woodland Peoples' *Northeast Indian Quarterly* 7(4):47-53.

Adovasio, J.M. 1977. *Basketry Technology* . Chicago: Aldine.

Adovasio, J.M., and R.F. Maslowski. 1980. 'Cordage, Basketry and Textiles'. In Lynch, T.F. (Ed.), *Guitarrero Cave*, 253-290. New York: Academic Press.

Allen, E. 1972. *Pomo Basketry: A Supreme Art for the Weaver.* (Ed. Brown, V.) Happy Camp, CO: Naturegraph.

Aschero, C.A. 1984. 'El sitio ICC-4: un asentamiento precerámico en la Quebrada de Inca Cueva (Provincia de Jujuy)', *Estudios Atacameños* 7, 62-72.

Bardwell, K. 1986. 'The Case for an Aboriginal Origin of Northeast Indian Woodsplint Basketry.' *Man in the Northeast* 31:49-67.

Barrrett, S.A. 1908. *Pomo Indian Basketry.* Berkeley: Univ. of Calif. Pub. in Amer. Arch. and Ethno. 7(3):134-308. repr. 1978 Washington: Mac Rae Pub.

Bedford, J. 1985. 'The June Bedford Collection'. In Bear, G. (Ed.) *Mohawk, Micmac, Maliseet and Other Indian Souvenir Art from Victorian Canada,* 5-10. London: Canada House

Beechey, S.A. 1831. *Narrative of a voyage to the Pacific and Beering's Strait...* 2 vols. London: H. Colborn and R. Bentley

Benavente Aninat, M.A. 1982. 'Chiu Chiu 200. Una Comunidad Pastora Temprana en la Provincia del Loa (II Región)', *Actas del IX Congreso Nacional de Arqueología,* 75-94. La Serena, Chile.

Benedict, S. & J. Lauersons. 1983. *Teionkwahontasen: Basketmakers of Akwesasne.* Hogansburg NY: The Akwasasne Mus.

Bird, J.B. 1943. 'Excavations in Northern Chile', *Anth. Papers of the Amer. Mus. of Natural History* 38, 179-316.

Bird, J.B., J. Hyslop and M. D. Skinner. 1985. 'The Preceramic Excavations at the Huaca Prieta, Chicama Valley, Peru', *Anth. Papers of the Amer. Mus. of Natural History* 62(1).

Blankenship, M. 1987. 'History of Qualla Arts & Crafts Mutual, Inc.' in Qualla Arts & Crafts Mutual, Inc. *Contemporary Artists and Craftsmen of the Eastern Band of the Cherokee Indians.* Cherokee, North Carolina: Qualla Arts & Crafts Mutual, Inc.

Boas, F. (Ed), H.K. Haeberlin, J. Teit & H. Roberts. 1928. 'Coiled Basketry in British Columbia and Surrounding Regions.' *Bureau of Amer. Ethno. 41st Annual Report, 1919-24,* Washington, DC: Smithsonian Inst.

Bockoff, E. 1977. 'Cherokee Basketmakers, the Old Tradition'. *The Explorer* 19 (4): 10-15.

Bolinder, G. 1925. *Die Indianer der Tropischer Schneegebirge.* Stuttgart.

Bolinder, G. 1926. *Snofjallets Indianer.* Stockholm.

Brandford, J. S. 1984. *From the tree where the bark grows ..North Amer. Treasures from the Peabody Mus., Harvard Univ.* Cambridge, MA.: New England Foundation for the Arts.

Brasser, T. J. 1971. 'The Coastal Algonkians: People of the First Frontiers' in E. Leacock & N.O. Lurie (Eds) *North American Indians in Historical Perspective*, 64-91. New York: Random House.

Brasser, T. J. 1975. 'A Basketful of Indian Culture Change'. *Nat. Mus. of Man, Mercury Series, Canadian Ethno.*

Service 22. Ottawa: National Museums of Canada.

Brawer, C. C. (Ed.) 1983. *Many Trails: Indians of the Lower Hudson Valley.* Katonah NY: The Katonah Gallery.

Brettes, J. de. 1898. 'Chez les Indiens du Nord de la Colombie'. *Tour de Monde*, n.s. IV, 61-96, 433-80. Paris.

Breunig, R. 1982. 'Cultural Fiber: Function and Symbolism in Hopi Basketry'. *Plateau* 53.4.

Bridges, E.L. 1948. *Uttermost Part of the Earth.* London: Hodder and Stoughton.

Butler, E. L. 1947. 'Some Early Indian Basker Makers of Southern New England'. In Speck, F. G. *Eastern Algonkian Block-Stamp Decoration...* 35-54. Research Series No. 1. Trenton: The Arch. Soc. of New Jersey.

Cahuachi, A. 1991. 'From bullets to tourists'. *Survival* 28.

Canadian Museum of Civilization. n.d. *Barbeau collection notes.* Quebec: Canadian Ethno. Service.

Cardale Schrimpff, M. 1979. 'Textiles arqueológicas de Nariño'. *Revista Colombiana de Antropología* XXI, 245-287.

Cardale Schrimpff, M. 1985. *Techniques of Hand-weaving and Allied Arts in Colombia* (2 vols). Michigan and London: Univ. Microfilms International.

Carrión Cachot, R. 1949. *Paracas Cultural Elements.* Lima: Corporación Nacional de Turismo.

Carse, M. R. 1949. 'The Mohawk Iroquois'. *Bull. of the Arch. Soc. of Connecticut* 23:3-53.

Carvajal, M. 1945 'Recuerdos arqueológicas de Santander'. *Estudio*, organo del Centro de Historia de Santander, año IX, nos. 105-107, diciembre, 303-334.

Chatwin, B. 1979. *In Patagonia.* London: Picador.

Coe, R. T. 1986. *Lost and Found Traditions: Native American Art 1965-85.* Seattle: Univ. of Washington Press and Amer. Fed. of Arts.

Cortés Moreno, E. 1989. *Así eramos. Así somos. Textiles y tintes de Nariño.* Pasto: Museo de Oro, Banco de la República.

Darwin, C. 1845. *Journal of Researches into the Natural History and Geology of the Countries Visited During the Voyage of H.M.S. Beagle Round the World...* London: John Murray, Second Edition.

Dauelsberg H. P. 1974. 'Excavaciones Arqueológicas en Quiani', *Chungará* 4, 7-38.

De Wald, T. 1979. *The Papago Indians and their Basketry.* Tucson: Terry De Wald.

Dixon, S. R. 1990. 'The Essential Spirit'. In Dixon, S. R. (Ed.) 'Unbroken Circles: Trad. Arts of Contemporary Woodland Peoples'. *Northeast Indian Quarterly* 7(4):2-12.

Donnan, C.B. 1964. 'An early house from Chilca, Peru', *Amer. Antiquity* 30(1), 137-144.

Douglas, F. H. 1939. *Indian Basketry East of the Rockies.* Denver: Denver Art Museum Leaflet 87.

Dransart, P. 1991. 'Llamas, herders and the exploitation of raw materials in the Atacama Desert', *World Arch.* 22(3), 304-319.

Duncan, P.B. 1836. *A Catalogue of the Ashmolean Mus. ..* Oxford: S. Collingwood

Eckstorm, F. H. 1932. *The Handicrafts of the Modern Indians of Maine.* Bull. 3 Bar Harbor, ME: Robert Abbe Museum.

Eisenhart, L.L. 1990. 'Hupa, Karok and Yurok Basketry.' In Porter, F.W.III. *The Art of Native Amer. Basketry: A Living Legacy.* Westport, CT: Greenwood Press Inc.

Ellis, F. H. & M. Walpole. 1959. 'Possible Pueblo, Navajo, and Jicarilla Basketry Relationships'. *El Palacio* 66 (6).

Emery, I. 1966. *The Primary Structure of Fabrics.* Washington D.C.: The Textile Mus.

Emmons, G.T. 1903. 'The Basketry of the Tlingit.' *Amer. Mus. of Natural History Memoirs* Vol. III: 229-277.

Elsasser, A.B. 1978. 'Basketry' in Sturtevant, W.C. (Ed.) *Handbook of North Amer. Indians*, Vol. 8, *Calif.* Washington: Smithsonian Institution.

Engel, F. 1966. 'Le complexe précéramique d'El Paraíso (Pérou), *Journal de la Société des Américanistes* 55, 43-69.

Farrer, C. 1991. *Life's Living Circle: Mescalero Apache Cosmovision.* Univ. of New Mexico Press.

Feder, N. 1933. 'Indian Basketry Varieties and Distribution'. Leaflet 58. *Dept. of Indian Art Leaflets.* Denver: Denver Art Museum.

Feest, C. F. 1980. *Native Arts of North America.* New York: Oxford Univ. Press.

Fields, V.M. 1985. *The Hover Collection of Karuk Baskets.* Eureka, CO: Clarke Memorial Mus.

Feldman, R.A. 1983. 'From maritime chiefdom to agricultural state in Formative coastal Peru'. R.M. Leventhal and A.L. Kolata (Eds), *Civilization in the Ancient Americas. Essays in Honor of Gordon R. Willey,* 289-310. Cambridge, MA: Univ. of New Mexico Press and Peabody Mus., Harvard Univ.

Fernández Distel, A.A. 1974. 'Excavaciones arqueológicas en las cuevas de Huachichocana, Dep. de Tumbaya, Prov. de Jujuy, Argentina', *Relaciones* 8 (N.S.), 101-126.

Fernández Distel, A.A. 1978. 'Elementos indicadores de pautas de vida migratoria en etnías del borde de la puna jujeña (Argentina)'. *Actas del V Congreso Nacional de Antropología Argentina* Vol. I, 99-101. San Juan.

Field Museum of Natural History. n.d. *Accession Records.* Chicago: Field Mus.

Field Museum of Natural History. n.d. *C.F. Newcombe collection notes.* Chicago: Field Mus.

Flores Espinoza de Lumbreras, I. 1969. 'Informe preliminar sobre las investigaciones arqueológicas de Tacna'. *Mesa Redonda de Ciencias Prehistóricas y Antropológicas* Vol 2, 295-302. Lima: Pontificia Universidad Católica del Perú.

Foreman, C. T.. 1948. *Cherokee Weaving and Basketry.* Muskogee, Okla.: The Star Printery.

Foster, G. M. 1967. 'Contemporary Pottery & Basketry' in Wauchope, R. and M. Nash (Eds.) *Handbook of Middle Amer. Indians,* Vol. 6. Austin: Univ. of Texas Press.

Freeman-Witthoft, B. 1977. Cherokee Indian Craftswomen and the Economy of Basketry', *Expedition* 19: 17-27.

Gettys, M. (Ed.) 1984. *Basketry of the Southeastern United States.* Idabel, Okla.: Mus. of the Red River.

Goddard, P.E. 1903-1904. *Life and Culture of the Hupa.* Berkeley: Univ. of Calif. Pub. in Amer. Arch. and Ethno. 1(1):1-88

Gold, T.S. 1903. 'Fostering the Habit of Industry'. *Connecticut Magazine* 8(3):452:54.

Gordon, J. 1990. 'Micmac Indian Basketry'. In Porter, F.W. III (Ed.), *The Art of Native American Basketry: A Living Legacy,* 17-44. Westport CT: Greenwood Press.

Gough, B.M. (Ed.) 1973. *To the Pacific and Artic with Beechey... 1825-1828.* Hakluyt Soc., Second series vol. 143. Cambridge: Cambridge Univ. Press

Grieder, T., A. Bueno Mendoza, C.E. Smith Jr and R.M. Malina. 1988. *La Galgada, Peru: a Preceramic Culture in Transition.* Austin: Univ. of Texas Press.

González, A.R. 1977. *Arte Precolombino de la Argentina. Introducción a su historia cultural.* Buenos Aires: Filmediciones Valero.

Guss, D. M. 1989. *To Weave and Sing: Art, Symbol and Narrative in the South American Rain Forest.* Berkeley, CO: Univ. of Calif. Press.

Hames, R. B. and I. L. Hames. 1976. 'Ye'kwana Basketry: its Cultural Context', *Antropológica* 44: 3-58.

Handsman, R. G. 1987. 'Stop Making Sense: Toward an Anti-Catalogue of Woodsplint Basketry'. In McMullen, A. & R. G. Handsman (Eds.),144-67.

Handsman, R. G. & A. McMullen. 1987. 'An Introduction to Woodsplint Basketry and its Interpretation'. In McMullen, A. & R. G. Handsman (Eds.),17-35.

Harrington, M. R. 1908. 'Vestiges of Material Culture Among the Canadian Delawares'. *Amer. Anth* 10:408-18.

Harrington, M. R. n.d. Field collection notes. New York: Mus. of the Amer. Indian, Heye Foundation.

Hauptman, L. M. 1979. 'The Iroquois School of Art: Arthur C. Parker and the Seneca Arts Project, 1935-1941'. *New York History* 60(3):282-312.

Henley, P. and M.-C. Mattéi-Müller. 1978. 'Panaré Basketry: Means of Commercial Exchange and Artistic Expression', *Antropológica* 49: 29-130.

Herold, J. 1984. 'Basket Weaver Individualists in the Southwest Today'. *Amer. Indian Art* 9.2

Hicks, G. L. 1977. 'Introduction: Problems in the Study of Ethnicity'. In Hicks, G. L. & P. E. Leis (Eds.), *Ethnic Encounters: Identities and Contexts,* 1-20. North Scituate, MA: Duxbury Press.

Hidalgo L., J., Schiappacasse, V., Niemeyer, H., Aldunate, C., and Solimano, I. (Eds.) 1989. *Culturas de Chile. Prehistoria desde sus Orígenes hasta los Albores de la Conquista.* Santiago: Editorial Andrés Bello.

Hill, R. & F. G. Semmens. 1980. *Mohawk Basket Making at Akwesasne.*

Hobsbawm, E. & T. Ranger. 1983. *The Invention of Tradition.* Cambridge: Univ. Press.

Hoffman, W. J. 1970 [1892-3]. *The Menomini.* New York: Johnson Reprints.

Holland, N. 1983. *Baskets of Akwesasne.* Lake Placid NY: Fine Arts Gallery, Centre for Music, Drama and Art.

Holmer, N.M. 1952. 'Ethno Linguistic Cuna Dictionary'. *Etnologisker Studier* XIX, Goteborg.

Hoskold, H.D. 1894-1895. 'Catalogue of a Collection of South American Indian Objects made in the Argentine Republic from 1882 to 1886..', *Proceedings of the Cotteswold Naturalists' Field Club* XI(3), 309-324.

Hudson, J.W. 1893. 'Pomo Indian Basket Makers' *The Overland Monthly* 2nd series, 21:561-578

Hudson, J.W. 1899 undated letter to Otis T. Mason. MS in Nat. Anth. Archives, Smithsonian Institute.

Hugh-Jones, S. 1979. *The Palm and the Pleiades. Initiation and Cosmology in Northwest Amazonia.* Cambridge: Cambridge Univ. Press.

Jahn, A. 1927. *Los aborigines del Occidente de Venezuela.* Caracas.

James, G. W. 1972 [1909]. *Indian Basketry.* New York: Dover

Johannsen, C. B. 1984. 'Efflorescence and Identity in Iroquois Arts'. Unpub. Ph.D. diss., Dept. of Anth., Brown Univ..

Johannsen, C. B. & J. P. Ferguson (Eds.) 1983. *Iroquois Arts: A Directory of a People and Their Work.* Warnerville NY: Assoc. for the Advancement of Native N. Amer. Arts and Crafts.

Jones, V. H. 1934. 'A Chippewa Method of Manufacturing Wooden Brooms'. *Papers of the Michigan Academy of Science, Arts and Letters* 20:23-30.

Kelemen, P. 1943. *Medieval American Art*. New York: The Macmillan Co.

Kelsey, V. & L. de J. Osborne. 1961. *Four Keys to Guatemala*. New York: Funk & Wagnalls Co.

King, J.C.H. 1982. *Thunderbird and Lightning: Indian Life in NE North America 1600-1900*. London: British Mus.

King, M.E. 1931. 'The Prehistoric Textile Industry of Meso-america' . In La Farge, O. & D. Byers. *The Year Bearer's People*. New Orleans: Tulane Univ. Middle Amer. Research Inst. Series No. 3.

King, M.E. 1965. *Textiles and Basketry of the Paracas Period, Ica Valley, Peru*. Ann Arbor: Univ. Microfilms Int..

Koelewijn, C. (with P. Rivière). 1987. *Oral Literature of the Trio Indians of Surinam*. Dordrecht and Providence: Foris.

Konrad, L.-A., with C. Nicholas. 1987. *Artists of the Dawn: Christine Nicholas and Senabeh*. Orono ME: Northeast Folklore Society.

Krieger, H.W. 1926. 'Material Culture of the People of Southeastern Panama based on specimens in the U.S. Nat. Mus. *Bull. U.S. Nat. Mus.* 134, Washington.

Kroeber, A.L. 1905. *Basket Designs of the Indians of NW Calif.*, Univ. of Calif. Pub. in Amer. Arch. and Ethno.,vol. 2(4):105-164

Kroeber, A.L. 1925. *Handbook of the Indians of California*. Bureau of Amer. Ethno., Bull. 78. Washington: Smithsonian Inst.

Kroeber, A.L. 1944. 'Peruvian Archaeology in 1942', *Viking Fund Publications in Anth.* 4

Kroeber, T., A.B. Elsasser and R.F. Heizer. 1977. *Drawn from Life: Calif. Indians in Pen and Brush*. Socorro, NM: Ballena Press.

Laforet, A. 1990. 'Regional and Personal Style in NW Coast Basketry.' In F.W. Porter III (Ed) 'The Art of Native Amer. Basketry. A Living Legacy.' *Contribs to the Study of Anth.* 5. New York: Greenwood Press.

Laforet, A. n.d. *Hats of the Central Coast*. Paper presented to the Native Art Studies Assoc. Annual Conf., Victoria, 1986.

Lamb Richmond, T. 1987. 'Spirituality & Survival in Schaghticoke Basket-Making' in McMullen, A. & R.G. Handsman (Eds.) 126-143

Lane Fox, A. 1874. *On the Principles of Classification adopted in the Arrangement of his Anth. Collection*. London: Anth. Inst.

Larsen, J. L. 1979. *Interlacing - the Elemental Fabric*. Tokyo, New York & San Francisco: Kodansha International.

Leftwich, R. 1970. *Arts and Crafts of the Cherokee*. Cherokee, NC: Cherokee Publications.

Lester, J. A. 1987a. *We're Still Here: Art of Indian New England*. Boston: The Children's Mus.

Lester, J. A. 1987b. '"We Didn't Make Fancy Baskets Until We Were Discovered": Fancy-Basket Making in Maine'. In McMullen, A. & R. G. Handsman (Eds.) 38-59.

Lismer, M. 1982 [1941]. *Seneca Splint Basketry*. Ohsweken ON: Irocrafts.

Lizarralde, R. & S. Beckerman 1982. 'Historia contemporánea de los Barí'. *Antropológica* 56, 3-52, Caracas.

Llagostera M., A. 1989. 'Caza y pesca marítima (9.000 a 1.000 a.C.)'. In Hidalgo L., J., *et al* (eds), 57-79.

Llagostera Martínez, A. and M.A. Costa Junquiera. 1984. *Museo Arqueológico R.P. Gustvo Le Paige S.J.* Santiago: Departamento de Extensión Cultural del Ministerio de Educación, Series Patrimonio Cultural Chileno, Colección Museos Chilenos.

Londoño, E. 1990. 'Santuarios, santillos, tujjos: objetos votivos de los muiscas en el siglo XVI.' *Boletin del Museo del Oro, Banco de la República* XVI, 93-119 Bogotá

Lopez, R.A. and C.L. Moser. 1981. *Rods, Bundles and Stitches: A Century of Southern California Indian Basketry*. Riverside, CO: Riverside Mus. Press

Lothrop, S.K. 1928. 'The Indians of Tierra del Fuego', *Contribs from the Mus. of the Amer. Indian,The Heye Foundation* 10.

Martinez Peñalosa, P. 1975. *Arte Popular Mexicano*. Mexico DF: Editorial Herrero, SA.

Mason, O.T. 1889. 'The Ray Collection from the Hupa Reservation' pp205-239 in *Annual Report of the Smithsonian Inst. for 1886, Part 1*.Washington, DC.

Mason, O.T. 1904. *Indian Basketry*. New York: Doubleday, Page.

Mason, O.T. 1988 (1904). *American Indian Basketry*. New York: Dover Publications Inc.

Massone, M. 1987. *Hombres del Sur. Aonikenk Selknam Yámana Kaweshkar*. Santiago: Museo Chileno de Arte Precolombino and Congregación Salesiana.

Mattéi-Müller, M-C. and P. Henley. 1978. *Wapa. La Comercialización de la Artesanía Indígena y su Innovación Artistica: el Caso de la Cestería Panare*. Caracas: Litografía Tecnocolor.

Mauldin, B. 1984. *Traditions in Transition - Contemporary Basket Weaving of the Southwestern Indians*. Santa Fe: Mus. of New Mexico Press.

McBride, B. 1990. *Our Lives in Our Hands - Micmac Indian Basketmakers*. Gardiner, Maine: Tilbury House.

MacDowell, L. W. 1982. (1904). *Alaska Indian Basketry*. Alaska Steamship Co.,Seattle, Wash.: Shorey Pubs.

McFeat, T. 1987. 'Space and Work in Maliseet Basket Making'. In McMullen, A. & R. G. Handsman (Eds.) 60-73.

McLendon, S. and B. S. Holland. 1979. 'The Basketmakers: the Pomoans of California' in Roosevelt, A. C. & J.G.E. Smith (Eds) *The Ancestors: Native Artists of the Americas*, 102-129. New York: Mus. Amer. Indian.

McLendon, S. 1990. 'Pomo Baskets: The Legacy of William and Mary Benson' *Native Peoples* 4(1):26-33.

McMullen, A. 1982. 'Woodsplint Basketry of the Eastern Algonkian. *Artifacts* 10(5):1-8.

McMullen, A. 1983. 'Tribal Style in Woodsplint Basketry: Early Paugusset Influence'. *Artifacts* 11(4):1-4.

McMullen, A. 1985a. 'Changing Views of Nineteenth-Century Connecticut Basketry'. Paper presented at the Connecticut Historical Soc., October. Hartford, CT.

McMullen, A. 1985b. 'Interpreting Woodsplint Basketry: Changing Traditions in Northwestern Connecticut. *Artifacts* 13(3):7-9.

McMullen, A. 1987. 'Looking for People in Woodsplint Basketry Decoration'. In McMullen, A. & R. G. Handsman (Eds.) 102-23.

McMullen, A. and R. G. Handsman, 1987. *A Key Into the Language of Woodsplint Baskets*. Washington, CT: Amer. Indian Arch. Inst.

McMullen, A. 1990. 'Many Motives: Change in Northeastern Native Basket Making'. In Porter, F.W. III (Ed.) *The Art of Native American Basketry: A Living Legacy,* 45-78. Westport CT: Greenwood Press.

McMullen, A. 1991. 'Native Basketry, Basketry Styles and Changing Group Identity in Southern New England'. Paper presented at the Dublin Seminar for New England Folklife. 29 June 1991, Deerfield, MA

Morgan, L H. 1962 [1851]. *League of the Iroquois*. New York: Corinth Books.

Morris, E.H. and R.F. Burgh. 1941. *Anasazi Basketry*. Washington D.C.: Carnegie Institute, Pub. No 533

Moser, C.L. 1986. *Native American Basketry of Central California*. Riverside, CO: Riverside Mus. Press.

Moser, C.L. 1989. *American Indian Basketry of Northern California*. Riverside, CO: Riverside Mus. Press

Moser, E. 1973. 'Seri Basketry'. *The Kiva* 38:105-140.

Mowat, L. 1989. *Cassava and Chicha. Bread and Beer of the Amazonian Indians*. Princes Risborough: Shire.

Muñoz O., I. 1989. 'El período formativo en el Norte Grande (1.000 a.C. a 500 d.C.)'. In Hidalgo L., J., *et al* (Eds), 107-128.

Museo Chileno de Arte Precolombino. 1985. *Arica Diez Mil Años*

Museums of the Andes 1981. *Museums of the Andes (Great Museums of the World)*. Tokyo: Newsweek, Inc. and Kodansha Ltd.

NENCATACOA. nd. *Estudio descriptivo de los diferentes modelos de tejido artesanal y de sus raices históricos y culturales en Cundinamarca, Boyacá y Santander*. Bogotá: Banco de la República.

Newman, S. C. 1974. *Indian Basket Weaving*. Flagstaff: Northland Press.

Núñez A., L. 1970. 'Algunos Problemas del Estudio del Complejo Arqueológico Faldas del Morro del Norte de Chile', *Abhundlung und Berichte des Staatlichen Museums für Völkerkunde Dresden* 31, 79-109.

O'Neale, L. 1932. *Yurok-Karok Basket Weavers*. Univ. of Calif. Pubs., Amer. Arch. & Ethno., Vol. 32.

O'Neale, L. 1949. 'Basketry' in Steward, J.H. (Ed.) *The Handbook of South American Indians* Vol. 5, 69-96. Washington D.C.: Smithsonian Institution, Bureau of Amer. Ethno. Bull. 143.

Ortiz, M.M. 1990. 'Cerámica y cestería: marcas de identidad en el Valle de Tenza'. *Memorias del V Congreso Nacional de Antropología, Villa de Leiva, 1989. Tomo* Curnaderismo II, 417-427.

Ortiz, S.E. 1937. 'La necropolis del "Cerillo": uno historia figurada'. *Idearium* año 1, no. 3, 143-149. Pasto.

Osborne, L. de J. 1965. *Indian Crafts of Guatemala and El Salvador*. Norman: Univ. of Oklahoma Press.

Parker, A. C. 1983 [1910]. *Iroquois Uses of Maize and Other Food Plants*. New York State Mus., Educ.Dept. Bull. No. 482. Albany.

Paul, F. 1944. *Spruce Root Basketry of the Alaska Tlingit*. Lawrence, Kansas: US Indian Service.

Pelletier, G. 1973. 'The Analysis and Classification of Malecite Splint Ash Baskets'. Undergraduate Honors Paper, Dept. of Anth., Univ. of New Brunswick.

Pelletier, G. 1977. *Micmac and Maliseet Decorative Traditions*. St. John: The New Brunswick Mus.

Pelletier, G. 1979. 'Micmac Splint Wood Basketry in Nova Scotia, New Brunswick and Quebec.' MS, Canadian Ethno. Service.

Pelletier, G. 1982. *Abenaki Basketry*. Ottawa: Nat. Mus. Man.

Peri, D.W. and S.M. Patterson. 1976. 'The basket is in the roots, that's where it begins' *Journal of Calif. Anth.* 3(2):17-32

Peters, R. M. 1987. *The Wampanoags of Mashpee*. Boston: Indian Spiritual and Cultural Training Council.

Phillips, R. B. 1989. 'Souvenirs from North America: The Miniature as Image of Woodland Indian Life'. *Amer.*

Indian Art Magazine 14(2):532-63, 78-79.

Pinton, S. 1965. 'La maison Bari'. *Journal de la Societé des Americanistes* LIV-2, 247-333. Paris.

Plazas de Nieto, C. 1979. 'Orfebrería prehistórica del altiplano Nariñense, Colombia. *Revista Colombiana de Antropología* XXI, 197-244.

Porter, F. W. III. 1985. 'American Indian Baskets in the Middle Atlantic Region: Material Survival and Changing Function'. *Material Culture* 17(1):25-45.

Porter, F. W. III. 1990. 'Introduction'. In Porter, F.W. III (Ed.), *The Art of Native American Basketry: A Living Legacy,* 1-16. Westport CT: Greenwood Press.

Preuss, K.T. 1926. *Forschungsreise zu den Kogaba*. (2 vols). Vienna.

Price, S. 1989. *Primitive Art in Civilized Places*. Chicago: Univ. of Chicago Press.

Purdy, C. 1901-1902. 'Pomo Indian Baskets and their Makers' *Land of Sunshine* 15(6):438-449 and *Out West* (formerly Land of Sunshine) 16(1):9-19; 16(2):151-158; 16(3):262-273. Los Angeles: Land of Sunshine Pub. Co.

Qualla Arts & Crafts Mutual. 1987. *Contemporary Artists and Craftsmen of the Eastern Band of Cherokee Indians*. Cherokee, N.C.: Qualla Arts & Crafts Mutual, Inc.

Quilter, J. 1985. 'Architecture and chronology at El Paraíso, Peru', *Journal of Field Arch.* 12, 289-297.

Reichel-Dolmatoff, G. 1945. 'Los Indios Motilones'. *Revista del Instituto Etnológico Nacional* II, i,15-116. Bogotá.

Reichel-Dolmatoff, G. 1946. 'Etnografía Chimila'. *Boletin de Arqueología* II, 95-155. Bogotá.

Reichel-Dolmatoff, G. 1949-50. *Los Kogi*. (2 vols). Bogotá.

Reichel-Dolmatoff, G. 1961. 'Notas etnográficas sobre los indos del Chocó'. *Revista Col. de Antropología* IX, 73-156.

Reichel-Dolmatoff, G. 1963. 'Apuntes etnográficos sobre los indios del alto río Sinú'. *Rev. de la Acad. Col. de Ciencias Exactas, Físicas y Naturales* XX, no. 45, 29-40.

Reichel-Dolmatoff, G. 1985. *Basketry as Metaphor: Arts and Crafts of the Desana Indians of the Northwest Amazon*. Los Angeles: Univ. of California.

Rivera, M.A. 1977. *Prehistoric Chronology of Northern Chile*. Ann Arbor: Univ. Microfilms International.

Rivera, M.A., Soto R. P., Ulloa T. L. and Kushner L. D. 1074. 'Aspectos de agriculturización en el norte prehispano, especialmente Arica (Chile)', *Chungará* 3, 79-107.

Rivière, P. 1969. *Marriage among the Trio*. Oxford.

Romoli, K. 1987. *Los de la lengua de Cueva*. Bogotá: Inst.Colombiano de Antropología, Inst. Colombiano de Cultura.

Rossbach, E. 1973. *Baskets as Textile Art*. New York: Van Nostrand Reinhold.

Roth, W.E. 1924. *An Introductory study of the Arts, Crafts and Customs of the Guiana Indians*. 38th Annual Report of the U.S. Bureau of Amer. Ethno. (1916-17). Washington D.C.: Smithsonian Inst.

Roth, W.E. 1929. *Additional Studies of the Arts , Crafts and Customs of the Guiana Indians*. Bull. 91, US Bureau of Ethno. Washington D.C.: Smithsonian Inst.

Rowe, J.H. 1979. 'Standardization in Inka tapestry tunics'. In Rowe, A.P., Benson, E.P., and Schaffer, A.-L. (eds), *The Junius B. Bird Pre-Colombian Textile Conference* , 239-264. Washington D.C.: The Textile Mus. and Dumbarton Oaks.

Royal British Columbia Museum. n.d. *Collection Notes*.

Rydén, S. 1955. 'A basketry technique from the Lake Titicaca region', *Antiquity and Survival* 1(1), 57-63.

Sanipass, M.A. 1990. *Baskadegan: Basket Making Step-By-Step*. Madawaska: St John Valley Pub. Co.

Santoro, C. and L. Ulloa (Eds). 1985. *Culturas de Arica*. Santiago: Departamento de Extensión Cultural del Ministerio de Educación, Series Patrimonio Cultural Chileño, Colección Culturas Aborigenes.

Sayer, C. 1990. *Arts and Crafts of Mexico*. London: Thames & Hudson.

Schon, M., P. Jam & J.M. Cruxent. 1951. 'Cultura material'. In Sociedad de Ciencias Naturales, La Salle, *La region de Perija yu sus habitantes*, Chapter 4. Caracas.

Schottelius, J.W. 1946. 'Arqueología de la Mesa de los Santos'. *Boletin de Arqueologia*. Bogotá.

Schroeder, R.F. 1983. *The Indian Arts and Crafts Board: An Aspect of New Deal Indian Policy*. Albuquerque, NM: Univ. of New Mexico Press

Sigourney, L. H. 1824. *Sketches of Connecticut Forty Years Since*. Hartford, CT.

Simons, F.A.A. 1885. 'An exploration of the Guajira Peninsula'. *Proceedings of the Royal Geog. Soc.*, n.s. VII, 781-796.

Skinner, A. B. 1913. 'A Preliminary Sketch of Lenape Culture'. *Amer. Anth.* 15:208-35.

Skinner, A B. 1924. 'An Ancient Village Site of the Shinnecock Indians'. *Amer. Mus. Nat. Hist. Papers* vol.27 pt.5.

Solano, P. 1974. *Artesanía Boyacense*. Bogotá: Artesanías de Colombia - Litografía Arco.

Speck, F. G. 1909. 'Notes on the Mohegan and Niantic Indians'. In Wissler, C. (Ed.) *The Indian of Greater New York and the Lower Hudson*, 183-210. Anth. Papers of the Amer. Mus. of Natural History 3.

Speck, F. G. 1915a. 'Decorative Art of the Indian Tribes of Connecticut'. Ottawa: *Canada Dept. of Mines, Geological Survey, Memoir 75.*

Speck, F. G. 1915b. 'The Nanticoke Community of Delaware'. *Contributions from the Mus. of the Amer. Indian, Heye Foundation* 2(4):1-43.

Speck, F. G. 1920. 'Decorative Art and Basketry of the Cherokee'. *Bull. of the Public Mus. of the City of Milwaukee* 2 (2): 53-86.

Speck, F. G. 1926. 'Culture Problems in NE North America'. *Proceedings of the Amer. Philosophical Soc.* 65(4):272-311.

Speck, F. G. 1947. *Eastern Algonkian Block-Stamp Decoration: A New World Original or an Acculturated Art*. Research Series No. 1. Trenton: The Arch. Soc. of New Jersey.

Speck, F. G. 1976 [1940]. *Penobscot Man: The Life History of a forest Tribe in Maine*. New York: Octagon Books.

Standen R., V. and L.Núñez. 1984. 'Indicadores antropológicos-físicos y culturales del cementerio precerámico Tiliviche-2 (Norte de Chile)', *Chungará* 12, 135-154.

Stout, D.B. 1948. 'The Cuna'. In Steward, J.H. (Ed) *Handbook of South American Indians* IV, 257-268.

Strong, W.D. and C. Evans. 1952. *Cultural Stratigraphy in the Virú Valley, Northern Peru: the Formative and Florescent Epochs*. New York: Columbia Univ. Press.

Swanton, J. R. 1946. 'The Indians of the SE United States'. *Bureau of Amer. Ethno. Bull. 137*. Washington, DC: Smithsonian Inst..

Tanner, C. L. 1983. *Indian Baskets of the Southwest*. Tucson: Univ. of Arizona Press.

Tanner, C.L. 1982. *Apache Indian Baskets*. Tucson:Univ. Arizona.

Tantaquidgeon, G. 1930a. 'Notes on the Gay Head Indians of Massachusetts'. *Indian Notes* 7(1):1-26.

Tantaquidgeon, G. 1930b. 'Newly Discovered Straw Basketry of the Wampanoag Indians of Massachusetts'. *Indian Notes* 7(4):475-84.

Tantaquidgeon, G. 1935. 'Notes on Mohegan-Pequot Basketry Designs'. *Indians at Work* 2 (17):43-46.

Tantaquidgeon, G. and J. G. Fawcett. 1983. 'Wussuckhosu'. *Artifacts* 11(5):2-3.

Tantaquidgeon, Gladys and J. G. Fawcett. 1987. 'Symbolic Motifs on Painted Baskets of the Mohegan-Pequot'. In McMullen, A. & R. G. Handsman (Eds.) 94-101.

Teit, J. 1909. 'Notes on the Chilcotin'. In *The Shuswap Jesup North Pacific Expedition* Vol 8, part 2, 759-789.

Trigger, B. G. (Ed.) 1978. *The Northeast*. In Sturtevant, W.C. (Ed.) *The Handbook of North American Indians,* Vol. 15. Washington, DC: Smithsonian Inst.

Tschopik, H., Jr. 1938. 'Taboo as a Possible Factor Involved in the Obsolescence of Navaho Pottery and Basketry'. *Amer. Anth.* XL.

Tschopik, M. H. 1946. 'Some Notes on the Arch. of the Dept. of Puno, Peru', *Papers of the Peabody Mus. of Amer. Arch. and Ethno. Harvard Univ.* 27(3).

Turnbaugh, S. R.P. & W. A. 1987. 'Weaving the Woods: Tradition and Response in Southern New England Splint Basketry'. In McMullen, A. & R. G. Handsman (Eds.) 76-93.

Vasco Uribe, L.G. 1987. *Semejantes a los Dioses. Cerámica y Cestería embera-chamí*. Bogotá: Centro editorial, Universidad Nacional de Colombia.

Villegas, L. & A.R. 1982. *Iwouga. La Guajira a través del tejido*. Bogotá: International Petroleum (Colombia) Ltd., Litografía Arco.

Voight, V. F. 1965. *Mohegan Chief: The Story of Harold Tantaquidgeon*.

Wafer, L. 1934 [1699]. *A New Voyage and Description of the Isthmus of America 1680-88*. London: Hakluyt Soc.

Wallace, D. 1962. 'Cerrillos, an Early Paracas Site in Ica', *Amer. Antiquity* 27(3), 303-314.

Wassén, H. 1988 [1935]. *Apuntes sobre grupos meridionales de indígenas Chocó en Colombia*. Bogotá: El Greco Impresores.

Waugh, F.W. 1973 [1916]. 'Iroquois Foods and Food Preparation'. *Canada Dept of Mines Geological Survey Memoir 86. No. 12. Anth. Series.*

Weinstein, L. 1986. '"We're still living on our traditional homeland"; The Wampanoag Legacy in New England'. In Porter, F.W. III (Ed.) *Strategies for Survival: Amer. Indians in the Eastern US*, 85-112. Contributions to Ethnic Studies 15. Westport CT: Greenwood Press.

Whiteford, A, H. 1988. *Southwestern Indian Baskets - Their History and Their Makers*. Santa Fe: SAR Press.

Whitehead, R. H. 1980. *Elitekey: Micmac Material Culture from 1600 AD to the Present*. Halifax: Nova Scotia Mus.

Wilbert, J. 1974. *Yupa Folktales*. Los Angeles, UCLA Latin America Center Publications.

Wilbert, J. 1975. *Warao Basketry: Form and Function*. Occasional Papers of the Museum of Cultural History, No 3. Los Angeles: UCLA.

Willoughby, C. C. 1902. 'Coiled Basketry'. *Science* XVI(392): 31-32.

Willoughby, C. C. 1935. *Antiquities of the New England Indians*. Cambridge: Peabody Mus., Harvard Univ..

Yde, J. 1965. *Material Culture of the Wai Wai*. Copenhagen: National Mus. of Copenhagen, Ethnographic Series 10.

Zaldivar, M.L.L. 1982. *La Cestería en México*. Mixcoac, DF: Fondo Nacional para el Fomento de las Artesanías.